D0875760

# MAD DUCKS AND BEARS

## BOOKS BY GEORGE PLIMPTON

*The Rabbit's Umbrella* • *Out of My League*
*Paper Lion* • *The Bogey Man* • *Mad Ducks and Bears*
*American Journey: The Times of Robert Kennedy*
(with Jean Stein) • *One for the Record* • *One More July*
*Shadow Box* • *Pierre's Book* (with Pierre Etchebaster)
*A Sports Bestiary* (with Arnold Roth)
*Edie: An American Biography* (with Jean Stein)
*Sports!* (with Neil Leifer) • *Fireworks: A History and Celebration*
*Open Net* • *D.V.* (with Diana Vreeland and Christopher Hemphill)
*The Curious Case of Sidd Finch* • *The X Factor*
*The Best of Plimpton* • *Truman Capote* • *Ernest Shackleton*
*Chronicles of Courage* (with Jean Kennedy Smith)
*The Man in the Flying Lawn Chair*

## EDITED BY GEORGE PLIMPTON

*Writers at Work: The Paris Review Interviews,* volumes 1–9
*The American Literary Anthology,* volumes 1–3
*Poets at Work: The Paris Review Interviews*
*Beat Writers at Work: The Paris Review Interviews*
*Women Writers at Work: The Paris Review Interviews*
*Playwrights at Work: The Paris Review Interviews*
*Latin American Writers at Work: The Paris Review Interviews*
*The Writer's Chapbook* • *The Paris Review Anthology*
*The Paris Review Book of Heartbreak, Madness,* etc.
*The Norton Book of Sports* • *As Told at the Explorers Club: More Than Fifty Gripping Tales of Adventure* • *Home Run*

# MAD DUCKS AND BEARS

## FOOTBALL REVISITED

GEORGE PLIMPTON

Little, Brown and Company
New York Boston London

Little, Brown and Company
Hachette Book Group
1290 Avenue of the Americas, New York, NY 10104
littlebrown.com

Originally published by Random House, 1973
First Little, Brown edition, April 2016

Little, Brown and Company is a division of Hachette Book Group, Inc.
The Little, Brown name and logo are trademarks of Hachette Book Group, Inc.



ISBN 978-0-316-32644-5
Library of Congress Control Number: 2015951332

10 9 8 7 6 5 4 3 2 1

RRD-C

Printed in the United States of America

. . . rage, rage against the dying of the light

—Dylan Thomas

# Foreword

## by Steve Almond

There is a fine late-night row to be had over which of George Plimpton's sports books ranks as his most daring. Plenty would nominate *Shadow Box,* in which our slender hero gets his nose flattened by light heavyweight champion Archie Moore. Others would agitate for *Open Net*—a perilous venture into the world of pro hockey—and still more, *Paper Lion,* which culminates with Plimpton nearly becoming the first quarterback ever decapitated during a scrimmage.

Fine and rousing as these accounts may be, I am here to tell you that the distinction belongs to the volume you hold in your hands. I assert this knowing full well that *Mad Ducks and Bears* is the author's most obscure athletic odyssey, little known even to devout Plimptonians.

In fact, what makes the book so courageous is that fact that it does not hang neatly on what we should probably dub the *Plimpton Hook:* that of the plucky amateur ethnographer sent hurtling into the hazards of professional athletic combat.

*Mad Ducks and Bears* is a much stranger and more improvisational composition, an extended suite of riffs that bop wildly in tone from madcap to mournful. The essential subject here is football, specifically the rigors of serving as a lineman. Plimpton's guides through this inferno are a pair of world-class bullshitters: Alex Karras, a motor-mouthed defensive tackle (dubbed "the Mad Duck" for his deranged pursuit of quarterbacks) and the infamously hirsute offensive tackle

John Gordy ("the Bear"). The initial aim of the project, as outlined by Gordy, is to provide a remedial guide for manhandling opponents.

I'm happy to report that the finished book contains precisely zero percent of such instruction. Instead, Plimpton allows these two to mouth off. There are long sections devoted to Karras and Gordy's disastrous business endeavors, including their devout and doomed efforts to peddle a high-end vibrator known as the Picomaster. (Karras winds up with a basement full of them.)

Many pages are spent at the annual Karras golf tournament, an endeavor of such startling and persistent oddity—midgets play a prominent role, as do llamas—that Fellini would have classified the event as implausible. We also get surreal excursions into the alcoholic adventures of the famously Texan quarterback Bobby Layne, and a portrait of his brutal hazing rites.

First published in 1973, seven years after the blazing success of *Paper Lion, Mad Ducks* offers us football not as a ritual of discipline and valor, but as a pretext for anarchy.

The book is also astonishingly forthright about the darker motives that roil beneath the pageantry of the gridiron. Here's Gordy explaining why he returned to football after being driven from the game by nervous anxiety:

> *"Oh Christ!" he said. "The best thing in football was to really* pop *someone. One of the great joys of my life was to get a bead on a guy and really put him out. Absolutely! To lift him up right under his chin, or under his throat with the top of your helmet and put him on his back on the grass. You've done your job, you've gotten your good grade. The movie's going to show it. That's it. Yes, that's why I came back to the Lions the next year."*

Do players speak like this anymore? Not often. The essential business of the league (marketing violent spectacle to the masses) has led us to an historic moment in which such candor is virtually verboten. And yet we now know—thanks to actuarial experts hired by the NFL itself—that up to 30 percent of all retired players will suffer "long-term cognitive ailments," which is lawyerese for "brain damage." To read *Mad Ducks and Bears* in this context is to understand that pro football has always been predicated on huge men who report to work every day with helmets, shoulder pads, and homicidal intent.

Even more piercing is Gordy's assessment of football fans. We watchers get off no easier, I'm afraid.

> *Gordy said intensely, "It's the frustration. They take out their frustrations through what we do on the field. They can't go around hitting people. They're scared to, or they don't want to—it's barbaric—so they pay football players to do it. But the trouble is that the game doesn't really rid them of their frustrations. I'm not even sure that a* win *satisfies them, but a loss makes them grotesque. They wait for you at the end of a game. They hang over the fence, their faces twisted with hate, and shake their fists—these* little *people."*
>
> *He was visibly upset. He began pacing around the room. "You can feel the mob rule ticking in these people."*

Because Plimpton is freed from the mission of documenting his own incompetence, he can devote himself to the larger universe of football. "I am an eavesdropper at heart," he tells us. And he makes excellent use of this vice.

Point Plimpton in the direction of a peewee game that Karras coaches, and he will return with this startling dispatch, one that speaks volumes about the medieval gender roles that football enforces, even among its youngest acolytes:

> *The teams churned back and forth, neither scoring. Behind the Jet bench a few girls stood watching the game, shifting their weight from one long, thin leg to another. "Is that your brother?" I heard one of them ask in disgust. "He fell down. He's gross."*

It can all seem that silly. But Plimpton is too sensitive a correspondent to overlook the fragile ego dramas that prevail. He devotes a full page to a postgame interview with one of Karras's charges, an overmatched player nicknamed Puffer:

> *I continued, "Puffer, did you put out any lightbulbs?"*
>
> *He did not answer. He walked with his head down. My heart sank.*
>
> *"No," he said softly. "I ran away."*

This is football, boiled down to its essence: to succeed you must fear the perception of cowardice more than you fear injury. The end result, in the here and now, is a game that devours its own players, even as it bathes them in luxury and fame.

I laughed so much reading *Mad Ducks and Bears* that my wife often made me get up and move into the other room. But I also found the book to be more searching and sad than Plimpton's others. Perhaps this was because of his deep love for Karras and Gordy, his willingness to elicit and record not just the hijinks but the elemental terrors of their trade.

I've quoted Plimpton extensively because the elegance of his prose demands transcription, not description. And so I must leave you with one final passage, the one that continues to haunt me. It comes late in the book, as Karras is sitting in Plimpton's apartment. The two are discussing the dead bodies that, according to local lore, sometimes float by on the Hudson River.

The general perception is that these are the corpses of criminals and stool pigeons. But Karras reveals the solemn truth:

> *"Well, look close the next time you see a bunch of floaters going by and you'll see they're all old washed-up football players. They can't afford cement boots. And they'll all be linemen," Karras said. He stared moodily down at the currents and sighed. "Quarterbacks and*

*tight ends die comfortably, in big beds, and the Irish setter is whimpering on the other side of the door, and someone is mowing the great lawn outside the big mansion. But the linemen give it up in these little rooms in the poor sections. They wake up on a cot in a room the size of a closet, and they look at their pushed-in kissers in the little mirror, and they pull out their old football jerseys with the number on the back out of the bottom drawer of the beat-up dresser, and they put them on and go up to the bridge there... and they drop off the Triboroughugh and float down here... There goes one. That's Ed Glurk, number seventy, good journeyman tackle for the Eagles in the fifties. Always was a nice guy. Look how he rides nice and high in the water. Just behind him, that's Al Wojciechowicz—good Polack kid who played guard for the old Yankees. He's got his jersey on inside out. Look at him turn in the water. He always had classy moves."*

Karras is just joshing around, of course. But he's also telling us the deeper truth about football, the one we prefer not to hear, about the disposable nature of its heroes, and our own habit of turning away from the human ruin.

We needn't dream up any Glurks or Wojciechowiczs. We've got our own Websters and Seaus and Duersons. New bodies drift past every year. And yet we stubbornly cling to football as a place of refuge. It's a tainted paradox. Or a dissertation nobody will ever read: *The Modern Killing Field as Personal Salvation.*

This is the small miracle Plimpton achieves in *Mad Ducks and Bears.* He makes us love football more deeply, for its rogues and its folly and its thrills. And yet he also gently reveals to us the depths of our own corruption, those moments when the game gives way to sorrow, when the floaters appear and linger in our periphery and we must face the cruel truth that, for a few seconds anyway, we are no longer children.

# Author's Note

## August 1993

I am especially pleased that this revised edition of *Mad Ducks and Bears* is being published. It rectifies an error of judgment on my part. Going over the galley proofs of the original version in the summer of 1973, I realized I had made an editorial blunder by including a "diary" kept during a participatory journalistic stint as the quarterback of the Baltimore Colts—a kind of repeat of what I had done a few years before with the Detroit Lions and written about in *Paper Lion*. I was doing this for the purpose of a television documentary. The diary I kept and put in the book had only a tangential relationship to Alex Karras and John Gordy, the two Detroit linemen who are the true subjects of *Mad Ducks* (Karras) *and Bears* (Gordy). True, John Gordy, out of football because of an injury, was my adviser for the documentary (rather charmingly entitled *The Great Quarterback Sneak*) and Karras, still with the Lions, was gunning for me when I quarterbacked for the Colts during an exhibition game against Detroit. Both appear from time to time in the diary, but they are overshadowed by what I had to say about the Colts, who were a championship team of the time—John Unitas, Bubba Smith, Bill Curry, Ted Hendricks, Tom Matte, Mike Curtis, et al.

So it seemed to me that summer day that the book was badly out of kilter. I went to my editor at Random House and said, "Hey, we have two books here." He looked at me—thinking of the printing schedule—and said, "No, we do not!"

So that was that. For years, when I spotted the book in someone's library, or thought about it, I felt the regret that it wasn't what I wanted it to be. Now it is.

If a reader is curious about the diary, it can be found in the original edition, perhaps in the stacks of a local library. Among other things, it describes the Colt-Lion exhibition game, which was played at Ann Arbor, Michigan, on a hot August day in front of 106,000 people, the largest crowd, I believe, ever to see a professional football game up until that time. Just as I had done with the Detroit Lions, I was sent in to quarterback a few plays... which I did, I must say, with considerably more effect than my performance with the Lions. With them I had lost twenty-nine yards in five plays. As the Baltimore Colt quarterback, darned if we didn't make eighteen yards in four downs—fifteen of them, I must admit, on a roughing-the-passer penalty!

Thus, there are things of value in the diary. Still, it does not belong here... rather like a guest who arrives on the wrong day and finds himself settled rather awkwardly into a family gathering. Best to focus on those remarkably entertaining if roguish linemen—Alex Karras and John Gordy.

# MAD DUCKS
# AND
# BEARS

# CHAPTER 1

This book was not my idea.

I had happened to be in Detroit watching the Lions prepare themselves for a Sunday game against the Chicago Bears. I had been invited to watch the practices, then the game, and to stay over the next night for the annual team hayride—a mid-season ritual initiated in 1960 by Darris McCord, the defensive end.

After one of the midweek practices John Gordy came up to where I was standing on the sidelines and started talking about his idea for a book. He was one of the offensive guards on the Detroit Lions, about the best in the league at that difficult position. During the time I had spent with the team, he had been a sympathetic friend and a lively source of information. He was called "the Bear" because his body was covered with a thick pelt-like thatch of hair, and on his way to the shower, a towel around his middle, one of his teammates would invariably lean out of his locker room stall and call out, "Hey John, don't forget to take off your overcoat!"

Gordy's notion for the book was simple and practical. It was to be about linemen. He had figured out that of the twenty-two different positions on a football team (counting both offense and defense) there are fourteen players who can be described as linemen. He was including linebackers, who do indeed often play head-to-head on the line of scrimmage. It was his conservative reckoning that at one time or another fifty

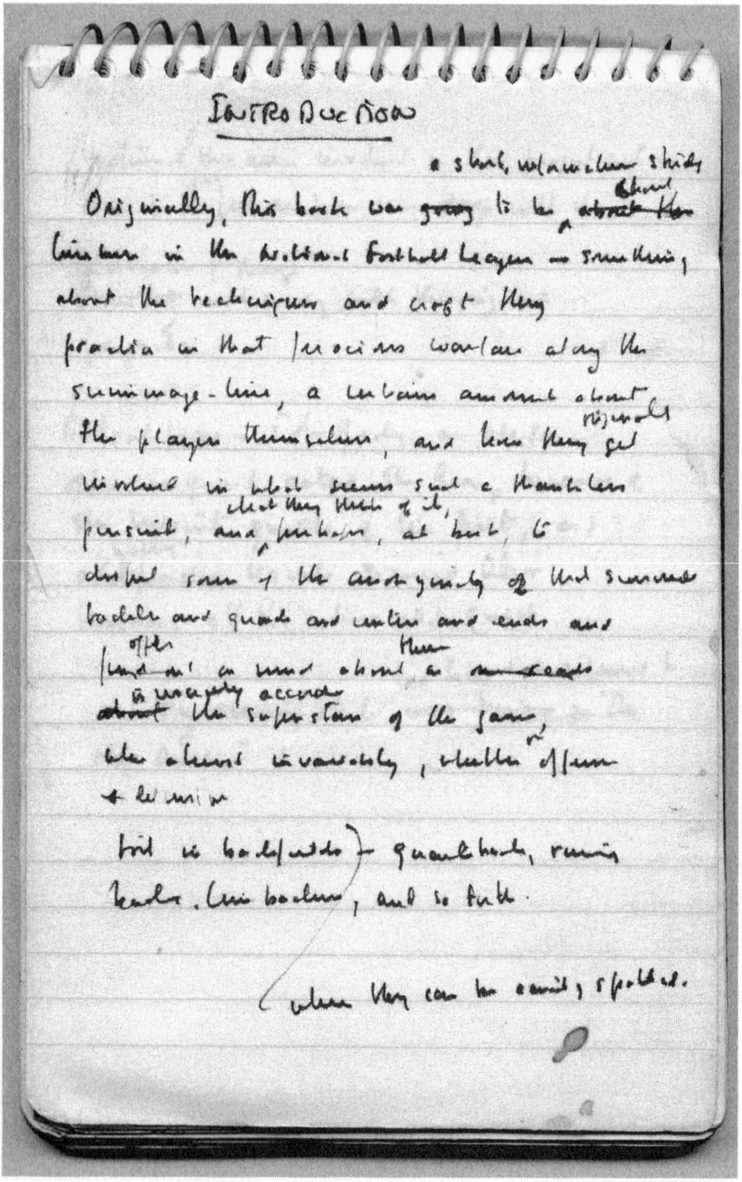

A handwritten introduction to *Mad Ducks and Bears* in the author's spiral notebook. (*Plimpton Estate*)

million Americans had played on the line of scrimmage, and that well over one and a quarter million active players (if one counted the nine- and ten-year-olds in the Pony Leagues) were colliding against each other every autumn weekend.

"That's a whole mess of people," he said. "Now my point is this: they're all potential readers. The people who are doing it now, those one and a quarter million, will want to know how to do it *better*. They'll have to get the book in order to survive against these linemen who *have* read it and put its theories in practice. As for the other fifty million, the retired linemen—well, they played in the line at some point in their lives, and it was the best thing they ever did, and maybe they've gone a bit to flab and they'll want to read the book to be refreshed by what it was they once went through. We'll cash in on the nostalgia kick."

I interrupted. "Maybe it *wasn't* the best thing they ever did in their lives. Maybe they hated it."

"Well, then they'll buy the book to try to figure what the hell they did it for," Gordy said. "They'll buy the book in droves—all those puzzled people."

"It all sounds very carefully thought out," I said.

I asked Gordy what he felt I could do to help. I could "put it together," he said. It wouldn't take much time. There would be some diagrams; it would be a sort of "manual." He would devote himself to the text on offensive line play, and for the defense he felt that his training camp roommate, Alex Karras...

I blinked. "Karras!"

In truth, Karras was an excellent choice. He was an All-Pro defensive tackle, relatively short for that position—being a massive hydrant-like figure of 245 pounds—but possessed of tremendous strength in the upper part of his body and a startling quickness of foot which carried him into opposing backfields in a savage bustling style of attack which caused some observers to refer to him as "the Mad Duck." Since he was not overpowering, but relied on deftness and guile to get to the opposition, his theories on defensive lineman technique would be valuable; furthermore, his mind was freewheeling, full of fancy, and he loved to drift into extemporized skits and monologues, which would help brighten the instructional text of the manual.

I told Gordy I'd think about it overnight, and the next day I went up to him during practice and said I would do what I could to help. The thought of working with those two friends was irresistible. Gordy grinned and said that was fine.

After the team practice I spoke to Karras. The locker room was almost deserted when he appeared; he had been sitting in the training room treating a bone bruise in the whirlpool. He liked the idea of the book. He said that he was very eager to get on with it. "It's important," he said, "that right off we instruct our readers that they should never be intimidated by the opposition." His voice rose in the empty room, and I knew that an impersonation was imminent. Reaching into his locker, he produced a golf hat with a decal which read JEWISH OPEN; he set it on his large pumpkin-shaped head and peered out through the black horn-rimmed spectacles he wore off the field.

"All right, men, listen up! As your head coach, with The Big Game coming up tomorrow, I'm telling you that I want this game. Why should we be scared? We're going out there tomorrow and we're gonna crack heads. They're gonna know they've been in a ball game, right? And the team I'm talking about is the Kansas City Chiefs, just in case some of you people didn't know. Now I understand that a lot of you guys are scared of the Chiefs. I understand there's been a lot of whimpering and players going and getting sick in the back of their lockers thinking about playing the Chiefs. Well, I don't think that's the proper spirit, men, and that sort of attitude is not in my book. There's no need to be scared. Their front four is big, but they can be dominated if we go out there and want to crack heads. Now let me diagram a play that'll show you how I want you to dominate these people."

Karras turned to the locker room blackboard and with a piece of chalk drew the traditional symbols for the offensive line.

He stepped back. "Okay. That's our offensive line. Now here's the Kansas City front four." He stepped forward again with the chalk.

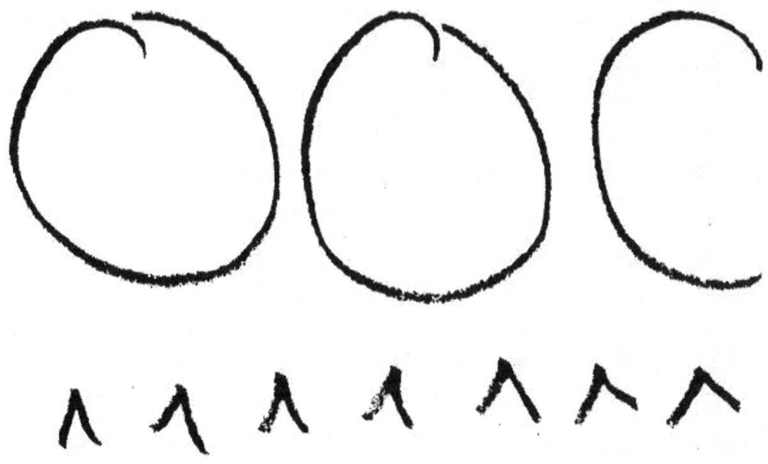

As Karras was halfway through drawing the absurdly outsized circles designating the Chief front four, Friday Macklem, the Lion equipment manager, came out of his office and said, "Hey, Alex, what are you fooling around with that blackboard for?"

"We're writing a book," Karras said.

Friday looked at the strange diagram. "Why not?" he asked. "The big question," he said after a while, "is whether the country is ready for it. What's the book about?"

"Well, largely about linemen," I said. "About their life, how they perform their skills..."

"You going on the hayride Monday night?" he interrupted.

I nodded.

"That's the best possible introduction to the behavior patterns of linemen you could ever ask for." He whistled and shook his head. "If you survive, you may want to take on another assignment."

* * *

I watched the Sunday game, in which the Lions beat the Bears, but I had an engagement that kept me in Detroit on the evening of the hayride. I told Darris McCord that when I was done, I'd drive out and try to find his party. He gave me directions to Howell, a small town twenty miles northwest of Detroit, to the Kaiser farm there. When I got to the farm I was to step out of the car and listen, and off in some direction I'd be able to hear the general hubbub from the hay wagons; even if the party was a couple of miles across the fields. I could strike out cross-country to meet up with them.

It was after eleven o'clock when I arrived at the Kaiser farm and got out of my car. It was cold and I could see my breath. A full Halloween moon was up, and underfoot a thin ice crust cracked as I walked across the farmyard. Sure enough, in the distance, beyond a dark line of trees at the end of the pasture, I could hear the hollering and the carrying-on—first a sharp scream or two, then a maniacal warbling laugh, as if someone, far across those frozen fields, was being tickled to death.

I started across the fields toward the tree line. The first Lion I met was Mike Lucci, the team's middle linebacker; he jumped when he saw me looming up. "Christ!" His wife was with him, a young girl, pale-faced in the moon and looking dazed, as if she could not rid herself of a disturbing mental image. Wisps of straw stuck to their clothing.

"You'll come to a road," Lucci said. "Turn down it toward the noise. They're on their way back to the farm. We couldn't take it any longer."

"The big ones are crazy," the girl said succinctly. "It's very scary."

It was easy to find the party. There were two wagons—one drawn by tractor, the other by a pair of horses—moving side by side to allow the players to leap, vast hurtling shapes in the darkness, from one to the other with great bellowing cries. The straw in the wagons was alive with motion.

A number of people were walking alongside. I joined Nick Pietrosante, the big running back.

"Who's up there?" I asked.

"Mostly the linemen," Pietrosante said. "Everyone else has got down and is walking."

Gordy's head appeared above the side of the wagon, his hair askew with straw. He asked me up; I declined. A pumpkin flew out of the wagon in a high arc and landed with a dull thud beside me in the darkness.

"We had a pumpkin fight down the road a piece," Pietrosante said. "There must have been twenty pumpkins in the air at the same time."

"Where's Karras?"

"He's probably up there in the straw. The Mad Duck's in his nest."

"The what? The Mad Duck?"

"They're *all* mad ducks, absolutely certifiable," Pietrosante said.

"Are there any girls still up there?" I asked.

"Maybe one or two have sifted down to the bottom."

Even when we got back to the Kaiser farm, the merrymaking continued in the wagons, standing huge in the center of the farmyard, rocking and squeaking on their axles. The horses were led away, moving swiftly from the traces, so that the farmhand had to trot hard to keep in front of them. A girl got down from one of the wagons, her dress bulging grotesquely where the players had stuffed her with hay. A beer can arched out after her and clattered tinnily at my feet, crushed in on itself by a hand of such enormous strength that the can was almost as flat as a shingle. In the farmhouse a vacuum cleaner started up; revelers were getting the straw cleaned off their clothes.

Darris McCord appeared at my side. "Well, what did you think?" he asked.

"It's a great party," I said.

"It's finishing earlier this year. Usually it goes on until dawn. We don't hardly ever lose a game after the hayride. Of course, maybe it's because everything seems easier after it's over. Most anybody who survives feels he can beat up on the world."

"I never actually got up in the wagons," I admitted. "I walked alongside. But the linemen certainly like it."

"Yes," said McCord. "For us, it's the normal way we live—in heaps."

I never saw Alex Karras at all that night. Somebody told me that he had fallen asleep in his hay wagon, tucked under a heavy blanket of straw like a huge mouse.

Afterward I kept in touch with both Karras and Gordy, but the manual never progressed the way I imagined it might. My original notion was that the two players would write, or perhaps dictate into a tape machine, various short essays on such topics as "The Pass Rush," "How to Brush-Block," "The Proper Three-Point Stance and Common Mistakes," and so forth. We would get someone to draw the Xs and Os of the necessary diagrams, and I would put it all together, perhaps in a month or so. It would be called *The Pit,* or *In the Trenches,* or perhaps *High Numbers* in reference to the 50s–80s category of numerals that linemen wear on their jerseys. We would add a catchy subtitle such as "Or How to Bite Through a Helmet." Then we would sit back and see if John Gordy's prognosis about the tens of thousands of potential readers had any validity.

But slowly the book became something else. Neither Gordy nor Karras did their obligatory essays. When I saw them in Detroit, or they came to the apartment in New York, there was very little discussion about the *technical* aspects of football. Sometimes Gordy rearranged the furniture, set up standing lamps, and rushed around indicating the various routes of the offensive guard. The apartment seemed very small at such times. Karras and I watched nervously. But he did this rarely, and I don't think Karras ever did any such demonstrations. Perhaps it did not really interest them.

What did begin to emerge when we got together to "work on the book" was an irreverent, roguish account of their lives as football players, full of anecdote, reminiscence, and story, often tempered by grievance, but always with an underlying attitude of humor—as if their occupations were only acceptable in that light. It was good that the emphasis swung away from the original concept, because I worked slowly with what they gave me, having other things to do, and finally Gordy quit football and Karras got into his twelfth year, which would have made our lineman's manual, if we had kept to that idea, as outdated as a book by Bronko Nagurski on how to play fullback.

Then something else contributed to the shift in direction of the book. Following my stint with the Lions in 1963—joining them to write a book about an amateur amongst great professionals—I thought I was done with such participation forever. But in the summer of 1971 I was coaxed "out of retirement" (as my friends put it) to do a television special—once again playing last-string quarterback, this time not with the Detroit Lions, who felt that television crews would disrupt their training season, but with the Baltimore Colts, who were the world champions and did not feel that my presence, and the television entourage, would unhinge them.

I trained with the Colts for almost a month—preparing to quarterback four plays against my old teammates, the Lions, in a preseason game at Ann Arbor. Right up through that confrontation I kept a diary and filled up an extraordinary number of notebooks, not because I had so much to say but because I dislocated the thumb on my throwing hand during practice, which necessitated holding the pen in my fist and writing the daily notations in an enormous scrawl which filled a page after a word or so.

Selections from the diary have been included in this book. It seems appropriate; Gordy and Karras were very much a part of the experience. Gordy (in his first year out of football) was my technical adviser at training camp, tutoring me endlessly in the plays the Baltimore coaches had devised, and also helping the television crew. Karras, of course, was still active, the first-string Detroit tackle, and he would be waiting for me at Ann Arbor. Someone asked him how he was going to react to my presence on the field. He thought for a while. He said finally, "I am primarily a very docile person . . . easygoing . . . very happy. The only time I am really violent is on the football field. I'm going to catch him and I'm going to knock his block off. It's as simple as that."

# CHAPTER 2

When Karras and Gordy turned up in my New York apartment, shucking their coats, and coming down the steps into the living room, it seemed to me that a proper starting place for their book was to get them both to talk about that moment when they knew they were going to become football players.

Whatever their professions, most people can recall such a moment, one special instant when they suddenly know what to make their mark in, as if someone had suddenly opened a door for them and said, "Well, there it is. It's in there." Perhaps a number of people slide into their professions without being aware of such a moment, but it turned out that for both Karras and Gordy there *had* been an occasion they could look back on and say that was the pivotal point.

For Karras it was a shot he made on a basketball court when he was in high school in Gary, Indiana. He was sent into a game against a team running third in the state. Karras had no particular wish to go into the game. He was a reserve; because of the athletic proficiency of his older brothers, he lacked confidence; furthermore, the pressure on him was inordinate, the game being extremely close and in its final minute.

"I went down the court," he said, "and they threw me the ball. I don't know what made me do it, but I said to myself that for once in my life I was not going to pass the ball off. That's what I generally did—I'd get the ball and throw it to someone else quick, like a bomb was ticking

~~I would guessthat~~ Most people, whatever their professions, can think back on some particular moment, one special instance, when they suddenly know what they would go on and try to make their mark in, as if someone had suddenly opened a door for them and said, "Well, there it is; it's in there." Perhaps there are a number of people who slide into their professions without being aware of such a moment, but for both Karras and Gordy there had been sharp instances which they could look back on, and say to themselves, well, that was the pivotal point.

For Karras it had been a shot he made on a basketball court when he was in high school in Gary, ~~Indiana~~. He was sent into a game against a team that was running third in the state, which, being Indiana, a stronghold of great basketball, would indicate the high standard of ~~basketball being~~ played. Karras had no particular wish to go into the game. He was a reserve; he lacked confidence ~~mostly~~ because of the proficiency at athletics practiced by his older brothers; furthermore, the pressure on him was inordinate, the game ~~was~~ being extremely close, and in the final ~~last~~ minutes, ~~which put inordinate pressure on him.~~

"I went down the court," he said. "And they threw me the ball. I don't know what made me do it . . . but something came into my mind. I said to myself that for once in my life I was not going to pass the ball off. Thatgs what I generally did. I'd get the ball and throw it to someone else quick, like a bomb was ticking in it. But this time I took a shot, pushed it up with one hand, and it went in, and we won the game."

Gordy was laughing. He was sitting on the living-room sofa, Karras was opposite. The two of them had come for lunch. "Oh God," ~~he~~ Gordy said.

"I'm serious when I say that," Karras said. He seemed hurt that this private divulgence was not being accepted solemnly.

"Basketball!" Gordy was finding it hard to contain himself thinking of someone of Karras' physique on a basketball court.

"No, I'm serious," Karras said. "That s when I found my con fidence."

An early draft on the process of becoming a lineman, complete with edits in the author's hand. (*Plimpton Estate*)

in it. But this time I took a shot, pushed it up with one hand, and it went in, and we won the game."

Gordy was laughing. He sat on the living room sofa, Karras opposite him. "Oh God," he said.

"I'm serious," Karras said. He seemed hurt that this private divulgence was not being accepted solemnly.

"*Basket*ball!" Gordy was finding it hard to contain himself thinking of someone of Karras's physique on a basketball court.

"No, I'm serious," Karras said. "That's when I found my confidence."

"Okay, okay."

"And if the shot hadn't gone in?" I asked.

"I probably would have ended up as an elegant fop," Karras said expansively. "Maybe I would have learned the harpsichord. At this very moment I might be the secretary of the interior, lolling on a sofa in Washington with an ecology student, reaching out from time to time with a long arm and hitting a sad chord on the harpsichord, instead of sitting around with you bums. Of course, *I* could have turned out to be a bum too."

"That's for sure," Gordy said.

"You want to know something?" Karras crossed his knees and put his fingertips together. "I don't think I would have been much of a football player if I didn't have a name like Karras. That hard *K* sound is the key. If my name was Harris, an *H* instead of a *K*, and they'd baptized me Alexander... with *that* name, 'Alexander Harris,' I'd never have made it as a football player—at least not as a defensive tackle. It's not a football player's name. Maybe I could have been a flanker with a name like that... but more likely I would have turned out to be the secretary of the interior."

"Would you say this theory was true of other football players?" I asked.

"Absolutely," he said. "John Unitas. Think of that name. It suggests authority and teamwork. Twenty percent of a football player's genius is the name he was born with. Leo Nomellini—what does that name bring to mind but power and an afternoon of terror for the guy going in against him? Sam Huff? A guy that's going to blow you over. Csonka? It sounds like a blow to the gut. Dick Butkus? Look at the collection of consonants—*that*'s why he's a great linebacker. If his name was Robin Jenkins, he couldn't have made it in the *Ivy* League."

"I see," I said. I was trying to think of a name in football that did not necessarily conjure up such associations.

"Or take the other side of the coin," Karras said. "Milt Plum. That's why Plum was never a great quarterback with the Lions, however gifted he was with natural ability. He was destroyed by his name. His parents probably wanted him to play the cello and take them for picnics up on the hill when they were eighty years old, so they called him Milt. You played bridge with him when you were at Detroit, right?"

"That's right," I said. "He was very good."

Karras nodded. "Of course, there's not much his parents could have done, given that name Plum, but suppose they took out the Milt and called him Jack and spruced him up with a good middle name. Suppose they called him Jack *Kong* Plum."

"Jack *Kong*?"

"Sure. Some of his aunts might have objected—on the grounds that there weren't any Kongs they could recall in the Plum family tree, but someone called Jack Kong Plum would have been a helluva quarterback. He'd talk different, and he wouldn't have played bridge, and he'd walk different with a name like that. He would have started out *right* in football."

"What about you, John?" I asked.

"My freshman year in high school," Gordy told us, "I was five feet two and weighed one hundred and nineteen, and I played trumpet in the band. We marched at the games. I didn't care at all about football. I ate hot dogs and looked at the girls. Then I changed high schools. I didn't have any friends in the new place, Isaac Litton High School in Tennessee, and I was lonely. Then one day a girl walked up to me in the corridor and told me that if I went and got a crew cut—this shows you how long ago it was—maybe some of them would start talking to me. A red-haired girl. Well, I hightailed it down to the barbershop and came back with a crew cut that apparently made me acceptable enough so that I was invited to the weekend high school dance.

"Well, that night I got into a fight. I was leaving the place with a girl who was a cheerleader. A guy by the name of Joe Henderson came running out and wanted to know what I was doing taking his girl home. He was a *huge* guy, about six foot eight—"

"Did he have hair under his arms?" Karras asked.

"He did," Gordy said. "He had a *lot* of hair under his arms. He grabbed me. Out of fright I swung a punch at him, and down he went, right there on the street under the arc light. I reached down and grabbed his jacket, and he busted out crying and carrying on and asking me to leave him alone. This big guy, and all of a sudden there he was on the ground.

"Well, I got this tremendous surge of confidence. After that, I didn't play the trumpet anymore. I didn't even know that professional football existed then, but I would guess that knocking down that guy put me on the road to it."

"To think," Karras said, "that you drove that poor nice Tennessee boy to an early grave."

"What are you talking about?"

"Probably a nice big gentle boy who kept canaries at home and took care of an elderly aunt who coughed a lot, and he went out every morning on his bicycle at six A.M. on the newspaper route, throwing the *Nashville Hillbilly* up onto front porches, and he only had one thing in life he truly loved, which was this pretty cheerleader, Margie, whom he dreamed about every night as he lay there hoping his aunt wasn't going to have a coughing fit, and you went and *popped* this guy."

"What do you mean?" Gordy said in anguish. "He was a big *thug.* Margie? What are you *talking* about?"

"...was forced to run away to sea," Karras was rambling on. "Completely driven out of that town. People kept coming up to him and yah-yahing at him for being beaten up by a hundred-pound trumpet player. His canaries wasted away. His aunt got so weak from worry that she died from the effects of lifting a cupcake off the shelf. He had nothing left. Shipped out of New Orleans, and the dope fiends got him in Hong Kong."

"Hong Kong?"

"...and his last words, just barely overheard, through the smoke of that dope den: 'Save the last dance for me, Marge.' "

"That's horrible," said Gordy. "Ridiculous."

"Hey, Alex," I asked, tapping a pencil. "What about childhood idols? Was there anyone in football you kept a picture of—something like that?"

"Hell, yes. On my bureau top when I was a kid I kept a picture of Bronko Nagurski. It was a sort of formal picture. He was dressed in a team blazer, wearing a big tie with a wavy design of flowers. It was the biggest picture in the room; you would have thought it was my dad. I wanted to be a fullback. In the dark his eyes followed me everywhere. He was the biggest idol I ever had."

"Did you ever meet him?" Gordy asked.

"Well, years later, the season I was suspended and went into professional wrestling, this one time I went up to Minneapolis for a match. I was late, and I came running into the place and the promoter said, 'You're on the tag team tonight.' 'Wonderful,' I said. He didn't mention my partner on the tag team. So I went down to the locker room. Locker rooms that wrestlers use are different from any other—dingy and small and dirty, and always with this very distinctive smell, a body smell that's worse than anything you find in places where football and baseball players have been. I don't know why. Maybe it's because a lot of wrestlers are big, haystack guys that sweat a lot and maybe take a bath once a month. The smell of wrestlers lies in these little rooms in layers.

"Well, I went down there to change my clothes, and in the shadows I saw this older man practicing with a pair of dumbbells, pumping his arms. I kept looking at him. A much older man. Suddenly it came to me that it was Bronko Nagurski, my childhood idol, standing over in the shadows and pumping these barbells toward the ceiling. I could hardly believe it. I went over and introduced myself; sure enough, it *was* Nagurski. He was my tag-team partner. I stared at him, bug-eyed. Hell, I knew more about him than *he* did."

"Was he that down-and-out that he had to wrestle for a living?" Gordy asked.

"I don't know why he did it," Karras answered. "I always heard he had a fortune salted away somewhere. Certainly he was the cheapest man who ever walked the earth. It's the God's truth that he was wearing the *same tie* he wore when he played with the Chicago Bears."

"Come *on!*" Gordy said.

"I swear. I saw it! It was hanging on a hook right there in the locker room, a big tie with a flower design—the exact same one that was in the picture on the top of my bureau."

"Go on," Gordy objected. "Nobody wears the same tie for twenty years."

"Nagurski does," Karras insisted.

"It would have rotted off his neck," Gordy said.

"Well, maybe this one was made of some special material—asbestos, or something—but sure as I'm sitting here it was the same one." He glared at Gordy.

"That's crap," Gordy said.

The tension in the room was eerie. I always remembered that while the two of them were roommates, and good friends, invariably they had a fight in training camp, exploding at each other on a hot August day—an annual event.

"Hold on," I said. I cast around for something to say. "Would anyone like a drink before lunch?" They grumbled out some orders and I went to the kitchen to fill them.

When I came back the two of them had calmed down and Gordy was just finishing a dissertation on the benefits of a beef and bourbon diet. Karras began talking about jockeys' diets. "You know what jockeys do?" he was saying. "They eat so much that they stuff themselves, and then they throw up. I've seen them do it. 'Give me some more broccoli... excuse me for a minute. I'll be right back.'"

"You've *seen* this?" Gordy asked.

"Well, there's not much to see," Karras said. "I mean, it's not like watching a five-hundred-pound Jap wrestler get sick." He shifted in his chair. "I'll tell you who *did* turn the stomach. That was Bob St. Clair of the 49ers. He used to eat uncooked steak. When I went out for the Pro

Bowl some years ago, I sat with him for the pregame meal. He said to the waitress, 'Bring me a cold steak.' She asked, 'What do you mean by cold?' He said, 'Cold and raw.' She looked surprised, but she went and got him a raw steak and he ate the whole thing."

"Yes, I've heard that about him," Gordy said.

"I'll tell you something else about St. Clair," Karras said. "He shot a deer one time—Leo Nomellini of the 49ers told me this—and when the deer went down, he ran for it. He dove at that deer and cut it open and grabbed at the heart and *ate* it. Ate it right out of the deer."

Gordy said, "Get out of here!"

"God's truth," Karras said. "Leo Nomellini told me. Ask him. Actually, St. Clair got sick that time. Not because of the deer's heart. Something else. He had the grippe or something. He really believes the raw food idea. Even his *kids* eat their meat raw. He takes the steak and cuts it in very thin pieces for them. It takes him a long time to eat, because there's so much chewing to do—maybe twenty minutes for each piece...

"The *biggest* eater I ever heard of," he went on, "was Mack Lewis of the St. Louis Cardinals. He was about six foot thirteen inches tall and he weighed about four tons. He was gigantic. He played at Iowa. He was a great, jolly giant. He laughed all the time. Everything amused him. Someone would say, 'Hey, it's three o'clock in the afternoon,' and that would just about double up Mack Lewis—he'd laugh for six minutes.

"Well, the coaches at St. Louis tried to pare some of that weight off him, so they put him at the Fat Man's table. He'd sit there, roaring with laughter, and they'd put a little thin sliver of steak on his plate. That's it. That's all he had—that, and a little glass of water. But the weight never seemed to come off him; he still weighed four tons. So the coaches followed him, and they discovered that fifteen minutes after his meal at the Fat Man's table, he was at the frozen custard stand down the road from the training camp eating these *pails* of ice cream. He couldn't help himself. The coaches kicked him out. I'm not sure he minded much. He was the best-humored man there ever was. He didn't care if he was in football or not, as long as he had something to laugh at."

"I don't suppose that laissez-faire attitude is at all typical?" I asked.

"It's better to be more positive," Gordy said. "And lay off the ice cream."

"But I always had doubts," Karras said. "Obviously I'm grateful for what football's done for me, but I wasn't so sure at the beginning. I hated high school and college football, mainly because I was constantly being pushed around and forced into it. I hated the whistles that are always shrilling in the background when you're being goaded. I assumed that in the pro leagues whistles weren't needed, so when I finished college football, that was what I hoped I'd heard the end of: whistles.

"But when I graduated I was picked for the All-Stars. I got to training camp, and Otto Graham, the coach of the All-Star team, called us together for a big pep talk. He had a whistle around his neck and he said we were going to beat the hell out of the Detroit Lions, who were the champions the year before, in the All-Star game. He said, 'We'll be the first All-Star team to win against the National League champions since... since eighteen oh three.' I wish coaches would all shut their mouths, so we don't have to run our asses off trying to keep them looking good because they've made statements like that. We had a hard day of scrimmaging. Charlie Krueger was on the team, and he had come from Texas where Bear Bryant is the coach and the whistles go from dawn to night. He kept saying, 'Man, this is easy. This is apple pie.' Meanwhile, I was dead. I'd been smoking three packs of cigarettes a day. But Charlie, he was in top form and he kept saying, 'Man, this is a breeze.'

"When the scrimmage was over, I started walking to the gym. But Otto Graham yelled, 'All right now, let's all line up at the goal line.' So I turned back and lined up on the goal line with the others. Then Graham said, 'Now when I blow this whistle—'

"Well, that was it, man. I knew what was coming next: grass drills. Sure enough. '—I want you guys to fall down and get up and fall down and get up, fast, real *fast,* until I blow the whistle. Then stop. When I blow the whistle again, I want you to run three steps forward, three back, then three forward until...'

"Well, that was it for me. I started walking out across the playing field for the locker room. Otto Graham saw me, and he blew his whistle—which was not good judgment—and shouted, 'Where are you going?' I said, 'I'm leaving. I've had enough.' He said, 'Where are you going?' His eyes were bugged. He looked like someone had hit him very hard in the throat. I said, 'I'm going to the Detroit Lions camp.' He said, 'You can't go there. You're supposed to stay here. You can't go to the Lions camp.' I said, 'Oh yes I can.' He said, 'Oh no you can't.' I said, 'Oh yes I can.'"

"Man, that was some dialogue," Gordy said.

"Everybody was standing on the goal line ready to do these grass drills and they couldn't believe their ears. So I said to Graham, 'I don't want to play in the All-Star game.' He said, 'What?' I said, 'I'm not playing.' He said, 'Well, what's the problem?' I said, 'I don't want to do any of this stuff—these drills.' He said, 'Wh—, wh—, didn't you do this in college?' 'Yes,' I said. 'But I'm not going to do it here.' That really threw him. He said, 'You've got a real bad attitude.' So I said, 'Yeah? How much are you paying me here in this camp? A hundred and fifty dollars to fall down. And stand up. And fall down again. I'm twenty-three years old. I'm going to the locker room.' I began to walk in, and one of the came running after me to get ahold of me. I said, 'Don't, fellow.'

"Well, they finally got me to hang around. The rest of the time in camp I had this bad shoulder. 'Oooh, my shoulder hurts.' Graham wrote the Detroit coach, George Wilson, a letter in which he said I had the worst attitude he'd ever seen in a football player. He had no idea how I'd ever gone as far as I had in football. I would be of no help to the Detroit Lions.

"Well, after the All-Star game I got to Detroit. Wilson told me, 'There's this letter,' and he showed it to me. So I said, 'Well, that's his opinion.' Wilson said, 'You're right.' I thought, This guy's got to be half-way decent. I got along famously with George. He was the only coach I ever got along good with... He didn't carry a whistle."

"So from that point on, there were never any doubts?" I asked.

Karras shook his head and sucked in his breath. "I'm telling you, I began wondering about the game again—the first time I ever started in a pro game. It was against the Chicago Bears in an exhibition game in Norman, Oklahoma. What a way to break in! What happened was that Jim David was playing cornerback for us, and he was the roughest who ever played that position. If a *line judge* wandered into his area he was looking for trouble. Well, Harlon Hill, who was playing flanker for Chicago, came into Jim David's territory on a little look-out pattern. The Chicago quarterback threw the ball to someone else, but that didn't make any difference to Jim David, no *sir*. Someone was in his area, so David took a few steps and *whack!* he broke Harlon Hill's jaw. Hill got to bleeding pretty bad, so George Halas, the Chicago coach, took him out and sent in some guy whose only function was to get revenge on Jim David. And he did, too. He hit Jim David and busted his teeth. All his teeth just fell out. I couldn't believe what I was seeing. David stayed in the game, wobbling around, his jersey just red with blood, and it was a horrible sight, especially to a rookie like me. Then Gil Mains, our big tackle, kicked somebody and somebody kicked Gil Mains, who fell over and dislocated his arm. He had to be taken out. Then someone from the Bears got hurt. They brought out a stretcher. By the time they got him off the field he was covered with these sweat bugs that live in the ground in Norman, Oklahoma. Then Rick Casares of the Bears fumbled the ball and their center picked it up and started to run. One of our people hit him with a flying tackle and completely compounded his ankle, just tore his foot all around. He was sick as hell. He was going *y-a-a-a-a!* The guy's name was Damone. I'd played against him in college; he used to play with Northwestern. I stood around and watched this with my jaw down to my knees. I mean, what was I getting into? It was the fiercest thing I'd ever seen. About eleven guys were hurt in that game in Norman, and on the way home in the airplane the public relations man for Chicago keeled over and dropped dead. Right out of his seat. So I said, Well, maybe I'll give this sport a year. Then I'll quit."

"Jeezus! What about you, John?" I asked. "Did you ever think of quitting?"

"Well, I *did* quit," Gordy said. "In nineteen fifty-seven, my first year, and I was playing first string, the Lions won the championship—the top of the world. But it wasn't for me. I had a horrible time. The pressures were so considerable. And the hassles! Bobby Layne was on my back all the time. I never felt a part of the team. I remember before the championship game we had a meeting in the locker room in Tiger Stadium to vote on the disposition of the championship shares. The lockers are wire mesh, and I was sitting in the back of mine, peering out and watching what was going on. Layne was running the meeting, and he began to yell at somebody. Hell, he was yelling at *me!* 'God damn it,' he said, 'are you going to vote or not?' I didn't think I could! I was the first-string guard, but hell—I was a *rookie.*"

Karras was clucking sympathetically.

"It wasn't only that," Gordy went on. "Every Sunday I had to play against these monsters. Twice a season I had to come up against Leo Nomellini and Art Donovan and get myself thrashed. It wasn't any fun at all. Well, after that first championship season, I went home to Tennessee and everyone I knew from my team was coaching, and they all seemed so happy. They walked around with big half-moon grins. They seemed so happy that I looked at myself, all smashed up and nervous, and thought, What the hell am I doing?"

"You couldn't come up with much of an answer, could you?" Karras said.

"Just visions of a future involving Leo Nomellini and Art Donovan," Gordy replied. "So then LeRoy Pearce, who was a young end coach at Tennessee, asked me if I'd like to take a job coaching the offensive line at the University of Nebraska. I was offered exactly what I was getting playing with the Lions: seven thousand. Well, how could I turn it down? It meant I wouldn't have to think of Nomellini or Donovan anymore. Of course, I had no crystal ball to see how big and lucrative professional football was going to become. In the back of my mind was always the notion that playing pro ball was just an interim before getting into coaching. So that when that job was offered, I jumped at it.

"Well, I discovered that the pressures are exactly the same in coaching. It was no fun at all. Every Sunday I sat in front of the television set and watched the fellow playing in my position with the Lions, and I felt sick that I wasn't out there. I was being eaten alive by nostalgia."

"What was it you were nostalgic for?" I asked. "The physical aspects?"

"That was a big part of it," he said. "A couple of times at Nebraska I actually *hit* the kids I was coaching. I got so mad that I'd line up opposite them and go at them to show them what it was like. I did it without any pads. It made me feel great."

He noticed me staring at him. "Oh Christ!" he said. "The best thing in football was to really *pop* someone. One of the great joys of my life was to get a bead on a guy and really put him out. Absolutely! To lift him up right under his chin, or under his throat with the top of your helmet and put him on his back on the grass. You've done your job, you've gotten your good grade. The movie's going to show it. That's it. Yes, that's why I came back to the Lions the next year."

"What about the pleasure of winning?"

Gordy thought for a minute, looking at his big hands, and then said a curious thing: "The great pleasure of winning was sitting next to Alex after the game on the stool outside the lockers and realizing that you were free the next day, and that you didn't have to spend twenty-four hours going through the nightmare of rehashing what you did wrong, or worrying why you lost, and that you didn't have anything to fear when it came time to watch the game films on Tuesday. What I'm saying is that part of the joy of winning was that you could just *forget* about it. That's odd, isn't it—that you would go through all that pressure and pain just to forget about it. And, of course, the horror of losing is just the opposite—that you're not going to be *allowed* to forget it. The nightmare. You're stuck with it. You're going to see it in the game films. It's only after the films and being made to run grass drills by the coaches—almost like doing a type of penance—that the nightmare begins to fade. That was the best part of football: not to have nightmares..."

Karras said, "That's right. It made winning awfully sweet. Of course, there were the obvious pleasures—the associations you made."

"That was the best part?" I asked.

He thought awhile. "I guess the best part for me was the thrill I got seeing what great football players can do physically—to see what they *really* can do. It's breathtaking to see Jim Brown do things that the normal player can't. That's why the Pro Bowl game means so much to football players: we get to see the sort of company we keep. I guess the greatest thrill I can remember happened to me in a Pro Bowl game, and hell, it was a play where I didn't do what I was supposed to do. I was the *goat,* really, and yet I'm not sorry...

"In their game plan," Karras went on, "the other team decided that they'd run takeoffs on me every once in a while—that is, influence me by pulling the guard opposite on a sucker play and hoping I'd pursue, which being an aggressive tackle I was likely to do, and then slipping the ball carrier, who was likely to be Jim Brown, into the hole I'd vacated. It's called the 'Oh, shit' play, because that's what the tackle says when he realizes he's been suckered and pulled out of position and the fullback's ripping through his spot.

"Well, I'd been out late the night before—when it's Pro Bowl time in Los Angeles the players aren't much tempted to be in bed at eight—and I'd had a few drinks and I didn't feel good. Consequently, I wasn't as aggressive as I would have been normally; I didn't feel like pursuing that pulling guard. Well, the other team didn't know that, so they called the 'Oh, shit' play, with Jim Brown carrying the ball.

"Next to me in the defensive line, I should add, was Gino Marchetti. Greatest, roughest end there ever was. Brutal. He'd been out with me the night before. *He* had a headache, and *he* wasn't going to be influenced either. So the two of us stayed, and they ran Jimmy Brown right at us. His guards were gone. He had no interference. It's the worst thing that can happen in the sucker play, that the tackle is not influenced. Not only did I have a straight, unimpeded shot at Brown, but so did Marchetti. My greatest desire was to *really* put Brown down—the greatest running back ever—and I was going to *kill* him. So I uncorked as hard as I possibly could. Marchetti must have had the same thought in mind, because he went at Brown like he'd come out of a cannon. Both of us, and we hit him *pow!* You could tell he was hurt. He was knocked back about ten yards, his head snapped, and he was like a buffalo going down; he still had the ball but he was shaking his head. The defensive backs, they saw it too, and they began to swoop down on him, like scavengers, to pick at him. They moved for him, but Marchetti and I, we were savoring what we'd done; we just stood there and gloated.

"Well, something happened. As Brown was going down, he caught himself. He shook his head a couple of times, and as the scavengers were barreling in on him, he regained consciousness and went eighty-six yards for a touchdown! The most fantastic, brilliant run I've ever seen in my life! I stood there, next to Marchetti, and we watched it like spectators. I suppose we should have finished him off when we had the chance. But I don't regret it. It was probably the greatest thrill I've ever had in football."

"I can understand that," Gordy said. "In professional ball, and especially in something like the Pro Bowl, you often ask yourself, What am I doing out here on the field with these great athletes?"

"When I was in the steel mills," Karras said, "the open hearths... well, I can *see* myself there, you know, with a shovel, and talking to Stashakowski. 'How ya doin', Stash?' He says, 'Okay, boy.' I can *see* that; it doesn't surprise me. But to see myself doing the same things those great football players are doing—none of us can really understand or believe that. I've never met a football player who could."

"Absolutely right," said Gordy.

# CHAPTER 3

Karras was staying in town the next day. Gordy was off somewhere, but Alex said he would turn up anyway. He might find some things to say.

When I had been at the Detroit Lion training camp in 1963, it was the year of Karras's banishment from football, for charges of placing small bets on other NFL games. This was substantiated by Karras himself on a radio broadcast, and he was suspended for a season. That summer his teammates did so much reminiscing about Karras that on occasion the training camp took on the aspect of a prolonged wake. Like an uninvited guest at such a ceremony I knew nothing of Karras except by reputation, but because of the endless stories about him he began to solidify in my mind so much that soon I felt a proper mourner at his absence.

The first story about his undergraduate days at Iowa I heard from Dick LeBeau, the cornerback and archivist who collected vivid portraits of his teammates. He would divulge them when he was of a mind—often at such unexpected moments as during a poker game in one of the dormitory rooms where everyone's attention was on the cards—LeBeau's story in his Ohio twang as much a background music to the football players hunched around the card table as the Muzak is to a factory worker.

"When Alex was at Iowa," he would announce abruptly as he sat with his back up against the wall, his guitar across his legs, "Forest Evashevski, the Iowa coach, took him under his wing and tried to make him more comfortable socially."

"Gimme two cards."

"This big homecoming weekend comes along, and Evashevski decides to take Alex to a big sorority dance. Big deal there at Iowa."

"Two dollars."

"He tells Alex to find something complimentary to say about everyone—*that* was the key to social behavior. So Alex arrives at the dance with a paper bag full of sandwiches. That was what *he* was worried about—going hungry..."

"Amos, you son of a bitch, I'm raising you two."

"Alex sits in the back of the dance hall looking out at the girls who all look like drum majorettes, and occasionally he dips a big hand into his paper bag and breaks off a bit of sandwich. All of a sudden—"

"I'll see you."

"—this big girl comes across the dance floor heading straight for him. She has a face that looks like it's blocked a punt. Maybe three or *four* punts. She's damn near bigger than Alex. He doesn't know what to do; he's trapped. So he gets up to dance with her. All the time they move around the floor he's thinking about what Evashevski told him—to find something complimentary to say. But he can't *think* of anything. The music stops, and the two of them stand there just looking at each other. So Alex finally says, 'You know something? You *sweat* less than any fat girl I've ever seen.'"

"Hey, LeBeau, pass me over that can of beer, willya, man?"

I had never asked Karras about that story. I knew it was suspect because Evashevski and Alex did not get along at all, certainly not enough for the Iowa coach to volunteer as social adviser. But it was too nice a line to lose ("You sweat less than any fat girl I've ever seen"), and it would have been a big wrench to have Karras say, "What's LeBeau *talking* about. I don't dance with fat girls—not unless they come up and grab me from behind. The only true part of that story is the paper bag and the sandwiches."

There were others who remembered him at Iowa. Jim Gibbons, who afterward became his teammate at Detroit, remembered Karras's arrival as a freshman. About a hundred of the freshman athletes were gathered for an indoctrination in Hillcrest dormitory when Karras blundered in, looking for his room.

"He'd just arrived," Gibbons told me. "He was overweight then, about two hundred and fifty pounds, but what I remember is that he was carrying his clothes in his arms. The guy had no suitcase. He was carrying his entire wardrobe the way you carry a tray. I didn't know him at all in those years. He was very quiet. You'd look around and he was there, but he was silent.

"The other thing I remember about him was when we filled in the questionnaire giving our background as athletes. Most of us had a line or two to write—State Honorable Mention, that kind of thing. When the rest of us were done, Karras was still slaving on his. He handed in *two pages*. Hell, he was the greatest athlete at any number of sports who ever came out of Indiana."

When Karras arrived at the apartment, we started talking about his early days, and I mentioned what Gibbons had said about him.

"That's right about the other sports," he said. "Wrestling, basketball, baseball. I was good at them." He'd enjoyed baseball and basketball more than football, he said, because his older brothers played very little of either sport, which left the field to him without the anguish of sibling rivalry. Football, on the other hand, threw him into direct confrontation with his brothers, both of whom were not only older but larger. Louis, seven years his senior, was six-four and 250 pounds, and Alex recalled him as "mammoth" almost from his first memories. He had an awesome reputation on the east side of Gary, which was the roughest part of town. "When Louis came around the corner," Karras said, "it was like a whole street gang had turned up. People backed into doorways." Louis went on to play football at Purdue, and then with the Washington Redskins.

The second brother, Teddy, was just sixteen months older than Alex, but also bigger, and tough on his younger brother. He was good enough to go on to play at Indiana, where he was captain, and then professionally with the Chicago Bears.

"I learned to run from Teddy," Alex said. "I hung around with his crowd, and when Louie played we'd go down to the football field to watch. It cost money to get in, so we sneaked in over a tall barbed-wire fence in the back of the stadium. Teddy and his friends would boost me up first, and I'd drop down, ripped by those barbs, and stand on the inside of the fence, waiting for the cops to spot me. Then my job was to run long enough and fast enough, staying ahead of them like the rabbit at the greyhound races, so that Teddy and his friends could get over the fence while the cops were occupied chasing me. Maybe it was the ham in me, but I really liked it—the dodging, the speed, the excitement of it, the crowd yelling and carrying on. It got to be quite a show. The crowd used to wait for me every game, because they knew I'd be dropping down over the fence, and I guess maybe the cops knew, too. They never caught me, but looking back, I guess they enjoyed being part of the show. They ran hard, but some of them wore these big grins..."

He winced. "But football itself—that was another matter. Teddy was real rough on me. I guess *he* was why I didn't like football then. Because though I was never worried about getting hurt, I *was* scared of doing something wrong which would mean that Teddy would sit on me. He was the disciplinarian. Perhaps he didn't want me embarrassing him in front of his friends. He was tough. In fact, Louie stood around and watched to make sure that Teddy didn't kill me."

Karras leaned forward out of his chair and put his hands on his knees. "I remember once years later when the Lions were playing the Chicago Bears, George Halas of the Bears substituted the guard playing in front of me. I was really taking off and popping this new guy, just murdering him. As you know, I don't see well; I just knew he was a guy in a Chicago uniform wearing a black helmet. But then after this real vicious pop I gave him, I heard this voice say, 'Hey Al, it's me. It's your brother. It's Teddy.'

"I've often wondered if subconsciously I didn't somehow know that it *was* Teddy, and that I was making up for all those horrors and that punishment, all those times he'd sat on my head back in those high school days. And maybe it wasn't only Teddy, but all the discipline guys, the guys who blow whistles... That was the man in front of me who I was beating up."

Despite his doubts about football, Karras admitted that he was wondrously good at it during those early years. His father, very weak then, dying of cancer and bundled up in blankets, used to sit out on the upstairs porch and watch his three sons playing in the parking lot, and once he told his youngest that he was going to be the best of them.

"I never could understand why he said that," Karras said. "I couldn't see myself doing as well as Louie and Teddy. I hardly remember my father—I was thirteen when he died—but I remember what he told me as something private we had between us."

By the time he graduated from high school Karras had been selected All-State *four* times—the only instance of this in Indiana—and what is more remarkable, he was selected in successive years at three different positions: guard, offensive end, and fullback in his senior year.

By his senior year over a hundred offers from colleges across the country had come in. "Favors" began to be bestowed. The people at Indiana University sent a crew of professional painters around to spruce up the Karras house; they put up ladders and painted the house from top to bottom. The most persistent offers kept coming in from Florida State, where a new coach had been installed and a crash football-building program was being initiated; letters arrived every week or so urging Karras to come down and see what they had to offer.

"It was very tempting," Karras said. "I'd never been out of Gary—except to Hammond, Indiana, which is eight miles away. I thought, Well, I'll go. I got off the plane in Jacksonville wearing Levi's and an Indiana Athletic Department T-shirt. I had my toothbrush in my back pocket. I don't believe I had any baggage. My idea was that if they saw my Indiana T-shirt they might think I was awful close to going *there,* like being rushed by a fraternity, and then they'd really put on a show to get me to change my mind—a big Cadillac to drive down the beach, pompom girls whisking their pompoms outside my door at night, and a lot of Florida State Athletic T-shirts to wear, along with maybe some nice Mister Jax slacks to go with them. So I got off the plane with no baggage and a big pop-eyed look of expectancy.

"Down at the foot of the ramp I could see the Florida State coach. There was no mistaking him; he was an enormous man, about six-eight, and he was close to three hundred pounds. He was looking eagerly at the door of the plane. At that time I weighed two hundred pounds and was about six feet tall. I thought I was pretty hot stuff, but when I stepped down the ramp, ready to greet this guy, I noticed that *he was looking intently over my shoulder*. He was still looking up at the entrance waiting for some mammoth guy to step into view, some guy who had to bend double to get off the plane and would then straighten up seven feet at the top of the ramp, his eyes blinking in the sunlight—*that* was the guy he expected. Well, I was terribly embarrassed. I didn't know whether to turn around and get back on the plane or pretend I was a porter. I decided I had to introduce myself, and when I reached the bottom of the ramp I walked up and stuck out my hand. His eyes dropped. I could see the tremendous disappointment in them when he realized that I was not the Karras that he had imagined. He drove me to the Florida State campus without saying a word. I stayed there for five days *alone*—nobody even looked in my direction. I never saw the coach again until I went out to the airport to fly home. He was there with some of the other kids from around the country who'd come to look the place over. I thanked him for the five days. 'Gee,' I said to him, 'you never did ask me if I could play football.' He looked puzzled. I think he'd forgotten who I was—somebody's fat cousin, perhaps."

"What finally tipped the scales in favor of Iowa?"

He stirred in his chair. "My brother Louie said it would be best for the family if I went to Iowa. That was all there was to it. There was no malarkey of following family tradition—going to Indiana because

Teddy was there, or Purdue because Louie had gone there. It was a question of expediency. I never asked about it because I didn't want to stir up any mess. The family hadn't had any money since my father's death—he was only forty-eight then—and it was decided that if I went to Iowa things would be easier for them. There was never any question."

"Alex, what would you have done if you'd stayed in Gary?"

"I'd probably be a first helper in the open hearth. I'd have three stripes on my Levi's. I worked in the steel mills every summer when I was a kid. I was a cinder snapper—which means that you bank the furnaces so they won't overflow. Also, you throw in minerals. After it's tested, you're told, 'It needs three teaspoons of zinc.' So you throw the zinc in with a shovel.

"I've had easier jobs. Just before I went to the University of Iowa I was filling doughnuts with jelly at Mister Donut's doughnut shop at two sixty-eight an hour. The owner of the place was a big Indiana booster, and he thought he was doing me a favor by giving me the job."

"How many could you do in an hour?"

"I got up to pretty good," Karras replied. "There was a little machine with a nozzle...I wasn't the manager's best doughnut filler, but I was coming along. Of course, that sort of job was rare. At that time everyone was interested in seeing me play football in college. Naturally they wanted me to be strong as an ox, so I had a lot of hard jobs. I worked for the city late that summer, and they gave me a big jackhammer to operate. I did that for three months. When I'd gone to see the mayor, he'd said, 'No soft job for you, Karras. What's this I hear about you filling doughnuts? Christ Almighty! Hey, Felix! Bring in that jackhammer for Karras. No, the *big* model. You can't lift it? Well, get Harry to help you. Bring that thing on in here. Look out for the coffee table! Now Karras, I want you to take this jackhammer home with you and carry it to work every morning, because we want you to be big and strong so we can be proud of you when you go off to college."

"Jim Gibbons told me that you arrived at Iowa carrying your wardrobe in your hands."

"I didn't have any clothes," Karras said. "I arrived there with two pairs of Levi's, three T-shirts, and my brother's black double-breasted suit I'd graduated in from high school. The kids would ride me, but what could I do? So I went down to the gym and stole seven T-shirts to improve my wardrobe. They had IOWA ATHLETIC DEPARTMENT stenciled on them, and they were brown-colored. The department thought maybe people wouldn't steal their shirts if they had these real shit-brown models. The shirts *didn't* look good, but they were better than what I had. Still, I felt real backward—and I *was* backward. I hated college. I was never part of the system at Iowa. Since I'd come there from a fairly poor family, I always had a chip on my shoulder about people who did have money. When I got there, I went into a shell and just rebelled against everyone. I skipped classes and sat in my room and talked to nobody. I was alone in the world and as glum as a loner can possibly be. The other Iowa players called me 'The Blue Boy.'"

"Didn't you have a roommate?"

"Eventually," Karras said, smiling. "Mike Nahod. 'Big Mesho' we called him. He looks like me, a lot of people think. He was my roommate one year. Big, heavy-set guy. Big Mesho. Yes, he got me out of my shell. But it wasn't very constructive. 'The Tons of Fun' they used to call the two of us. We got kicked out of the dormitory because we tore the place up. We had this big feud with these guys who lived two rooms down the corridor. In between the two rooms was a premed student from Hawaii. A wonderful guy. Every night he was in his room trying to study. We drove him crazy. We were always having these water fights with the guys down the hall, and this premed student would hear something and think there was someone at his door who wanted to see him, maybe a chemistry professor who wanted to compliment him on a paper, and he'd step out... 'Yes?' And *boom!* he'd get hit with a bucket of water, first from one side and then from the other. He was always stepping out into a heavy crossfire. I warned him all the time. He was a terrific guy, but his luck didn't run good. Every time he came out of his room he got hit. I mean, he'd open the door of his room just to sneak a look, just peering down the corridor to see if the coast was clear, and *boom!*—first from one side and then from the other. He was always wet, this guy.

"Finally we got into trouble with the authorities. They said, 'That's enough. There's too much water in the halls. The floors are getting warped. We'll give you one more chance. No more of this or you'll get yourselves kicked out of the dormitory.'

"Well, about a day after we got this ultimatum, Big Mesho and I came in very late, maybe three-thirty in the morning, and we didn't feel much like sleeping, so we dropped in on a friend called Sharman—a gigantic guy, mammoth, about six feet eleven in height—and we borrowed an overcoat of his. Then I got up on Big Mesho's shoulders and I put on this coat so that it hung down over the two of us, and made me about twelve feet tall. It was the damnedest sight you ever saw in your life! We lurched down the corridor and Big Mesho reached out of the overcoat and pounded on the door of the dormitory proctor. He was a sort of Mister Peepers character, about five feet one and he weighed thirty-three pounds. It took quite a while for him to answer the door, and we waited there, rocking back and forth. Finally, he opened the door. He had this little kimono on, and from Big Mesho's shoulders I could look down and see the top of his head. Then he looked up the long length of this overcoat, and when he saw me looking down at him, his mouth opened and out came this little high scream. 'Waaaaa!' It scared Big Mesho. He turned and began running. I hollered, 'Big Mesho, look out!' But he couldn't see where he was going, or maybe he forgot that with me on his shoulders the two of us were ten or twelve feet tall, and he ran me right into a gigantic light fixture hanging from the ceiling. I hit it with my head, and the whole damn thing came down—a beautiful thing, about five hundred dollars' worth of light fixture. Well, that was it. They gave us the thumb.

"I finally found a place to live over an Italian restaurant where I set the all-time record for eating submarine sandwiches. Ten, I think it was. That's when my weight began to balloon up. The college authorities began to worry. They could see that I was getting so huge that I'd be useless as a football player. So they set these conditions. My place was about six miles from the campus. So the authorities made me run to class. Then I ran to the stadium for practice. Then back to class, then back to the stadium for more practice, and then finally home. The authorities were very pleased. The trouble was that when I got home I went down to the back of the Italian restaurant where I hoped nobody would see me and ordered up ten submarine sandwiches."

"What sort of campus jobs did the authorities have you doing for your scholarship?" I asked.

"I was very much into the arts," Karras said.

"The arts?"

"That's right. I was an usher at an art-film theater. I spent twelve hours a day watching foreign movies. In fact, I got my foreign language credits—French and German—out of that experience. It was a lonely time, a real lonely scholarship. I spent all that time in the movie house with six people with long hair and thick glasses staring at films where these very sad men and women wandered around in large gardens among the statues. Sometimes they actually spoke, and that was when you had to really pay attention, though it was all right if you missed it because they were almost sure to say the same thing again.

"But I was also into the other arts at Iowa—especially painting. One of the scholarship jobs I had during the summer when I came back to the college to make up the courses I'd flunked during the winter was to paint the football stadium. The authorities gave me a bucket and a brush—a long green brush. I went out to the fifty yard line and looked up at all those seats—fifty thousand of them—and it was there that I coined the phrase that all stadium painters use to this day: 'My God, where do I begin?' "

"Where *did* you begin?"

"I painted the base of the goalposts. I painted a few seats. I wasn't in any big rush. My idea was to paint one seat with a lot of care, six or seven coats, so that the son of a bitch really *glowed,* rather than do a half-ass job on a lot of seats. That summer I only worked on one or two seats."

"I see."

"I was also into sculpture. In fact, I was enrolled in a sculpture course. The authorities gave me a job in that class. There was a big wooden box with water and clay in it, where the clay was kept moist overnight, and my job was to dig out a big lump of clay for each student as he came by on his way in. I wore a little bib. That was my job; it was all I had to do in the course. The instructor said, 'Come in every day, Karras, and pass out the clay. That's all you have to do to get through the course satisfactorily. You'll get a good passing mark.' He didn't think I had any talent for sculpture. He didn't try me out or anything; he just figured that I was a football player and couldn't do anything else. Well, that was all right with me. So the students would disappear with their lumps of clay behind a partition, and when they were all in there with the instructor I would take off my bib and have a couple of Cokes down at the local drugstore. I'd check my watch from time to time, and when the class was over I'd be back at my wooden box with my bib on to get the clay back from the students. I did okay, and one day the instructor said, 'Karras, you're doing fine. The way you're coming along you'll be getting a better grade than just passing. Keep it up.'

"For five weeks I never went behind the partition. Then one day this girl came hurrying in. She was late. I'd noticed her before, though she'd never come by my box and asked for a lump of clay. She was very strange-looking and beautiful, and she wore a long housecoat that came down below the knees. Well, as she rushed into the room behind the partition she shucked off this coat; it just fell away from her shoulders to a heap on the floor behind her, and she was *bare naked*. I mean, there was her ass twinkling into the other room.

"Well, I went rushing in there behind her, with my bib on and all, to see what was going on—the first time I was ever in the classroom—and she was in the middle of this huge circle of little tables, with a student sitting at each one with his lump of clay in front of him, and they were *sculpturing* her. They had been doing that for five weeks and I didn't know it!

"I rushed out and got myself a lump of clay and I took over one of those little tables right up close and started working. No more cokes down at the corner drugstore, nossir! I didn't know what I was doing, but I had a good time. That's the truth. I got a B in that course. It was called Anatomical Sculpture."

"Did you ever turn out a sculpture?"

"Of course I did," Karras said. "I did a frog."

"A frog?"

"The lump of clay looked a little like a frog when I set it down on the table. So I punched at it a bit and painted it green and sent it to my mother in Gary. She still has it. It sits in the house somewhere. It's huge—about ten inches across and quite flat. It weighs seven or eight pounds. People ask my mother, 'What's that thing over there?' 'That's Al's frog,' she says. She's very proud of it."

"What other courses did you take?"

"It always seemed like I was in the basic courses. I was in basic English for three years. I was in general math for three years, too. I flunked the final exam so badly that they kicked me out and made me come back to summer school. What happened about that final math exam was that I was in a fraternity with this math whiz named Phil Lawson. He was a real tall guy, with big thick glasses, and he was a typical fraternity brother—I mean he just loved it. He was a real *good* guy; he got straight As and Bs, and he came from a fine family and all that. Well, I was having such trouble with math that on the final test I had to get a B to pass the course. There was just no way I could get a B in that exam on my own. In fact, on my own I would have been pushed to get a D minus. I was horrible at math. So I went to Phil and said, 'Phil, if I don't get a B in this final, I'm going to flunk the course. And if I flunk the course, then I won't be eligible for football, which will be bad for the fraternity.' He said, 'Oh my.' He was one gigantic dope. So I said, 'Here's what we're going to do. We'll go to the examination together. You get an exam and I'll get an exam. I won't put anything down on my exam paper. You put my name down and *you* do my test paper. Make sure you don't get an A. Just get a solid C for me, and then I'll talk my way into a B for the course.' He said, 'Oh my!' I kept conning him, and finally he said, 'All right.' He was a real fidgety guy, but I kept calming him down. I said, 'Don't worry, Phil. You'll be all right. All you got to do is get a C.' He said, 'That isn't what's bothering me. It's the *principle.*' I said, 'Think how bad it will be for the university, and for the *fraternity,* for Chrissakes, if I can't play football. *There's* your principle for you.' For a week I kept talking to him in order to build up his confidence.

"Finally the day came for the examination, and we went in together and got our exam papers. I whispered to Phil to sit way in the back and I'd go sit in the front row. So the exam started, and all these students started scribbling away in their books. I scribbled away too—playing tic-tac-toe, and drawing some rabbits, and thinking of the girl in Anatomical Sculpture, and just smearing up the paper because what I was going to do when the exam was over was hide mine and hand in Phil Lawson's with my name on it.

"So we're all slaving away, me with my rabbits and tic-tac-toes, and Phil up there behind me working on my solid C, when all of a sudden I heard this *proctor,* some assistant instructor who'd been prowling up and down the aisle making sure that students weren't cheating—I heard him say in this terrible loud voice, 'Phil Lawson, what are *you* doing here?' It was a good question, because Phil was an advanced mathematics major and was into calculus and crap like that, so it was a big surprise to find him taking an exam not much more advanced than long division. My heart just about stopped. I heard Phil say, 'Oh my. I'm sorry, I'm sorry. I'm in the wrong place,' and I turned around in time to see him bolting from the room. He just ripped out of there like a big dog was after him. So what was I to do? I had to hand in the paper that was covered with rabbits and tic-tac-toes. I used to wonder what they made of it—the professors—sitting correcting the papers and mine coming up. 'Hey Charles, I wonder if you'd take a look at this.' So I flunked that test and they kicked me out and made me come back to summer school. Poor Phil was scared half to death."

"What was it about the football program at Iowa that was so dismaying to you?" I asked.

"The coaches," he said. "Forest Evashevski was the head coach, and Bob Flora was the line coach, a big bald-headed man who always rubbed his neck with his hand as he talked to you. He'd run it right around his shirt collar like it was strangling him. We didn't get along from the start. Maybe he resented Iowa paying so much to get me to go there—I don't know. Anyway, the first time he saw me he called me 'Grease-ball' because he knew I was Greek. The next time he saw me he called me 'Poolroom Johnny' because he found out that I was from Gary. There wasn't any humor in this; he was trying to make me feel low. That was a characteristic of his, and I think what he liked best in life was being Evashevski's hatchet man and being asked to tell a player that he was being cut or losing his scholarship money. He always did this with a tremendous smile on his face."

"What about Evashevski?"

"A big, tall, egotistical blond," Karras said, "who had this enormously low voice that used to scare the hell out of people. He always told you first thing that he was the blocking back in the Michigan backfield who'd made Tom Harmon great. That always got into the first or second minute of conversation, whether he was talking to a thirteen-year-old kid or a grandmother in her nineties. You'd see these people getting puzzled as they listened to him, like he was talking in some weird code. They probably didn't know who Harmon was—or what a blocking back was, for that matter. His ego came on especially strong on the day of the games, when he dressed up in a long tan coat with a fur collar. The team would spend its last hours before a game lying on mattresses in a sort of ballroom at the local motel, looking up at the ceiling and getting psyched up for the game, and then Evashevski would make this tremendous entrance, striding through the double doors with his tan coat and fur collar and that voice that sounded like the bottom notes on an organ. He and I didn't get along. He started siding with Flora and began calling me 'Greaseball.' He called me that once in the locker room, and I threw a shoe at him and got up to go after him. But everybody grabbed me. I don't know why he thought he had so much social status that he could look down on me like that. He comes from Detroit, and I called up a friend from there once when I was at college and found out that he was Polish. So I said to him, 'Why do you call me Greaseball. Hell, you're a Polack!' 'The hell I am,' he said. 'I'm *Russian*.' "

"Russian!"

"Correct," Karras said.

"When did you begin to have trouble with Evashevski?"

"In my sophomore year," Karras said. "When I got back to school I was fifteen pounds overweight, and he and Flora began blowing whistles at me—making me run in place, stopping and starting, stopping and starting, for half an hour after practice to try to get that weight off. They seemed to enjoy doing it—Flora especially, who had this big wide grin on his face like he'd stepped out of a Nazi horror film. You know my hatred of whistles, how when anybody blows a whistle—even a little girl with pigtails—I'm like as not to rear up and *stomp!* All that first month they blew the whistles. Then in a scrimmage I cracked my ankle. It never got better and for weeks I limped like crazy on it. They kept me going. I played the entire opening game against Wisconsin on that ankle. Bobby Knovsky was opposite me—we teamed up later when I got into wrestling—and he beat the hell out of me, the worst physical beating I ever got in my life. I don't know why they didn't take me out. I was embarrassing, pathetically bad. Flora had to be nuts."

"What did Evashevski do?"

"He benched me. He came around to my locker after the game and said that he had never seen anyone play so bad. So I asked him why he didn't substitute me. That was the end for me that year. He benched me, and the team began to slide downhill."

Sitting in his chair, Karras looked distraught. "Those were the blue times," he said. "I spent those long times lying on the bed in my room and looking at the ceiling and thinking those bad thoughts about Evashevski and Flora."

"What happened the following year—your junior year?"

"Well, I came in at two hundred and ten pounds and a thirty-two-inch waist, and no one on the team recognized me. That wasn't surprising, because no one knew who I was anyway. They said, 'Who's that flanker standing over there? Who's the thin bird?' They started me out on the fourth string. I was eager for it. I wanted to show Evy and Flora what a pair of clowns they were. I tore up a guy's knee and went to the third string, then to the second, and in the final scrimmage I played such a great game that those two dummies told me I was going to start against Indiana.

"It was one of the first times I ever felt good about anything at Iowa, especially since my brother Teddy was the captain at Indiana. The newspapers were full of it—how the two brothers would be playing against each other in the line. My mom came down for the game, and so did Louie, and I knew they were watching me, and then just before kickoff Evy hollers out 'Burroughs!' and they start Burroughs at my tackle spot.

"I died—I absolutely just died. I sat there in this cold rage on the bench. Then after about two minutes Evy walked over and sent me in and I played for fifty-eight minutes. I played both ways, offense and defense, and I just slaughtered the people opposite. I played a little opposite Teddy, but not as much as I would have liked because I owed him a few whacks. We won the game, thirty-five to nothing.

"Afterward Evy came around to my locker. I was still in a rage about his sending in Burroughs, and I told him so. He grinned and he said that he had done it for psychological reasons. Well, I came off my stool and I told him that he could take his psychological crap and shove it back where it came from—real *pissed* I was, and damned if I didn't leave the campus and take off for Gary. I was real screwed up, and thinking back on it I must have been close to a nervous breakdown."

"How do you make any sort of accommodation with someone who drives you to a condition like that?"

"I told Evy that I would only come back to Iowa and play football on the condition that he and Flora laid off me. In fact, the condition was that they could not say *one word to me.* So they promised. And they kept to it, too; they left me alone. It worked fine. I made All-American and we won the Big Ten title and the Rose Bowl. As a coach Evy was fine. That team, and the one he put together the next year, in fifty-seven, were as good as any in the history of football."

"And he never said a word?"

"Finally after my last game Evy came up as we were walking off the field, and he talked to me for the first time in a year. He said, 'I want you to know that when you first came up to the varsity as a sophomore I wouldn't have taken ten cents for you; now I wouldn't take a hundred thousand dollars.' I looked at him and said, 'Evy, as far as I'm concerned, you're still a dumb Polack.' "

Not long after that conversation, I found out where Forest Evashevski was living—now out of football, he had settled down in Petoskey, Michigan, where he was in the real-estate business—and one morning I could not resist calling him up on the phone. I had mixed feelings about doing so, because he was so definitively established as a thorn in Karras's attitude about football that I did not relish having it blunted by whatever his old coach might say.

When Evashevski came on the phone his voice was deep, and I jotted down "organ-like." I told him I wanted to ask him some questions about Karras and he said he'd answer them, though he seemed slightly reserved at the start. Karras had published some reminiscences about his Iowa days in a Detroit newspaper, in which he had publicly criticized Evashevski. The silences at the other end were long and cool. I wondered vaguely how long it would be before he warmed up enough to tell me that he had been Tom Harmon's blocking back.

I began by asking him about Dick LeBeau's story—whether he had indeed taken Karras under his wing at Iowa and tried to help him socially. But I wasn't more than halfway into the story about the big sorority dance and the fat girl when Evashevski interrupted. "Is that the story with the line, 'You sweat less than any fat girl I've ever met'?"

"Why, yes," I said, surprised. "That's right. Then it's true?"

"No," he said. "That's a real old chestnut. That's a story that's been around for years. I'd be very surprised if it originated with Karras."

"Oh? Well, I'd never heard it," I said lamely.

I could hear him breathing easily on the other end of the phone.

"What about the relationship between you and Alex?" I asked after a pause. "I understand that it was... well, *strained.*"

"I've heard and read all those things in the Detroit paper Alex has said about me and about Flora. There's not much truth to them. Sometimes I think he went to a different school and played under different coaches."

"Oh?"

"I can't pretend that I was easy on him that sophomore year. I never lettered him. That hurt. Perhaps I invited his antipathy," Evashevski went on somewhat formally, "by riding him into greatness. He could have remained fat and sassy and coasted through life if someone hadn't come along to goad him. Perhaps his reaction is based on resentment that he ever *had* to be goaded."

"What happened in his sophomore year?"

"I think someone did Alex a terrible disservice," Evashevski said. "After his freshmen year he must have been told that if he wanted to go on into professional football he was going to have to put on more weight—that to be a defensive lineman you had to be real big and weigh two hundred and seventy pounds. That was crazy advice because Alex's God-given natural ability was based entirely on quickness and agility, not on strength or weight. Whether someone actually *did* advise him to put on weight or not, I don't know; I *do* know that in his sophomore year a football player that I expected to come in to school at maybe two hundred and twenty pounds turned up a fatty at over *two sixty.* His ankles gave out; they couldn't hold up all that weight. We were rough on him. Once I put a hunting jacket on him with fifteen pounds of lead weight in the pockets and made him wear it through practice, just to show him what *fifteen* pounds of extra weight felt like. He resented all that—who wouldn't? But I don't apologize for how I handle football players, much less Karras."

"What about the time you started Burroughs against Indiana?" I asked. "The psychological move that got Karras so angry he went back to Gary after the game."

"I don't remember that," Evashevski replied. "I certainly wouldn't have done it for psychological reasons. I suspect that we must have received the kickoff and our offensive team went out on the field first. Alex played both ways, but he really wasn't very good as an offensive tackle. His great true gift was to move and pursue. Burroughs was probably a better equipped offensive player."

"What about the conditions that Karras laid down in his junior and senior year? That he'd only play if you laid off him, and that no words—"

"That's not true," Evashevski interrupted. "No player who ever played for me laid down conditions. He played only under my terms."

"Oh?"

"No coach could operate under such conditions—players telling him what to do. It never happened."

"What about calling him Greaseball, and a shoe being thrown and all that?"

"Never happened. Perhaps Flora called him one, but I doubt it. After all, Flora's Italian..."

"Well, I really don't understand," I said after a long silence.

Evashevski could sense my distraction. "I'm sorry I have to discredit what he's been telling you. I should say that I have complete respect for Karras as a football player. He was a *fine* player. That part of him I understood."

"I wonder if some players to be truly great need to do this sort of thing—construct a collection of fall guys, some sort of imaginary nemesis they can challenge and overcome."

"I don't know," said Evashevski. "The psychological aspects of football are invariably puzzling. I've misread players and teams so many times. There are some players who can sing songs in the shower before a game. All I say is, 'Bless 'em!'—for whatever it is they have to do to prepare for a game as long as they can execute for you."

"One last question," I said. "What is the extraction of the name Evashevski?"

"You mean what nationality?"

"Yes."

"It's Polish," Evashevski said.

"What?"

"That's right. Polish. My mother's side of the family was Scottish, and my father's Bohemian and Polish. You sound surprised."

"No," I said. "Not really."

# CHAPTER 4

Gordy was saying, "The first time I ever saw Karras at the Detroit Lions, I remember thinking that he should have been wearing a beanie with a propeller on it."

The author poses for a photo with his subjects, Alex Karras (middle) and John Gordy (left). (*Walter Iooss Jr.*)

Karras stirred in his chair. "What the hell are you talking about?"

"That's right. You came in and sat down on the team bus. Your hair was real short and your face was round as a pumpkin, and I remember thinking how round and big it was and that it needed a beanie and propeller on top. You also looked scared."

"All the new people were scared," said Karras. "We were scared of the veterans, and especially Bobby Layne."

Bobby Layne was the team leader then, a veteran Texas-gamecock quarterback whose imprimatur on the team, a type of roustabout devil-may-care attitude, lasted long after his departure. He was a supreme individualist, even to his equipment on the field—delicate little pasteboard shoulder pads and an old-fashioned helmet that looked as if it had been plucked off the head of Red Grange.

"Know something?" Karras said. "The coaches never liked Layne much. He trampled on their authority. When he was on the field, it was his field, not theirs. The coaches would work these plays out on the blackboard, precise diagrams which they'd copy into the playbooks for the players to study and learn, and then down on the practice field Layne would give a little yawn and say, 'Hey, George, tell that boy over theah when he makes that outside cut, to take it about fahv more feet deep. Heah?' The coaches didn't like that sort of thing. It made them look like fools. But they went along with it, because they knew that nobody knew quarterbacking like Layne."

"He knew that," Gordy said. "*That's* for sure. But what he especially knew was how to make life miserable for the rookies. Jesus!"

Karras nodded. "My rookie year in training camp Layne got ahold of me and he said, 'Rookie, from now on you just follow me around like a puppy.' In fact, that's what he called me for a while: 'Puppy.' Then he changed it to 'Tippy.'

"I was his personal chauffeur. He'd come out of the team meeting and holler for me down the dormitory corridors. I tried to hide from him. Under the bed—anywhere. But he'd find me and I'd have to pick his car up and bring it around front. We'd start off at nine o'clock and go downtown and hit about thirteen bars. He'd drink nothing but Cutty Sark whisky and water ('Jes' pass me along a Cutty and water') and he'd make me drink with him. I never drank like that before in my life."

"Did you have to pay for all that booze?" Gordy asked.

"I never paid for a thing; I just had to chauffeur. Sometimes he'd drive—mostly when I was too sick from drinking to be the chauffeur. One night he was driving and I was sitting beside him holding my head in my hands. He was happy. He was singing 'Ida Red.' That was his favorite song, though he only knew two or three phrases from it, which he'd sing over and over. I looked across at him and when my head cleared I could see that he had his right foot up on the dashboard, and his left leg *out the window*. He had something jammed in the accelerator which held it right to the floor, because we were doing about one hundred miles per hour, the car just shaking itself to pieces, down the expressway, and there he was, leaning back in his seat, his legs straddled out in front of him, singing 'Ida Red' to beat the band, and I'm telling you I got down off the seat on my knees and *begged* him to stop the car. But he wouldn't.

"We survived that trip, how I don't know. I woke up for a few nights screaming at the ceiling. So after that I tried to chauffeur no matter how much Cutty and water I had in me. Sometimes I rested my chin on the steering wheel and drove four miles an hour. He didn't seem to mind. He used to sit in the backseat alone sometimes, and sometimes up in the front with me. There'd be maybe two or three guys he used to run with, but most of the time we were by ourselves. He always liked me for some reason. I guess I showed him a lot of respect. I just stayed drunk. For six weeks of training camp I was drunk all the time—drunk and *sick*. We never got any sleep. We'd come back at six in the morning and climb in the goddamn window. I'd get an hour's sleep. Breakfast at seven-thirty. Morning practice. Then I'd get a few hours of sleep before afternoon practice. I used to reek, just *reek* of booze. People thought I liked it. I hated it, but I had to: Cutty and water, hour after hour. The crazy thing was that *he'd* turn up at practice and it was, 'Let's go, men. Let's go here. Snap. Snap. Let's get *going* here.' He'd work his ass off, just cool and rough, while I was reeling around and breathing hard and throwing up all the time.

"He never could go to bed. He told me a number of times, 'I don't like the dark. I'm scared to go to sleep.' Someone told me once that when he was a kid, about seven years old, a car he was riding in with his father turned over out in the Texas backcountry, and his father was killed. Layne spent two days and two nights sitting by that upside-down car with his father inside, until they found him. I don't know if that story's true, but if it is, I can imagine why the dark scared him and he didn't want to sleep."

"Where'd you used to go with him?" Gordy asked.

"After afternoon practice I'd drive him—he had this old Pontiac—to a place called the Bar-B-Que, which later burned down, and he'd drink six or seven Cutty and waters. Then I'd drive him back to camp and we'd eat the evening meal. After that, we'd set off again and drink until it was time for the team meeting. Then after the team meeting we'd go out into the night and hit any number of places. One of them was this wild place called The Flame, and when we walked in, the crowds would stand up and yell, 'Mr. Layne's here!' and they'd go crazy. Nobody took any note of me. I was just a flunky. That's what you had to go through as a rookie."

"Remember Birmingham, Alabama?" Gordy asked. "First pro football game I ever started in. Layne was the quarterback. They had no facilities at the ballpark, so we got into our uniforms in the hotel and rode out to the stadium in a bus. An exhibition game against the Washington Redskins. I had to play against Gene Brito, the great end. He was on my back that whole game. I couldn't pass-block worth a damn. He just killed me. Layne kept yelling at me in the huddle, 'Hey, keep that guy *off* me!' Well, I'd been in the Lions camp two weeks and I didn't know anything. I was just being humiliated. I never wanted to kill anyone so much in my life.

"After the game we got on the bus to go back to the hotel. I sat there, blood all over me, and sweat, with my mouth hanging open, and thinking how bad I'd been humiliated. Then, as we're getting off the bus in front of the hotel, Layne says to me, 'Gordy, you're going downtown and buy us a case of beer.' I wanted to punch him right in the mouth."

Karras laughed. "Yeah, I'll bet that's just what you did—belted him one."

"So I said, 'Yessir,'" Gordy continued easily. "'I'll go upstairs in the hotel and change out of this uniform—'

"'No,' Layne said. 'To hell with changing. Go out and get me a case of beer. I want it *now*.'

"Well, I had to walk the streets of Birmingham, or Montgomery, or Mobile, some damn place like that..."

"One of those 'I hate everything' towns," Karras said.

"...looking for a case of beer in my football outfit. Carrying my helmet by the strap, the cleats of my football shoes making this big clopping sound against the pavement, covered with blood, everyone on the street staring at me, you know, and when I turned into this store the guy in there almost fainted dead away. I still had my teeth out—they were back in the hotel room—and when I asked the guy 'Could I have a case of beer?' he must have thought it was a robbery or whatever. He said, 'Here, take it.' I said I'd come back and pay as soon as I got to the hotel and changed into street clothes. It didn't seem to make any difference to him. 'Here, take it,' he kept saying.

"So I took the case back to the hotel. I delivered it to Layne, and then I went upstairs to my room, lay down on the bed, picked up the phone, called my wife in Nashville, and said 'I'll be home next weekend.' Swear to God! And I started crying. I did! I thought I'd let my father down. I'd let my mother down. I'd let my wife down. I'd let everybody down. I'd been chewed out by Bobby Layne. And now I was supposed to go back to Detroit to training camp and sleep on the third floor of a boys' school on a mattress shaped like a hayloft and get up the next morning and stand on a chair in the dining room and sing 'Oh

Tennessee,' the veterans all yelling at me, and go to practice and try to learn how to pass-block when I knew damn well that I could *never* learn such a thing. I'm telling you, sometimes football is the toughest thing in the world to make yourself continue to do."

Karras stirred. "One time we were in Norman, Oklahoma—you remember that game against Chicago I told you about when all those guys got hurt. Well, I have a real phobia about bugs and mice and stuff like that."

"About what?" I asked, startled.

"Bugs especially," Karras said. "I just go crazy with that stuff. Well, there we were—in Norman, Oklahoma, in August. It must have been a hundred and ninety-five thousand degrees hot. I started sweating my ass off as soon as we arrived there. I was wearing a heavy pair of pants—my old woollies. I had on a sports coat about an inch thick. I was really living.

"Well, we got to the hotel, which had a screen door in front which was covered with these giant green grasshoppers—it looked like an army of praying mantises! They were all going *z-z-z-z-z-z-z*. Jesus Christ! So I got by them into the hotel, and I said, 'That's it for me. I'm not going anywhere. I can't stand those bugs.' So I went up to my room, and I decided to stay there all night. I had a hamburger sent up. To show you how cheap the hotel was, the hamburger only cost twenty-three cents. I got undressed. There wasn't even a TV set in the room. I turned on the radio. 'Howdy folks. This is your ol' pardnuh . . .' I lay on the bed just sweating my ass off. There was no air-conditioning in that place, and the sweat just poured off. I was thinking about the Chicago Bears. About two-thirty in the morning I was just getting ready to go to sleep when the telephone by the bed rang and it was Bobby Layne's ol' gravel voice at the other end. 'Tippy,' he said, 'get up here.'

"I said, 'Yes, sir. Where are you, sir?'

"He said, 'I'm up on the sixth floor.'

"So I said, 'Okay, sir. I'll be right up there.'

"So I put on my old woollies and the sports coat that was one inch thick, and my big tie, and I gave myself a quick glance in the mirror. My! I had a flattop haircut. I really looked terrible—though at the time, of course, I thought I looked real flashy."

Gordy laughed. "You with a round face and a flattop!"

"And this huge wide tie," Karras went on. "Which wasn't 'in' at that time. It was Teddy's old tie. I scampered up the stairs about four flights and knocked on the door. Harley Sewell answered it. Offensive guard. He just hated me—always detested me. I don't know why, but he did. They were drinking beer. Cans all over the place. How they could drink that beer! Jesus! They were all sitting around, all that clique. I walked in with my head down, and Layne said, 'Tippy, we want hamburgers.'

" 'Yes, sir,' I said. 'The hotel has them. They cost twenty-three cents.'

" 'The hotel kitchen's closed down,' he said. 'You'll have to go out for them.'

" 'Yes, sir,' I said. 'How many hamburgers would you like?'

"Well, they ordered up about fifteen of them, all different, some with pickles on the side, relish, cheeseburgers, every variety they could think up. Layne gave me some money. I said, 'Sir, do you know where in Norman there are any hamburger places open?'

"He said, 'No, goddamn it, find one.'

"They closed the door on me. I thought, Well, here I go. I had to walk out where those bugs were. It was about three in the morning by then. I gave myself a little running start and got out through the door with the praying mantises waiting on the screen. But outside these other bugs started hitting me. They started pounding off my glasses. They got into my sports coat that was one inch thick. They landed on my brother's old tie. I tried brushing them off as I walked. I said, 'Oh man. Where am I going?' There was nothing. I looked around and all I could see was darkness, maybe a streetlight shining way off in the distance. A quiet Southern town, except for a freight train miles away and the humming of the bugs. Boy, was I hot! Finally I took my coat off. I began to trot along. I thought of those guys waiting back in the hotel, drinking out of the beer cans and getting hungry and looking at the door, waiting for it to open with me there, holding a big paper bag with their hamburgers. After I'd covered about two miles, I saw this little beat-up place that said EAT on it. Now it was three-thirty or four. So I went in — there wasn't a soul in the place, just this thin guy with glasses behind the counter — and I ordered up fifteen different kinds of hamburgers. The guy really looked scared. He knew I hadn't come in by car or anything; he'd have heard the motor. I'd just come in out of the night. What did he think, seeing this big guy standing there with these wool pants? Maybe he thought I was going to sit right down there at the counter and eat my way through all those crazy sandwiches, all fifteen of them. He cooked them up, though, and then he handed me this big paper bag, with the grease beginning to stain the bottom. Man, that was a bad place. I said to myself, 'I'm late. I'd better run back.' So I started running. Hot as a bitch. Bugs all over me. I'm just dying. I got to the hotel and through the screen door with all the praying mantises on it and ran up to the sixth floor.

I knocked on the door for about five minutes, and Harley Sewell finally opened it.

" 'What do you want?' he asked.

" 'I've got all these hamburgers,' I said.

" 'We all went to bed,' Sewell said. 'Goddamn it.' And he slammed the door on me.

"So there I was with this big bag of burgers at four-thirty in the morning, standing in the hotel corridor, looking at a closed door. I went down to my room, threw the paper bag in the corner, and went to bed. I suppose the cleaning woman must have found them the next day when I was out playing the Chicago Bears. I wonder what she thought. Jesus! Maybe she thought the guy who'd been in that room was a real big eater, some guy who weighed about five hundred pounds, and in this paper bag was a sort of snack he'd left behind by mistake."

"Maybe the bugs got to the sandwiches," Gordy suggested. "Maybe there wasn't anything left in the paper bag."

"Wouldn't surprise me," said Karras.

"I'll never forget the bugs in Norman, Oklahoma," Gordy said. "We played the Philadelphia Eagles there. Remember? The playing field in Norman looks nice and fresh and green, but when you hit the ground on a tackle or a block, it comes alive—*z-z-z-z-z*—these bugs coming out of there. Sweat bugs, I think they are. You get terribly tired playing in that awful heat in Norman, but you don't relax lying around on the ground, nossir! The bugs will get you. If you get hit to the ground, you jump up as fast as you can. God's truth! You hardly ever see anyone lying on the ground in Norman, Oklahoma."

"We got beat horrible in that Eagle game," Karras said. "I recall it."

"It was the biggest Chinese fire drill I've ever been in," Gordy said. "We got beat so bad it was funny. Earl Morrall and I, the only veterans, and *nine* rookies started the game. Nineteen fifty-nine. I was playing left tackle and the defensive end opposite me kept spinning in one place, and then hitting me again. I never did figure that out. He'd hit, spin in a circle, and then hit again. We were all horrible. The defense had to come in every two or three downs. And most of *them* were rookies, too."

"Yeah, I remember," Karras said. "I did a lot of laughing behind my hand."

"And it was hot," Gordy continued. "But the place was packed with people. Big occasion in Norman. Right behind our bench was a box with the governor in it, and the lieutenant governor, and Bud Wilkinson, who was the Oklahoma coach then, and Gomer Jones, who became the head coach later on, and all their wives. These dignitaries were practically on the bench with us, watching us getting beat, and Joe Schmidt, sitting right in front of them, was getting more and more embarrassed. He and the other regulars hadn't played. He kept shouting at Coach Wilson, 'Haven't you seen enough of those goddamn rookies?'

"Finally, along in the fourth quarter, Wilson says, 'Okay, Joe, get your group in there.'

"Joe jumps up. 'About time!' he shouts. He's really ready to go. He's going to show everybody, especially those dignitaries. He looks around. 'Where's my helmet?' He looks under the bench. 'Who's got my helmet?'

The players are all looking at him—*they* don't have his helmet. What do they want his helmet for? They've got their helmets on. They're ready to go out on the field. Joe's looking everywhere."

"He must have thought the bugs ate it," Karras said.

Gordy could hardly tell the story he was laughing so hard. "Oh Christ!" he said. "Oh my. 'Where's my helmet?' Joe kept shouting. Oh Jesus! What the dignitaries had to be thinking! Schmidt began looking in their *box,* which was right there. He was frantic. 'Where's my motherfucking helmet?' he shouted. 'Who's got it?' The wives all shrank back. They didn't want to have anything to do with him."

"Yeah, that was funny," said Karras. "Norman was some town—something crazy always happened when we went there, especially if Bobby Layne was along."

"What about today?" I asked. "Do the rookies defer to you like you did to Bobby Layne in those days—I mean 'Yes, sir' and all of that?"

"No respect," said Gordy. "They come equipped with these huge egos, big money and reputations, and they're not going to take any nonsense." He got up and began pacing around the apartment. "What they're chiefly rebelling against is that first restrictive year we all went through—under the rule of those authority figures like Bobby Layne who made us get up in the dining room and sing our school songs and generally treated us like dirt. The rookies today refuse to do that, and it's a shame because it made you feel a much stronger part of the team after you'd gone through it. The greatest thrill of my life was coming back my second year and suddenly being patted on the back and *accepted,* even by Layne."

"Didn't *anyone* rebel in your day?" I asked.

The two looked at each other. "Remember Carl Smith?" Gordy asked. "He played fullback at the University of Tennessee. He came to training camp in nineteen fifty-four. The singing was going on in the dining room, but Carl was never there. So a group of us looked in on him in his room and he was sitting at a desk, without a plate or anything, eating out of a brown paper bag! In it were mashed potatoes."

"And gravy!" Karras added.

"Yes, and gravy, and meat—all jumbled up in this brown bag, and he had a spoon in his drawer. It still had food on it. He would eat his food there simply because he didn't want to get up and sing in the dining room. The only time he ever wanted to face a veteran was on the football field. There, at least, he was confident of what he was doing. Of course that's a mild sort of rebellion compared to today."

"Did he ever make the team?"

"Never made it," said Karras. "Probably ate too much paper."

"Were the veterans ever helpful in your first year?" I asked. "Gil Mains was your predecessor, wasn't he?"

"Yes, 'the Horse' we called him," Karras said. "I remember the first league game I was going to start as defensive tackle was against the Cleveland Browns. At that time they had an offensive guard named Harold Bradley. I knew about him. He'd played at Iowa—it seemed like at least twenty-five years before *I* got there. A big black guy. Just huge! I remember he used to come back to Iowa every once in a while, and I'd hang around and just *stare* at him.

"Well, I went into consultation with the Horse. I was embarrassed to ask him because he was hurt, and he was probably figuring I was trying to take his job, but I reckoned it was a question of survival. So I asked him, 'What can I expect?' He started talking about Bradley. 'Alex, he's probably the strongest guard I've ever seen in my life. He's going to kill you. You're not going to get past him. He's going to make you look foolish.' Well, *that* wasn't the sort of stuff I wanted to hear. I began thinking of leaving camp!"

"Didn't he give you any advice?"

"Yes. He said that the only thing I was never going to have to worry about playing against Bradley and the Browns was traps. 'Never worry about traps,' he said. 'They never trap.' Well, when I got in that game, they trapped me forty-three times, I swear."

"That's typical," Gordy said. "Those guys really made you work things out for yourself. It wasn't easy, but maybe you were the better for it."

The two of them sat quietly, thinking back on those days. Finally Karras said, “You know something crazy? Bobby Layne was traded away by Detroit to the Pittsburgh Steelers. He ended up his career there. We played them one Sunday, and this play came up where he was chased out of the pocket and ran out-of-bounds. I was chasing him, really reaching for him, and when we got out-of-bounds I still went for him. I racked his ass. Back behind the bench somewhere. Knocked a water bucket over, I remember. I don’t know why I did it. It was crazy. We got a big penalty and I was chewed out plenty.”

“What about Layne?” I asked.

“I can remember him looking at me out of that crazy helmet he wore. ‘Hey, what did you do that for?’ he says.

“I couldn’t have told him. No way.”

# CHAPTER 5

A year or so after Karras and Gordy had talked about him I met Bobby Layne. I was giving a lecture at Texas Tech, which is in Lubbock, where Layne had settled down in somewhat restive retirement from football, working in real estate, oil wells, and one thing or another, and every once in a while collecting himself a big night or so on the town in Austin, Houston, or Dallas which got into the news. I heard stories about him from my Texas friends. Certainly in Lubbock he was an institution that ranked with the college itself, or the empty skyscraper downtown that had been nearly destroyed by a tornado, or the big cotton silos. "Mr. Layne?" the cabdriver said on the way in from the airport. "He's the biggest baddest thing there is around here. When he dies, they should stuff him and set him up out on Route 70, just outside town, with a sign hanging from him. People would come for miles around to look. Some sharp boy could make a heck of a lot of cash running a concession like that. 'Course I'll tell you something else, which is that Bobby Layne ain't never going to die off. He's one tough sumbitch."

Just before I went off for the lecture, I looked in the Lubbock telephone directory and found two numbers for a Robert Layne. It seemed too formal a listing for a man known so universally as "Bobby," but it turned out to be the right one. When he came on the phone we made an appointment to meet at my motel after I had finished with the students, and he'd show me Lubbock.

He picked me up at ten o'clock in the evening. We shook hands. He seemed very fit, just as I had remembered him from photographs: the large strong face, the sandy hair close-cropped. He was holding a glass in his left hand, and his voice was high, slightly nasal and querulous as he urged me to get a "leg up"; we had a big evening ahead and no time to lose.

"We're going down to Neal's Barbeque in the colored section," he said. "I'll tell you who's going to be there—Wyatt Ward, that's who. Everybody calls him 'W.W.' I knowed him ever since he was a shineboy at the country club. I like him because he *acts* dumb, but he's smart. He was a tremendous football player, a great running back when he was in high school, but he never went further because he was no good when the quarterback called 'automans'—which is his word for automatics. He says, 'Those automans, they mess up my mind.'"

We drove into the east part of town, with its blocks of one-story white windowless buildings with narrow doors that open directly onto the dirt street, each place identified by a neon sign with a fancy design blinking swiftly on and off, and a grandiose name—The Thunderbird, The Top Hat, The Tuxedo Club. We parked the car and walked into one called The Glass Hat. Part of the building was set aside for Neal's Barbeque. The proprietor, a diminutive black named Shorty, came forward to greet us. He had a single tooth in the front of his mouth. He showed it in an enormous grin. He was delighted to see Layne. Layne pummeled him, which unleashed a short fit of coughing. Layne pummeled him some more. "Shorty, you goin' to put the hurt on my stomach with some ribs?" Shorty showed us the ovens where the spareribs glistened in the heat. "He started out bootlegging," Layne told me. "His stuff costs you two forty-five a pint. *Good* stuff. Right, Shorty?" He pummeled him again.

The sound of a jukebox drifted through a door at the far end of the room. I wandered around while the two of them chatted and laughed. Layne ate some ribs, and also a pie, and then some more ribs, picking the ribs off the oven grill, smacking his lips, and mopping his hands on a paper napkin. We walked into the nightclub, our eyes adjusted to the soft pink jukebox glow, and we could see a couple moving on the little dance floor and one or two people sitting on the bar stools. Layne found a table, reaching for it with pale hands that shone, along with the white of his shirt cuffs, in the darkness.

"Where's W.W.?" he called.

A man slid off a bar stool and joined us at the table. "Goddamn it, W.W., you're so black I can't scarcely see you," said Layne. He slapped him delightedly across the shoulders and introduced us. Ward sat down next to me.

"Hey, W.W.," said Layne. "Tell George why you never stayed in football."

Dutifully, it seemed to me, Ward said, "Aw, those automans messed me up real bad."

Layne yelled with laughter. " 'Automans'! Oh, goddamn it, Wyatt, you are something else. What'd I tell you?" he said to me happily. "W.W.'s something, right?"

Drinks arrived. Layne took a gulp of his. "Hey, W.W., listen to this. When we come in here, Shorty was out in front, standing by his ovens, and he was standing there coughing and wheezing. So I ask him, 'Hey, Shorty, you got the whooping cough?' You know what Shorty says? He says, 'No, man, I got the *measles!*' God Al*mighty*. Ain't that grand? I ate one of Shorty's pies when he said that about the measles. That was the greatest pie I ever ate. Look at my stomach." He leaned back in his chair and pushed his stomach out at us. "Shorty put the hurt on me real good with that pie."

People began to collect around the table, and when the chairs were gone they stood on the perimeter like ranchers around a campfire. Layne would squint in the darkness to see who they were, and then would give a whoop of recognition and ask how their babies were doing, or Aunt Sue, or what was going on in their lives. The voices rose, and it was hard to hear.

To my left W.W. said in my ear, "The word's around the East Side.

There'll be people comin' on in heah through the night to see Mister Bobby. That man is a whizzer. I don' think he know that a man is supposed to sleep."

Layne was telling a story. "I was standing out in front of the hotel and this guy stepped up in front of me and took my cab. Well, I didn't like that nohow. I got into a big ruckus about that. So the next cab that came around had a colored light circling on the roof, and for generally disturbing the peace they took me off to a li'l bitty ol' jail no bigger than that dance floor..."

At this point a man wearing a white hat leaned over the table. His hat floated eerily above his dark face, barely distinguishable in the gloom of the nightclub. I could see the pale white of a toothpick working in the corner of his mouth. He started to tell a story, interrupting Layne's—he just *began,* with no prompting, his voice suddenly cutting in on the table conversation as if a connection had fused in an old radio and somehow the instrument had turned on. We all looked up.

"I want W.W. to hear this," he was saying. "It's a true story. I'm telling you no lies about this."

"Who's this guy?" someone at the table asked.

"The man came out of that saloon with a *wheelbarrow.* Now that's no lie," the man said. He shook his head solemnly. "Right into the main street of Yuma. That's the point. There was an old man wearing a bathing suit in that wheelbarrow. He had a beard. What was going on? Now *where* was they going with that wheelbarrow...?"

Layne was twisted around in his chair. "My ear bones hurt. You talk too much."

The man with the hat lowered his voice, but he leaned in on the man standing alongside and pressed the story on him. The toothpick worked busily. I would have liked to hear about the wheelbarrow in the streets of Yuma, but to my left W.W. leaned in and began talking about Layne again. "He has no patience with someone like that. He don't mind strangers, but he's happiest with friends. We don't talk about football. I mean, he don't take to it at *all* when folks come up and says, 'You was the greatest *this* and you was the greatest *that*.' There is two things that he don't like. One of them is being annoyed by people like that, and the other is not having something to do. He is some lively man. When he takes a trip outside of Lubbock, this town curls up and is daid. Nobody moves. Everybody's resting up. You can tell when he comes back—it's a *feeling*. 'Course now he's slowing down some. He's much more of a family man. Why, the other night he went to bed at one in the morning, and he was still sleeping at four the next afternoon, and I thought he was plumb daid, but he was just getting himself ready and revvying up because for the next few nights he didn't go to bed at all.

"What do we do? Oh, we sit around in clubs like this. Sometimes we disconnect the jukebox and the speakers and just sit and talk. It's real quiet. We talk about his oil wells—he's drilling over there in Oklahoma—and he draws these diagrams on the tablecloth which I don't understand nothing about. What do I know about oil wells? He gets real mad when I tell him I don't understand."

It was getting difficult to hear Wyatt, for the noise around the table, now ringed two deep, was cacophonous. Layne was trying to press some money on a bystander. He literally pulled the person's trouser pocket ajar and stuffed in some bills. "Now you go and buy yourself six hogs, heah?"

"Oh, Mister Layne, I dunno."

W.W. said in my ear, "He and I had a big discussion about carrying too much money around. If he had as much money as Mister Howard Hughes, why there wouldn't be a po' person in the Southwest. He always had a big roll of bills at the beginning of an evening. I kind of broke him of the habit. He was going to get himself robbed; he's so generous a man that the word'd get around. We got an underworld here in Lubbock, sure enough—some characters'll entertain you real good and smart."

Layne caught the end of W.W.'s remarks. "You tellin' him about the Lubbock underworld? Oh my!" He slapped the table with the palm of his hand. He leaned across, and when everyone had quieted down he told how when his son, Robert Jr., had got married, W.W.'s pals had broken into the biggest clothing store in Lubbock and fetched out a fancy pink oxford suit, very lively threads, which they thought W.W. should wear to the wedding. But W.W. turned out to be very particular. The pink suit didn't please him. There was a green suit in that very same store which he'd seen; why hadn't they picked *that* one? So his friends got in there a second time, a risky business since they had removed not only the pink suit the night before, but some more stuff too, so that the store management knew the place had been ripped off severely enough to arrange for more security, such as perhaps a pair of trained guard dogs. But W.W.'s pals got in there successfully again, and there were no dogs, and they found the green suit, though being a particular man W.W. had grumbled that it didn't fit properly along the shoulders.

The circle of onlookers laughed, and in the darkness I could hear the slapping of hands against knees. It was a story they must have heard many times, but it was a classic, and it was being told by Mister Bobby, and W.W. hung his head modestly. As the chuckling died away, the man in the white hat suddenly started off again: "When the man got into the rowboat, why the water come flooding right in over the back and down she went, right there in the Municipal Boat Basin three miles outside of town . . . that's the point—"

Layne spun in his chair. "Who is that talking? Man, you are *messing* with people's ear bones."

A chorus of agreement arose. The man in the white hat raised his hands in protest. "That's the point," he said mysteriously.

Another round of drinks turned up. I began to worry about the time; I had not had much sleep the night before. Layne saw me glancing at my watch. "I never wear a watch," he said. "When you look at a watch you see that time is going by, and what's the use of that? Besides, I know what time it is, anyway—just by the *feel* of things. It's eleven-twenty right now. Right?"

He was about twenty minutes off. "Just about right," I said.

Layne nodded and began telling me about his ranch near a town called Jayton—how time didn't make no difference there, the one place he loved to go to get away from it all, where he and his pals had these great cookouts, and every season a big shoot, gunning at quail over bird dogs brought down from Oklahoma.

"Hey, what are you doing tomorrow?" he asked.

I told him that I had a one o'clock conference with some students at the university, and then an afternoon plane to catch back to the East.

"Why, we'll fly out to the ranch in the morning. It's just an hour out. I'll be pounding on your door at eight in the morning. You ain't leavin' Lubbock without seeing the ranch."

"Don't go shooting out there," W.W. warned me. "The gunfire can be goddamn heavy. I got a pellet here in my knee from an over-and-under shotgun some friend of Mister Layne's was waving around."

"Hell, I remember that guy," Layne said. "You're talking about that weak-stomached sumbitch who got sick when a bourbon bottle was passed under his nose."

"You recall when McCade shot the hell out of John Murphy?" W.W. said. "Why, with all that buckshot in him, Murphy real quick weighed two pounds more than when he arrived at the ranch."

Layne roared with laughter and pounded the table.

"It sounds pretty dangerous out there," I said to W.W.

"Aw, you'll have a good time," he said. "He loves that place. You'll have a *good* time out there."

Layne turned up at the motel room just when he said he would, knocking loudly on the door. It was very bright outside, especially after the dark of the room with its thick curtains drawn against the dawn, and I squinted for a while. On the way out to the airport Layne talked about the Lubbock tornado—still the big topic in town, though it had happened two years before—and how it had ducked into the community one rain-swept night with quick massive devastation. He pointed out the tallest building in town, a fifteen-story insurance building, which he said had been "bent crazy" by the force of the wind, and was now inhabited only by pigeons. We drove out past the country club, where the funnel had touched down in the darkness and killed twenty-six people. "Out by the airport the planes were blown right up on roofs," he said. "Why, out there the wind was so strong that it blew a straw right plumb through a windshield so it stuck there."

"No kidding."

"Damn right. That's true."

We drove in silence for a stretch. I noticed a rushing liquid sound when we rounded curves, and Layne told me it was a large thermos jug on the backseat filled with ice and cans of beer. "Pearl," he said. "I cut my teeth on Pearl when I was sixteen and weighed a hundred and sixty pounds and ran like a deer."

I asked, "Bobby, what do you remember about Gordy and Karras from those days when you were with the Lions?"

"Oh hell, man, I don't remember them worth a *damn*. Why, they were *rookies*. Nobody remembers rookies. Gordy? 'Gorday,' we called him, giving him the French accent. Don't ask me why. 'John Gorday from Tennessee.' We thought that was very funny. Broke us up. That's the only thing I remember about Gorday—that it was funny to think of him as a Frenchman. But, you see, it was important not to get to know rookies, so we didn't pay them much attention."

"Why was it a bad idea?"

"Well, hell, they were trying to take jobs away from the people that you knew for a long time and sat around and played cards with and bullshitted with—and the rookies, hell, they were trying to break up the family. When Dick Flanagan, out of Ohio State, who played middle linebacker for us, why when he got beat out of his position by Joe Schmidt, well, we thought Joe Schmidt was some sort of sumbitch. He'd done in our friend. So it was the rule that you never spoke to a rookie, 'cept to tell him to get you something, like a pizza or a beer. That went on until the first exhibition game of his second year, when it looked like the boy was going to stick around. Then, if you felt like it, you could say 'howdy' to him."

"Was it the same when you broke in as a rookie?"

"The treatment's always been the same." He pounded the steering wheel with his fist. "I broke into the league with the Chicago Bears. The guy I recall was Bulldog Turner. He was the Main Man. That year he came in overweight and the Bear coaches—George Halas was some sumbitch strict man—they put him at the Fat Man's table to get the pounds off him. Hell, they fed him *lettuce.* Well, at night he and Ed Sprinkle and J. R. Boone, a li'l bitty back from Tulsa, they'd play hearts up in their room. It was my job as a rookie to stuff food into Bulldog Turner, who had an appetite that a couple of *heads* of lettuce wasn't going to do nothing to solve. He'd sit there looking at his cards and bawl for food. They made me break into the commissary to get him stuff."

"Do you suppose Bulldog Turner would remember you?" I asked.

"I'll tell you that if you went and found yourself Bulldog Turner to talk to—why, he wouldn't remember me at *all* when I was a rookie. Hell no. And if you went further and asked him about *his* rookie year—why, he'd remember some guy who horsed him around when *he* was a rookie, Christ, some ol' Indian chief who wore no helmet. And if you could find *him,* sitting in front of some damn tepee, and asked him if he could remember anyone called Bulldog Turner—why, he'd look at you and say, 'Boy, what sort of a grab-assing question is that?' He wouldn't know. What I'm saying is that you pay a rookie no attention at *all.* Why for?"

We arrived at the Lubbock airport. Layne's pilot was waiting by a single-wing Cessna and rushed forward to help him with the green thermos.

"I know you?" Layne asked.

"Nossir," the pilot said. "The regular guy you use is sick—flu or something." He was a young man, just barely out of high school, and obviously pleased to have Layne in his care.

"You want me to stow this job in the back?" he asked about the thermos.

"Hell," Layne said. "We're not delivering it to nobody. Set it alongside me in the seat."

We took off. The flight was over flat country to start, the huge cotton fields laid out in regular rectangles and squares below, but then the land gave way to arroyos and gulches, and the cultivated areas became smaller and irregular in shape. An occasional turkey vulture, almost at our level and turning slowly in a thermal current, streamed past below the wingtips. The roar of the engine and the rush of air were soothing, and I half dozed in the backseat while the pilot and Layne chatted in the front.

I heard the quick hiss of a beer can being clicked open.

I heard the pilot ask, "Hey, Bobby, are you a Leo?"

"A what?"

"A Leo?"

"What the hell are you talking about?"

"It's an astrological sign. When were you born?"

"Oh yeah," said Layne. "You're one of those guys. I was born in December."

"A Sagittarius," said the pilot. "That's very interesting. Very."

"I'm sure it is," Layne said. "Very big deal." He looked back over his shoulder at me. "See that mountain off there? Sammy Baugh's got his spread in the foothills."

This was how they ended up, I thought drowsily: the famous Texas quarterbacks, sitting out on their front porches gazing at their acreage, their jaws moving on chaws, their spurred boots up on the rail, and their gnarled hands, which had made them such fortunes spiraling footballs, resting now on the noble brow of a bird dog. I remembered Baugh at the Detroit Lion camp where he was an assistant to Harry Gilmer, also from Texas. They wore white cowboy hats on the sidelines, and Baugh, who chewed tobacco, carried a Dixie cup with him to spit into when he went indoors, and when it was full he left it on a coffee table, or on the piano, or in a corner by the grandfather clock, and went off to find another. The plane was wobbling now as the pilot turned it for the landing at the Jayton strip. Feeling queasy from that quick recall of the detritus of Baugh's chewing habit, I was relieved when the wheels touched down.

"Hey, d'ja see that?" the pilot called out. "Damn near got ourselves a rattlesnake with the right wheel. D'ja see him? Right out there sunning himself."

Layne's jeep was parked off to one side of the field. My ears buzzed in the abrupt silence after the pilot cut the engine. Back up the strip there was no sign of the rattlesnake. The heat rose in waves off the tarmac. The pilot put the thermos in the jeep and Layne drove. The pilot came with us, sitting in the backseat with the beer. We came around a bend, past a water tower standing at the edge of the cotton fields, and drove into Jayton. A sign announced its population: 703. The next town down the line was Spur, forty miles across the flatlands. The speed-limit signs brought us down to thirty miles per hour. The shop fronts were one story high with signs tacked above the door: CHUCK'S SWAP SHOP, PETE'S. The cars out front had their side and back windows soaped with various slogans; GO TOUGH, one of them read.

"Look there," Layne said. "This town is all fired up about the Jayton Jayhawks, the high school team. They got a big game tonight against Rule."

"Rule?"

"Town of about two hundred folks. What'd that sign back there say 'bout Jayton's population? Seven-oh-three? Well, that means nine hundred and three folks'll be seeing that game tonight over on the high school field."

The pep signs were everywhere along the main street. The town barber had soaped the front window of his shop (which was called Sleepy's Barber Shop) with the exhortation, SLEEP SAYS SHAVE'M!

Layne said, "Texas football, let me tell *you*. This town is riled up fierce." He slowed the jeep down and shouted at a group of men lounging by the gas pump of a filling station. They all wore pale blue coveralls—the old-fashioned switchman's model with the big back pockets, and the suspenders crossed over their shoulders. "You go git 'em, heah?" Layne shouted, his voice high and reedy.

The men waved at him.

Layne turned back to his driving. "Best doggone li'l ol' town in Texas," he said.

"How many of your friends come out here during the shooting season?" I asked.

He replied that the group hired out the bungalows in the little motor court ("The Jayton Hilton," they called it) and at the peak of the festivities perhaps twenty or thirty men were on hand out at the ranch. Of course, they didn't all shoot. Many of them sat out in the front yard, and smoked and talked.

"What's the general talk about?"

"Oh, football," Layne said. "We tell about the funny things that happen. Don Meredith ever tell you 'bout the time he quarterbacked for the Cowboys against that great Giant team that had Katcavage and Robustelli and Huff and all those people?"

"Not that I can remember."

Layne pounded the wheel. "Sam Huff damn near fell over on his back he was laughing so hard. What happened was that Meredith called this play in the huddle and when he got onto the line he took a gander out over the defense and he saw Huff and another linebacker move into the gaps and hell, man, he knew those cats were *coming*. So he decided to call an automatic at the line—a quick trap, which is the best thing you can call against the blitz, and he opened up his mouth and shouted, *'Red! Green! Blue! Shit! Time!'* and he stepped back and made the signal for a time-out. Christ, he couldn't remember how to call the automatic, but what he did say came out in the right sequence, like it was a signal: *Bam, bam, shit, time!*"

The pilot in the backseat was laughing hard.

"Some story, eh, Jim? Damn right that's some sumbitching story. True, too.

"Hey, you know what Meredith once said on the Jack Paar television show?" Layne went on. "Paar asked him if he came back in the afterlife what he would come back as, and Meredith thought for a spell and then he said that he'd like to come back as Bobby Layne's *cabdriver.* That's something, eh? So Paar asks, 'Why do you want to come back as Bobby Layne's cabdriver?' and Meredith says, 'Well, he tips good, and boy, you sure go to some interesting places!' "

"That's quite a compliment," I said.

We passed a sign that read SPUR 35 MILES.

The pilot leaned over the back of the front seat. "Hey, Bobby, you ever say anything to Huff and people like that on the other side of the line?"

"Naw," Layne said. "I'm not saying it don't happen though. Norm Van Brocklin, when he was quarterback, had this trick he played on Art Donovan of the Colts, who was maybe the best defensive player in the league and it was worth trying stuff on that boy—*any*thing. His father was the famous boxing referee, and Brocklin's trick was to come up to the line of scrimmage and call down to where Donovan was waiting, all poised to wrastle some poor sumbitch: 'Hey Al, how's your daddy?' And then in the next beat set loose the play right *at* Donovan. What he was hoping was that Donovan was going to hear the question 'bout his pappy and maybe turn it over in his mind and say to himself, 'Well now, how sweet of ol' Norm to ask about Daddy,' or even better, that maybe he'd come up out of his stance and look up into the sky to ponder the question, and then *boom!*"

The pilot in the backseat was captivated. "Hell, what an idea. Did it work?"

"Naw," said Layne. "Hell, I don't know. I wouldn't think so. Not on Donovan. Oh no. But that was all right. You had to try things. I'll tell you 'bout a play we had when I was with the Pittsburgh Steelers. It was called the 'What's the matter' play. What happened was that a situation came up against those same damn Giants—Huff, Robustelli, Katcavage, Roosevelt Brown—and we had fifteen yards to go for a touchdown. Those cats were real poison when you got down close, so in the huddle I called the 'What's the matter' play. What happens is this. I walk up behind the center but I keep my hands tucked in my crotch. I call out 'Red!' which begins the signal count, but all of a sudden John Henry, the fullback, calls out of the backfield behind me, 'Hey, wait a minute.' So I stop the count and rear up and I turn toward him and I sing out, 'What's the matter?' Across the line the Giants begin to relax and they think, 'Oh man, what a bum team *this* is,' and they stand up to enjoy the confusion, when suddenly, two beats after the word 'matter' the ball is hiked right past my hip to John Henry and he takes off—I mean like he just tears!"

The pilot pounded the back of the front seat. "Well, what about *that* one?" he cried. "Did it work?"

"Damn sumbitching *right,*" Layne said. "Sam Huff was laughing so hard he could hardly run after John Henry. He run like he was crazy drunk in some cabbage patch, just stumbling along holding his sides."

After our own laughter had died down, we drove along in silence for a while.

"Hey, Jim, you say there was a rattlesnake back on the strip."

"Yes*sir,*" the pilot said. "Almost got him with the right wheel."

"*God*damn."

Layne asked for a beer, and I reached back into the bucket, where the ice was sluicing back and forth, and opened a can for him.

"What was the point of keeping your hands in?" I asked.

"How's that?"

"On that 'What's the matter' play."

"Hell, man, if you put your hands under the center, you're not allowed to bring them out again, 'less you want to have a time-out called against you." He looked at me aggrieved, as if not knowing about that rule was a reflection on the quarterback fraternity, however limited my own involvement in it.

"Oh yes," I said.

"Here's the turnoff," he said. He whipped the wheel around and the jeep turned onto a dirt road. "We're just about getting there. I'm telling you, this is the best damn place in the world." The jeep swayed between the high red-dirt banks, over which the cotton fields had given way to a lumpy expanse dotted with mesquite bushes. We turned off on a track that rose up precipitously and the jeep's tires spun and threw back stones.

"Let's walk up," Layne said.

The camp stood on the brow of the hill—a low cabin, with a fenced yard at one end in which bird feathers, the residue of countless pluckings, stirred slightly in the soft air. Back of the cabin, sitting in the backyard, was a large gold and black school bus, its wheels gone, resting on its undercarriage amongst the weeds. HILES BAPTIST CHURCH read the letters along its side, with the additional legend above the windows: LUBBOCK'S FASTEST GROWING SUNDAY SCHOOL. Most of the windows were gone, or the glass shattered into white sunbursts by the impact of rocks or gunfire.

"Guns," said Layne. "Bought that sumbitch from the Baptists and fixed it up nice, four bunks in there for the hunting folk, and then the kids came up and shot the hell out of it... my *own* kids," he added ruefully.

Around the front, the land fell away steeply into a canyon. On the edge was a skeet trap, with boxes of clay pigeons set alongside. Layne cocked the arm back, loaded it, and pulled the lever: the clay pigeon sailed out over the gulch, black and gold, spinning prettily until its momentum failed and it dropped from sight and we heard it tinkle faintly on the rocks below.

The slight wind, hot and sweet, stirred the feathers in the yard. We looked across the canyons at a distant curve of brown barren hills. "Isn't that some country?" Layne asked.

"Yessirree," the pilot said.

Layne strode into the house and we could hear him puttering around inside. The pilot and I stayed in the yard and talked about astrology.

"I've been studying the occult for three years," the pilot said.

"What do you make of Layne?"

"Oh hell, he's sure your basic Sagittarius, all right. He's either jovial or he's against you. There's nothing halfway about him. He's great, isn't he?" He peered at Layne's cabin with a delighted smile, as if he had a prime specimen trapped in there.

"What made you think he was a Leo?" I could not resist asking.

The pilot glanced over. "Well, he has some of the characteristics of the Leo. I mean, I've been observing him. But it's better that he's a Sagittarius, much better. He takes nothing at face value. That's Sagittarius. I'll tell you something else: Sagittarius rules the legs, anything that's outside in the open air—dogs, horses, football... Of course, it depends on where the planets are in his chart. Neptune has to do with high spirituality. He might have a bad hookup with that. But if Neptune is in a good position, he could be tuned in to being a great artist—a Picasso or a Leonard Bernstein."

Layne began yelling from inside the house. "Hey, where the crap are you guys?"

We went inside to join him. The place was musty, long closed against the air; the furniture had bottoms that sagged; the beds were double-deckers; some bird feathers had drifted in and one of them floated between us, stirred up by the draft from the door. "Can't get this place too cleaned up," Layne said. "Or the women'd get to like coming out here, and it wouldn't be the same."

"Man, not much chance of that," the pilot said. He poked at a beer can with his foot. Layne looked at him sharply.

I shuffled my feet uncomfortably and said that I was worried about getting back to Lubbock in time for my conference with the Texas Tech students.

Layne looked out the window. "It's getting along about eleven o'clock."

I glanced at my watch. This time he was about a half hour off. "I can't be late for them," I said.

"You'll come back here to Jayton when we have a shoot," Layne said.

"Damn right," I said.

We walked down the road toward the car, the pilot behind us humming a country-and-western tune.

"Bobby," I asked, "do you remember a game when you were playing for Pittsburgh in which you were run out-of-bounds, and Alex Karras came out of nowhere and really belted you one? They damn near threw him out of the game for it? A water bucket went over. It was way out-of-bounds. Do you remember that?"

Layne was silent for such a long time that I thought he had his mind on something else and had not heard the question.

"Naw," he said finally. He reached for the door handle of the jeep. "Naw, now what would I want to remember a thing like that for?"

# CHAPTER 6

John Gordy and I were sitting in the apartment waiting for Karras. I was still trying to return to the original concept of the book, and my plan was to spend the morning talking to the two of them about the technical aspects of line play. I had a clipboard ready with some questions on it.

"Where do you suppose he is?" I asked.

"He was sleeping in the hotel when I left," Gordy said. "He sleeps late sometimes. He has his own time clock."

"You were roommates right from the start, weren't you?"

"I'd have taken any sort of roommate," Gordy said, "because before Alex joined the team I roomed with Gil Mains, a wild horse, the weirdest, wildest man in the world. Just crazy. He'd come in late sometimes, and I'd be sleeping, and he'd turn on the lights and whistle and stamp around and sing, just to aggravate me. He'd pick the most solemn moment of the day, like when I was sitting and writing an old aunt who was dying of something, and he'd throw a firecracker under my chair."

I got Gordy a soft drink and we looked out the windows and watched the boats work the currents of the East River.

"Hell," I said finally. "Let's get started. He'll be along." I sat down and looked at the questions on the clipboard. "What about some general questions—what sort of player is the toughest for an offensive lineman to play against?"

Grady settled himself in the chair opposite. "The quick ones," he said. "Like that guy sunning back there in the hotel. Or Art Donovan of the Colts. Leo Nomellini of the 49ers. He was a horror. When I signed with the Lions I knew that one day I'd be playing Nomellini. I had a chance ~~late my last college year~~ to watch the Rams play the 49ers, with one of the best guards in the business, Harris Putnam, going against him. Putnam was an awfully good guard—all-Pro—something I aspired to be. I looked up to him. He was my hero. Well, he just had a horrible time with Nomellini ... as everyone was having ... just humiliated ... and I thought, 'Good God, here's Putnam, all-Pro, and he's having this rough time with Nomellini. What the hell am I going to do?

"One time in San Francisco, Earl Morrall, who was quarterbacking for us then, came out in the papers the day before the game and said that Leo Nomellini was over the hill. I gave this big yell when I read it and I said, 'If you think he's over the hill, you go and play against him.' Nomellini was a raving maniac ~~that afternoon~~ ... trying to get to Earl that afternoon. Of course, to get to him he had to get through me, and oh Christ!

"What could you do?"

"You could just hope for the best," he said. "It meant—if you

An early draft from Chapter 6 (*Plimpton Estate*)

Gordy settled himself in the chair opposite. "The quick ones," he said. "Like that Alex sleeping back there in the hotel. Or Art Donovan of the Colts. Leo Nomellini of the 49ers. *He* was a horror. One time in San Francisco, Earl Morrall, who was quarterbacking for us then, came out in the papers the day before the game and said that Leo Nomellini was over-the-hill. I gave this big yell when I read it, and I said, 'If you think he's over-the-hill, *you* go and play against him.' Nomellini was a raving maniac trying to get to Earl that afternoon. Of course, to get to him he had to get through *me,* and oh *Christ!*"

"What could you do?"

"You could just hope for the best," he said. "If you had to play against Leo or Donovan, one of those great cats, it meant that for five days before the game, from Tuesday on, it was very hard to sleep nights."

He grimaced. "The worst thing about playing Leo Nomellini was that he had these eyes that crossed. He had no teeth either, and his mouth was always open, so that behind the bars of his helmet he looked like a death's-head. But it was the eyes that were the worst—those awful crossed eyes. Sometimes you can pick up from a guy's eyes where he's going to make his move; he'll flick a look, and you can read him. But Nomellini's! One one way, one the other. Hell, if you ever looked at those eyes, you could feel the strength drain out of your kneecaps—like a sparrow facing up to a cobra. It was not a heartwarming sight."

"Jesus! Well, what *do* you look at?"

"The best thing to watch is the number on his jersey. Never the hips or the head, which can fake and throw you off."

"What do you see in your mind's eye as you start to pull and run interference?"

Gordy answered obliquely. "Once I asked John Brodie, the San Francisco quarterback, about what he pictures as he swings at a golf ball. He's a helluva golfer and I'm a horrible one. I'm always picturing my grip, or the stance, or bringing the hips around. But for him, it wasn't that at all; it was the ball leaving the club and its flight to the green. That makes sense—though it's never helped *my* golf any—

because I realize that I do the same thing in football. Leading interference on a running play I have three routes as a pulling guard—a short pull, a long pull, and a deep pull—and in each case I can picture in my mind a sort of quick flash, what's probably going to happen. I've watched the movies, so I have a preconception as to how the defensive players are going to attack the play. Of course I can't be sure. I may have to hook the linebacker in, or the cornerback out, or vice versa. My moves depend on them. But you get to learn their methods of attack; they'll come at you a certain way. In some cases they'll look like they're really going to hit you, then they'll try to dodge around you. In that instance, you've always got to take an inside-out angle and pop the guy, and the runner behind you is a schmuck if he doesn't get out and away. Here, let me show you how it works." He stood up and mentioned me out of my chair. I demurred.

On occasion, when Gordy wanted to make a point, rather than use words or draw a diagram on a piece of paper, he would stand me up, moving chairs and standing lamps around to represent tackles and defensive ends, and then with quick darting hops and feints would simulate the moves on the line of scrimmage. Occasionally, an end table would go over or a lamp would sway alarmingly. He was always very intense when he demonstrated his skills, and a sort of way-ward look came into his eye which made me wonder nervously, on those occasions when I stood in front of him representing a defensive tackle, if it wasn't the turf of Kezar Stadium that he imagined underfoot and someone like Leo Nomellini opposite him.

"I got to keep notes," I said. "Truly."

He looked miffed.

"How many options," I asked, sitting back, "does a defensive man have?"

"They can do one of three things," Gordy said, settling down again. "They can meet you head-on, in which case it depends on who gets in the best licks. Or they can try to rip you out by hitting low; then you've got to keep your knees together and try to bowl *them* over. Or finally, they can try to dodge around you. We call those people *olés*. Like the *olé* the crowd gives when the bull goes by the guy, they'll give you an *olé*."

"Which are the most difficult to deal with?" I asked. "The *olé* people?"

"They're not harder, but it's frustrating. You want to hit someone, and you can never get a good lick in on an *olé*. But actually there's not too many of them. An *olé* is usually a guy who doesn't want to hit. He'll never strip the interference, which means he can put the defense in a lot of trouble. If he gets around me and then misses the tackle, his people are in a jam: I'm still on my feet, still in the play, and looking for someone to pile into and create a lane for my runner. We called Lem Barney, our cornerback, an *olé* for his first year. He understood what we were getting at and he changed his ways. Of course, sometimes the *olé* gets away with it. There's nothing more embarrassing than one of those guys getting around you, making his tackle on the runner, and there you are thundering along, assuming your guy is still on his feet behind you, looking for people to knock down, really eating up ground—like a locomotive barreling along without any cars attached. You run a long way in a play like that before you pull up, and when you get back in the huddle, you're the last man there, and some guy looks up, real cynical, and says, 'Give John the ball; he's really *eating* up ground.' "

"What about the guy behind you, running with the ball—can he help you?"

"Oh my, yes," Gordy replied. "A good halfback can fake the defensive man right onto your shoulder. Mel Farr, who's as good a runner as Detroit or anybody ever had, would stay long after practice, and we'd run the routes so he knew my moves and I knew his—the two of us working together so that the defensive man *would* end up on my shoulder. I never worked with anybody as good, as fast as Mel. That year he gained almost a thousand yards, and he was out of two games. God, that was fun!"

"Did you ever touch the football?" I asked. "In all those years?"

"Very rarely. On fumbles. When I was at Tennessee I caught a fumble in the air and ran eight yards for a touchdown. Don't laugh! We won, twenty–fourteen. We were undefeated that year. In the pros I only ran with a fumble once. I got killed. The only thing to do if you see a football rolling around is just to fall on it. It saves a lot of wear and tear on the head."

"Is what you're talking about typical of all offensive line play?"

"Well, all of them except the center, who has it easier," Gordy said. "On pass protection he doesn't usually have a man playing on his nose. His job is to take two steps back and help the guard if he's in trouble, or a tackle, or to cut down a linebacker's charge if he sees it coming. There are a lot of possibilities. Centers get kidded a lot because they don't have any specific opponent on pass protection. But a good center can really help you out."

"What about snapping the ball?"

"That's not hard. But I don't want to demean what centers do. I've never done it when it's twenty below zero and the wind is coming across Lake Erie into Cleveland's Municipal Stadium, and I've never had to do it consistently sixty times a game for twenty games a year. I wouldn't want to degrade a center because one or two bad snaps a year at the wrong time can cost you the whole season. The pressure can get awful rough on a center. But they practice, over and over again, a relatively simple act, until it gets grooved and they can do it whatever the pressure."

"Why is it that centers seem to last so much longer in the leagues?"

"They don't take that physical beating—that pounding, play after play. I've only seen one play in which the center was required to pull and run interference. The Chicago Bears had it in their repertoire."

"Tell me about your own rituals and procedures and thoughts with a game coming up," I said.

Gordy reflected. "I follow a very set and thought-out plan. I go to the stadium very early, and never in the team bus, which takes so damn long and has all those players sitting in rows staring straight ahead looking as though they'd all just lost their mothers. So I go alone, or with

Alex, by car, and when I get to the locker room I take off my clothes and leave my shorts and T-shirt on. Next, I get my ankles taped, one of the first people up on the training table, and then I sit in the locker cubicle and read the game program. There's one in each cubicle. All game programs are exactly the same. For years I haven't been surprised by anything in a game program. But reading them passes the time."

"Not much conversation?"

"A certain amount. There are only a few players there at that hour—just the early arrivals, the guys who don't like the bus. They kid the trainers and everybody laughs."

"Is the humor rich?"

"Rich? I don't think that would be my word for it," he said. "Let's see. A typical crack that would get everyone laughing might be to work a couple of pieces of the tape on your ankle loose, and then you go up to the trainer and say, 'Real good job on the tape. My little boy could have done better.'"

"Is that it?"

"Well, it's not one of your great funnies. But it's typical. The situation in the locker room before a game is so tense that almost anything will produce a sort of nervous laugh."

"I guess so," I said. It seemed such an odd scene—the guffaws starting up over "My little boy could have done better." A football player hearing the laughter from up by the training table would look up from reading the game program in his cubicle and call out, "Hey, what's so funny?" One of the tackles comes toward him, his shoulders still heaving with laughter, and draws up a stool to sit down and tell him. "It's a real beaut," he says. "Gordy comes up to the... the... training table." The tackle can hardly control himself. "Oh, Jesus."

"Yes? He comes to the training table. And?"

"Haw haw haw."

"Then what happens?"

"So Gordy hops up on the table. Right?" The tackle buckles over again. "I can't *bear* it."

"You want some water?"

"No . . . no . . . So Gordy . . . he says to the trainer . . . haw haw haw."

"Yes?"

"I forgot . . . I forgot a part. Gordy has . . . oh, Jesus! . . . worked some tape . . . loose on his foot . . . so it's . . . oh, Christ . . . *hanging* there . . ."

"Yeah, yeah."

"And . . . Gordy puts his foot . . ."

"Yes?"

". . . up in the trainer's . . . face . . . and . . . oh, Christ . . . he says . . . he says . . ."

"For Chrissake, *what* does he say?"

"He says . . . 'My . . .' "

"Come *on*."

". . . 'little boy . . .' "

"Yes."

". . . '*could have done better.*' Haw haw haw haw . . ." The tackle wipes the tears from his eyes.

"Is that it?" The player in the cubicle looks down at his football shoes. "I don't get it," he says. "Tell me again."

But the tackle has gone down the line to tell someone else, so the player in the cubicle shakes his head and picks up his football game program to begin to read it for the third time.

I looked across at Gordy. "That sort of funny mood doesn't keep up for very long, does it?" I asked. "I mean all the laughing and carrying on?"

"Christ no," he said. "In fact, the mood really begins to change when the bus pulls up outside and those guys start to file in with that look on their faces—that grimace, that pregame look. Then I know it's time. But I have a strange psychological edge, which is that I've been in the locker room for a while. These newcomers are the recruits and I've been there, in military training, for a week—that's what it's like. It gives me a sense of power and responsibility. So I walk around like a sergeant and tell everybody 'Let's go . . .' because I've already been there. Does that make sense?

"Then I go back to my cubicle and I put my jock on," he continued. "And my T-shirt, if it's not too hot in there. I put my hip guards on. I slide the pads into the pockets built into the pants for them, sliding each one in with care to get it just in place. Then I belt the hip guard tight. After a while I slip on my football pants, but I don't pull them up; I just keep them around my knees. I sit there. Then the pregame nerves start."

"Alex is sitting next to you?"

"He has the next cubicle. Sometimes he'd wait for the bus because he didn't want to leave the hotel room. He probably felt more secure in there. I always had to get the hell out of our room. I'd been there all night, and to stay around the next morning was like sitting at the dinner table with dirty dishes after you've eaten a meal. But it was always an effort for Karras to get out of there and to the ballpark. You remember how nervous he was before a game? Sometimes, sitting next to each other in the cubicles, we'd find something to say, but when you're getting down to it...that time coming up...it's real quiet in there. You remember it," he said.

"Oh man, do I," I replied, thinking back on that sepulchral silence in those big locker rooms crowded with men sitting in front of their cubicles, the only sound the water dripping in a shower at the far end.

"Then at the last moment I put on my jersey," Gordy continued. "It's a very special one, the last one at Detroit after Joe Schmidt, who used one before he retired from the game. It has a long tail in the back that comes around between the legs and buttons up in front."

"Why that sort of jersey?"

"I never like my shirttail coming out, which always happened when I wore the usual model. If you have a shirttail floating out behind you, someone's likely to grab it."

"Big Daddy Lipscomb's tail used to come out," I recalled.

"True," said Gordy. "But there weren't many people around who wanted to grab ahold of *that* one. The kind of jersey I wore not only kept the shirttail from coming out, but it kept the material fitting very snug and tight on the body so that no one could get ahold of it. Then I put the Vaseline on—rubbing it over the shoulders and down the arms, clear, for a white jersey, dark for the dark-colored jersey—so that when a defensive guy grabs you, his fingers slip and there's nothing to catch on to. Then I took my teeth out and wrapped them in a Kleenex to give to Friday Macklem for safekeeping."

"Vaseline's illegal, isn't it?" I asked.

"Oh, I imagine it is," said Gordy decorously.

"Are there other tricks like that? For instance, do running backs put Vaseline around their hips?"

"Yeah, but it doesn't help them much, because no tackler is ever going to hang on to a running back's hips with his fingers. A running back's not going to go down unless he's arm-tackled. So it's not much use. But for me it's important, because defensive players can legally grab at me to try to throw me away. When they get a fistful of Vaseline they bitch like hell."

"Do the nerves really get bad just before the game?"

"I had a really bad time," Gordy said. "You see, the only way I can ever work up enough confidence to get on the football field at *all* is to watch the films of the guy I'm going to be playing against. Starting Tuesday I watch those films over and over until I know every move he's going to make. I watch the films so often that after a while I'm physically *on* that film and matching and beating him. Then for a night or so before the game I don't need the film anymore. It's all there in my mind, and I can lie in bed and mentally see myself through a game against him. Sometimes I catch myself moving my body so hard that the bed thrashes across the floor, and I've always got him beat. But you know something weird? Just before the game starts, I don't think I've got a *chance* against him. I feel I'm going to get licked to pieces and humiliated."

"Why is that? Do you forget everything?"

"No, fortunately that stays there. But what's happened is that I've goaded myself into being tough, and yet I still haven't performed. Talk is cheap; now I've got to go out there and actually *do* it. Can I? I get absolutely scared to death. The most scared I ever got was the Pro Bowl game. Then I didn't even have the security of a game film to help prepare myself. I had no idea what I was going to face."

"Do you ever think how *big* the guy opposite is?" I asked, moved to ask because it was the first thing *I* would worry about, and secondly because Chuck Walton, an offensive lineman on the Lions, had once told me that he *preferred* playing against the bigger man. "He's just not going to move as fast," he'd said. "At least you can find him and hit him a lick. The nightmare people are the quick fast ones like Karras. Look at Lee Roy Jordan, the Dallas linebacker. Two hundred and fifty pounds. Well, I could never *find* that guy to hit, which was what I was supposed to do. I knew he was on the field somewhere because I'd keep hearing his name over the public-address system."

I told Gordy this. "Oh yes," he said. "The big tough guys who rely on their strength are by far the easiest. The play that you hope for is from the guy who *thinks* he can bowl you over because he's so much stronger and bigger than you are. That's what Merlin Olsen of the Rams used to do when he started. He came into the league at six foot six, two hundred and ninety pounds, and he spent the first year trying to run over me because I'm only six foot four and two hundred and fifty pounds. But I *love* that situation. I'll be bruised and beaten up for sure, but a player with that one single obsession will never get to the quarterback. He's easy to deal with. Every year when I start against a new player, whatever his reputation, that's how he behaves: he bulls straight ahead. The next year I watch the films of his early games to see if he's starting to make any moves yet. After about five plays I can tell if he's developing his technique. If not, then I'm pretty safe for another year."

"Why don't the coaches try to teach those first-year players?"

"They just don't, for some reason," Gordy said. "Maybe there are some that try, but I've never seen them. They make you learn by yourself, by experience. It's ridiculous. Of course, many of the great moves can't be taught; they're close to instinctive. I mean you couldn't lead a grandmother out to the line of scrimmage and expect her to learn to get through into the secondary, not if you spent a year teaching her fundamentals. You have to have the essentials. But I've never known why coaches don't go to work on rookies, especially the great ones. You should have seen Olsen his first year. He just stumbled around."

"Couldn't their mistakes be corrected?"

"Maybe," he said, "with defensive people. But I know that for offensive linemen it's hard. The mistakes and bad habits seem so insignificant—a slight dip of the shoulder or the head, or even the blink of an eye—that they're hard to spot and correct."

"The blink of an eye?"

"A *flinch*. If you blink or flinch when the tackle makes his move, if he's a quick one like Karras or Donovan, he's gone. You never saw him, or even touched him."

"What about the drills? Do they help?"

"Almost all the drills in football are a waste of time," Gordy said. "For years, a lineman had this drill where he hit the tackling dummy and bounced back and dug his feet in and then hit the bag again. That's fine for getting the legs in shape, but no lineman ever *blocks* that way. The proper position for an offensive lineman is to have his knees crouched, rear end low, back straight, his neck arched back because he mustn't ever duck his head or flinch, and his fists right in front of his jersey numbers so he can balance himself and is ready to punch away..."

"What do you mean by 'punch away'?"

"Stand up." This time Gordy wouldn't listen to my excuses. "To hell with your notes," he said. "You'll remember."

He pulled me out of my chair.

"Okay," he said. "I'm an offensive lineman set up properly. You're coming at me. Now put your hands on me. Try to throw me one way or the other. No, no, really work on me. Pull me *this* way."

I grunted and wrenched at him.

"Now watch how I counter." A fist flew out and thumped against my chest. I staggered up against a wall.

"See that?" Gordy shouted.

"Yeah, sure," I said.

"That's the move," he went on, brimming with enthusiasm. "Did you catch how I kept my balance and threw you off yours?"

"Yeah, that certainly was something," I said.

"Okay, now you try it. You be me, you be the offensive lineman. I'm Karras or Nomellini, trying to get through you. Right. Now move around this way."

"Look out!"

"What's that?"

"That's an ashtray. It's all right, it was just a small ashtray."

He put the pieces on the table. "Okay," he said, "now let's get in the proper position."

"Right," I said with no enthusiasm. I dropped into an approximation of the crouch he had demonstrated, fists cocked at my chest ready to shoot out at him.

At that moment Maria, the woman who comes in to clean the apartment a couple of times a week, materialized at the door, stared briefly at the two of us poised like wrestlers, and cleared her throat to announce that there was someone at the door downstairs. It was Karras. In the nick of time, I thought. He was wearing knit wool slacks and a stylishly cut jacket—one of the first of a number of mod outfits that he had begun to cultivate, none of which seemed to suit his big squat frame, or the round pale face with big spectacles that floated above the ensemble like a moon.

"Sharp," said Gordy in admiration.

Karras sat down in the armchair. "Has he been telling you lies?" he asked. "All linemen tell lies—especially offensive linemen."

"We were talking about linemen's techniques," I said. "But now that you're here, perhaps we could get into something else—perhaps the *psychological* aspects." I was eager to protect the furniture and lamps from the *two* of them demonstrating the physical particulars of their crafts.

"He's not a collision man," Gordy said, looking at me with mock despair.

"He's going to be the assistant secretary of commerce," Karras said.

"Alex, what about your position?" I asked. "Do most defensive tackles play the same way?"

"We all play a little differently," he said. "I'm very aggressive, and I try to move forward all the time, to go as fast as I can through the head of the guard opposite so I can get on the other side of the line and start feeling for who has the ball. Many linemen tend to lay on the line of scrimmage and move along it laterally, like fingers on a piano, to work an opening."

"Can the opposition take advantage of your type of play?" I asked.

"What I have to look out for is the quick trap. This means that the lineman opposite, usually the offensive guard, releases me and lets me move into the trap where I can be cut down from the side, usually by the offensive tackle. I can't ignore the possibilities of the trap play, but I can't get so leery of it that it affects the aggressive type of football that I like to play. Actually, what makes a trap play work is the running back. The best one I ever saw at it was Gale Sayers of the Bears, because there wasn't anyone could hit a hole as fast as he could. He could have had the worst blockers in the league, executing the sloppiest of trap plays, but all they had to do was breathe some bad breath on you for two seconds, and he was by you and gone."

"Do you have any mental exercises you go through before a game to stir yourself up?"

"Well, I'm not normally an aggressive person, so I compensate by working up antagonisms, like against good-looking quarterbacks. A lot of it is psychological. I tell myself before a game that I'm Paul Bunyan. I wake up in the hotel room in the morning and say to myself, 'Paul, we're going to have ourselves a game this afternoon. We are going to remove the stuffings from people.' I can feel myself inflate. When I leave the hotel bedroom I crouch down so my head won't hit the top of the bedroom door. Down in the lobby the players say, 'Hey, Alex, what are you bent over like that for? You got a stomach cramp or something?' 'The name's Paul,' I say."

He picked up a glass and turned it in his hand. “That’s ‘compensation,’ ” he said. “I do it a lot.”

“Do you think the mental preparation required is different for different positions?”

The two of them looked puzzled.

Somewhere in my notes, I explained, Merlin Olsen of the Rams had told me about the different temperaments of football players. For example, linemen, “our people,” were more “self-motivated” than backs and receivers. His point was that linemen do not perform their skills under the sort of public scrutiny received by a back, who runs the ball in an open field and, say, fumbles it. “Our work is done in close quarters,” Olsen had said. “You can make a serious mistake, but it won’t be noticed. Linemen are motivated by a more complicated, self-determining series of factors than the simple fear of humiliation in the public gaze, which is the emotion that galvanizes the backs and receivers.”

The two of them nodded and agreed that it was an interesting speculation.

“Are there differences between the basic temperaments of offensive and defensive linemen?” I went on.

Both Karras and Gordy considered this and seemed to think there were.

“First of all,” Karras said, “our jobs are so different. An offensive player like John has to concentrate much more. He has a certain assignment to perform, and he must do it on a certain signal. So in a sense he’s confined; he’s geared to a type of machine; he must function and mesh with others. Whereas defensive linemen like myself, we can express ourselves more fully. Our moves, our attack, is more freewheeling and extemporaneous.”

“That’s right,” Gordy said. “Most of the time—and always on pass-blocking—the offensive guard’s job is passive. If the guy trying to get to the quarterback goes to the left, we go the same way. If he goes the other way, so do we. If he loafs, we can loaf. Everything is dictated by what the guy opposite does. Most of the time, of course, shielding the quarterback means that you've got to take a beating—it's like being a dog cowering in a corner. The only time we can get in our true licks is when the quarterback calls a running play which requires that the guards pull to run interference. Then you can go out and smack down a little cornerback and have some *fun*." He made a rumbling, keening sound in his throat.

"Why wouldn't Alex's job be more complicated?" I asked. "After all, he has to make the first move."

Karras explained. "It's natural to knock over a guy. It isn't natural to have to stand there and let the other guy deliver blows to your head."

"As well as kicking and gouging and kneeing," Gordy added.

"And do you think these two postures affect the players involved?" I asked.

"The defensive linemen are more temperamental, more sadistic than the offensive people," Karras said, "and uncontrollable. It's because of the nature of what each does. The poor offensive lineman can't get violent and kick and bite and scratch; if he does, he gets a penalty for it. A defensive lineman can do just about anything. He can damn near haul an ax out of his jock and slash around with it before he'll be called for anything."

Gordy nodded his head. "I think of the defensive lineman as an aggressor," he said. "The two terms 'offensive' and 'defensive' are really inaccurate as regards what actually happens during a play. I'm called an offensive lineman because our team's on offense, but what I'm trying to do is keep an aggressor from knocking me down and getting at my home and family. I'm defending."

"Does that image actually exist in your mind out on the playing field?" I asked. "The home?"

"When I was at college," Gordy explained, "I imagined that my mother and father were in the backfield behind me sitting on little stools, and that I was protecting them from someone trying to do them harm. When I got into the pro leagues, what I imagined back there was my baby son, lying in a little cradle. You can imagine to what heights of protectiveness *that* image pushed me."

"I should say," I agreed, impressed.

"But, you see," said Karras, "that's all defensive and frantic. The defensive lineman, the guy John calls the aggressor, has for *his* impulse something quite different. I would guess that if you looked through their backgrounds, you'd find that the majority of defensive linemen have been rejected somewhere along the line, even if they're hardly aware of it. They make a vendetta out of it; most of them have chips on their shoulders. There's somebody they're trying to get back at by taking it out on the quarterback. I'm not the only one."

"And the image that kicks off this aggression?"

"For me, my simple hatred of quarterbacks," Karras said, "is because I see them as 'goodies,' people who've had music lessons and a barber who calls them 'Master Harry,' and they go on to eastern colleges and talk snuffy, and their hair is groomed flat against their heads, and they have these thin, delicate noses, and they take their girls on picnics with big straw hampers to hold the dishes, for Chrissakes, and *napkins,* and they're so polite, they kiss on the cheek in public, and hell, I don't think they *piss* or anything. Of course I know where this all comes from; it's because I grew up in Gary, with all its horrible roughness, and there had to be someone you took it out on, some glamour cat with all the luck. It burns in you if you're brought up in a neighborhood like that, like a fever, and so its opposite becomes the target.

"I've *never* liked quarterbacks. Sometimes I can't bear to watch them play because they're so bad, especially the ones we had on the Lions. If I were a coach and saw some of the things that quarterbacks do, I'd call a time-out and motion the quarterback over to the sidelines. He'd come over, ambling the way they do, very cocky and slowly because he knows that sixty thousand people are watching him, and the television cameras too, and everyone is admiring him—this general, this goddamn *field* marshal, this big deal *cat.* Everybody in the stadium knows that the coach is going to put an arm around this kid's shoulders and whisper in his ear, and everybody's looking and thinking, Oh, that's great—the Old Man and the Whiz Kid, look at the two of them. Well, that's not what *I'd* like to see. If I were the coach, I'd motion him over and wait for him with my head down, and he'd shuck his helmet off just as he got to the sidelines so everybody could see he had this terrific crop of golden hair down to his neck, and he'd lean forward so that I could get my arm up around his shoulder and whisper to him, and right then, when he was in range, I'd rear back and let him have it with a left cross—*pow!*—right in the kisser." Karras thumped a fist into his other palm with concussive force. "Damn right. And then when he was lying on the ground I'd stand on him for a while and look out on the field with my arms crossed."

"But suppose the quarterback you're trying to get to out there on the field also comes out of an environment like Gary? I mean, most of them *do*—John Unitas, say, out of the sandlots of a Pennsylvania steel town. So many of them are products of the same background."

"It's curious," Karras said. "I have my worst games against Unitas. Something happens. I can almost feel myself stop reaching for him because I can't make that proper adjustment in my mind."

"What do you see out there, Alex?" I remembered how bad his eyes were. "I mean, can you actually see the guy about whom you've worked up all this venom?"

"I can distinguish color. And movement, of course. I mean, I really do have bad eyesight. My vision is zero-thirteen. I mostly see shadows and fuzzy masses unless I'm wearing glasses. I can't see the stadium. But I've never felt sight was very important, since the main thing I have to do is get past the man in front of me and that's a question of reacting to pressure—*reading* him, so that it's not unlike types of Oriental wrestling. Sight isn't as important as touch."

"But once you're past that man, don't you have to see who you're going to tackle?"

"Well, you can sense that from the flow of the play, and what other people are doing. Being half blind is actually *helpful,* because all the faking and spinning around back there and cleverly executed handoffs are supposed to fool someone who can *see.* They don't fool someone who's *feeling* his way into the backfield. I used to call my technique a Braille system, and everybody would laugh. But it's really true. A blind man is incredibly sensitive because he's so attuned to what's around him. He's all nerve ends, and quick, like the way a person's perceptions are very sharp moving around a dark room. The slightest touch or shape makes you jump; you're like a cat."

"Did anyone ever try contact lenses on you?"

"I wore them for part of the nineteen fifty-nine season. Coach Wilson called me up and said, 'You're having so much trouble following the ball that I've arranged for you to see an eye doctor and get a set of contacts.' I got them, and I was just horrible. I saw so well that it destroyed the whole way I'd learned to play the game. I wandered around in the backfield looking at things. I relied too much on what I saw, and I lost those good instinctive moves—I wasn't so *sensitive* anymore.

"Besides, one of the advantages of bad eyesight is that everything seems a little smaller. With the contacts, I didn't like what I saw out there—I mean those big guys. I didn't like that much at all. You can't be too scared of what you can't see."

"What about when you're on the bench? Can you tell what's going on?"

"I don't see very much of what's going on out there. On the bench I try to sit next to someone with good eyesight. Once I sat next to Bill Swain, who played linebacker, and he'd lost his contact lenses. He sees worse than I do, and we sat there and joked about it. Swain said to me, 'Hey, do you think we're facing in the right direction?'

"You know, I'm an entirely different person with my glasses off," Karras said, abruptly shifting tack.

"In what way?"

"My voice gets much lower, for one thing." He took off his glasses. "Like *this,*" he rumbled. "My whole character changes. I become a football player. I turn mean. I can feel the hair growing in my armpits."

"Suppose your glasses fall off by mistake?"

"It's happened. At a birthday party right in Bloomfield Hills. I was leaning over the birthday cake trying to read what was on it, and my glasses fell off. They bounded on the cake and fell to the floor somewhere. Right away I felt different. I looked around, squinting, trying to see. There had to be a football game going on. I could hear the cheering from the stands. It sounded like they were singing 'Happy Birthday' to someone—probably the rival coach. Apparently there was a time-out—the players across the line were just standing around waiting for time to be called back in. Who were they? I strained to see. The Green Bay Packers, probably. Sons of *bitches*. I could feel myself puffing up with meanness. Then the referee—who seemed to be wearing a black and white striped dress, very odd—lifted his hand to his mouth to blow the whistle and I knew that with time back in I was really going to knock the stuffing out of someone."

"Well, what happened?"

"My wife caught sight of me without my glasses and knew instantly what was going on. She came running over and found the glasses and slapped them on just as I was beginning to breathe heavily and reach for someone."

"That's pretty frightening," I said.

"Damn right," he said.

"You wouldn't be invited anywhere anymore," I said.

"It's rare enough as it is," he said.

"Alex, what are you thinking about at the moment that the quarterback begins to call the signals?" I asked.

"Well, if it's fairly sure to be a pass play, *he's* the one I'm thinking about. The quarterback. He's the guy I've got to get to. I can't think about the man in front of me; I've got to get around him as quickly as I can. If John's the guy opposite, and he's dropping back on pass protection, for me he's just kind of a little peg I've got to get past. One could say that the offensive lineman has no more significance than the fence you climb over to get an apple off the neighbor's tree. The apple is what has all your attention. Any time I begin to think about killing the man in front of me, then I'm not going to be able to rush the passer."

"And that's what *I* have to do," Gordy said. "Make him look at me; make him fight *me*. I remember the first time I played Alan Page of the Vikings. The game started and he's like I'm not there. *Whack-whack*. But I remember thinking at the time that he was *going* to be a great tackle. He wasn't yet; there were still a few things that he had to learn. So I went to work on him. Pretty soon, like a bite that a person starts scratching, this damn peg that he was trying to get around began to get on his nerves. He looked at me, and then all of a sudden I had him. He took a full-bull inside charge, and I ran him across the line. He stopped and started to go the other way. Look, like this..."

He got up. Again he made me stand opposite him and began shoving me around the room. "Look, look...like *this!*" A lamp tottered. Karras watched solemnly. "See? See how it works? He went here; I was there. Suddenly he realized I was the jerk who'd been keeping him from what he wanted to do, and from down by his shoe tops he began to swing a stiff-arm, like a big club, to pop me in the head, and I ducked. I had him. I was in good shape. He might hit me and maybe I'd get stitched up now and then, but he wasn't going to get to the quarterback. He was near berserk. He was staring at me. He shouted to the line judge, 'He's holding me! He's holding me!' Well, I *wasn't* holding him. He just had to assume that, because he wasn't getting in to smack that quarterback down and there had to be some reason."

"He wasn't getting into that house of yours," I said.

Gordy was grinning. "No, he wasn't. I was slamming the door on him and he was feeling the pain in his fingers."

"Does the offensive guard, this guy who's supposed to be passive, ever lose his cool? I mean, go berserk the way Page did?"

"Obviously he shouldn't," Gordy said. "But I've done it. Les Richter, the Ram linebacker, blindsided me once—that is, he blocked me damn close to a clip when I was moving away from him, and when I pulled up he swung around and hit me in the face with a *cast*. He had this cast on from his wrist to his elbow, and it drove my teeth right through my lip and blood just went all over the place. Well, I busted the next two plays trying to get to him. It must have looked crazy—some idiot running amok on every play. I mean, I just moved from my stance at the quarterback's signal, and my head came up, looking for Richter, and I went for him. If he'd been sitting in Section E, forty rows up, I'd have gone for him, I swear."

"Did Richter know you were after him?"

"Sure he did. We kept it up for seven years. To block Les I would do anything. There were no holds barred. He runs a racetrack at Riverside now. I've done some things socially with him, and we enjoy each other's company. But on the field, ever since that particular time when he hit me with the cast, I've always gone over the side after him."

"So there are personal duels?"

"Absolutely."

"You had a pretty good one with Mike Pyle, the Chicago Bear center," I remarked to Karras, remembering a number of incidents between them.

Karras stirred. "Yeah. He's one of the goodies. He's the kind of guy that gets along with the coaching staff. I never heard a coach say a bad word about him. He's that kind of guy."

"I met him once in Chicago," I said. "He seemed a very agreeable cat. He's from Yale," I added, grinning.

"He gets along with everybody. I'm always leery of guys like that," Karras said. "But my feuds were mostly professional rather than emotional. For years I had one against Alex Sandusky of the Colts, who's the best guard I ever played against. We had great respect for one another. We never said a word to each other all those years, except at the very end. I'll never forget. It was a real bang-up affair. I was trying with anything I had to kill him, and so was he from his side. I got my nose broken. After that game was the only time we ever talked. We came off the field together and he said, 'Boy, am I ever tired.' I said, 'Me too.' He said, 'This is it for me. I can't take this beating anymore.' And that was the last. He retired."

Evening had come, and the river flowed fast and dark beyond the windows. Gordy began chewing noisily on some crackers. "Chow time?" he asked. "Shall we go out and get a bite somewhere?"

"Sure," Karras said.

"Do you ever see him socially, Alex?" I asked.

"Who?"

"Sandusky."

"No. He wrote me a letter after he saw the movie of *Paper Lion*. He said he thought I was good in it. He wrote, 'When I come to Detroit, we'll go out and have a drink.' He never came. I never said a word to Sandusky all those years, except for the last. All those years and he never said a word to me, one way or the other. And I did some bad things to him, and he did some bad things to me. But we had great respect for each other."

# CHAPTER 7

One spring day, Alex Karras called me up and invited me to come out to Flint, Michigan, to play in a golf tournament bearing his name—the Alex Karras Golf Classic.

"It's *your* tournament, Alex?" I asked. "A *golf* tournament?"

"That's right. It's been put together in three weeks. It's to benefit victims of cystic fibrosis. I don't know what it's going to do to my bad-guy image. Maybe I can run away with the proceeds," he said. "Well, are you coming?"

"But you know my golf," I said. "It's awful. It's about as bad as yours."

I had played golf with both Karras and Gordy. I doubt that among athletes there is any group as inept at golf as football linemen. That generalization may be as unsteady as the one which states that there are no pianos in Japan, but I have never seen a tackle or a guard on the golf course whose caddy for safety's sake didn't tend to keep the golf bag between him and ball when the lineman was sashaying back and forth getting ready to hit.

Gordy used to speculate that linemen were poor golfers because they spent so much of their time down in a three-point stance. Their backs were bad. But they kept at the game because every once in a while all that strength would flow properly into a golf swing, everything just right, and a titanic shot would result. Still, even Gordy's best remembered shots had a mournful duffer's quality to them. Eight or nine times he had told me about a 280-yard drive to the green, his best ever, that he had made on an Air Force course outside Nashville, but when it landed it had hit a colonel on the ankle. "Got him on the first bounce," Gordy said proudly.

Karras was as undistinguished a golfer as his friend. His actions on a football field were as confident and quick as the motions of a dragonfly above a pond, but on the golf course an earthbound quality and something of the hermit crab seemed to take over. His golf swing was a heavy swooping snatch at the ball, and from a distance it looked as if he were flailing at something that had got inside his shoe; invariably at the conclusion of his swing a large piece of turf was dislodged from the fairway and sailed into the air with his ball perched on it like a decoration.

It always surprised me that a man possessed of such satanic, if controlled, fury on a football field could keep himself contained playing such awful golf. But on the few occasions we played together, the sole impression Karras gave was of enjoying himself hugely, even when he disappeared into the deepest rough to flail away at an errant shot.

Still, I could not have been more surprised by his phone call asking me to play in his tournament. "You'll have a great time," he said. "My tournament is going to be different. No one's going to play good golf. The whole tournament has been set up as a duffer's revenge on the game.

"We've got these gags," he explained, "that are going to bring good golfers right damn down to their knees. We've hidden these tape machines around the golf course. There'll be these terrible noises coming out of the woods—cars crashing, elephants screaming, things like that, all on tape and amplified to really make the golfers jump. We thought of mining the greens so they'd blow up. Tiny Tim is going to rush out and carry on, and strum his ukulele, and we've got parachutists..."

"Tiny Tim!"

"He's been asked to the tournament. No kidding. He agreed."

"And you put all this together?"

"Pete Buterakos and me," said Karras.

"Holy smoke," I said. "Pete Buterakos? Well, I guess I'd better arrange to come."

I had never met Buterakos, though I had heard members of the Detroit Lions talk about him. Football was his passion, and he was around them often. He was a salesman who had made a fortune selling cemetery plots. His sales pitch combined quantities of zest and lunacy, coupled with self-confidence; his lectures on motivation were famous throughout the Midwest. I had once heard the tape of a speech he had given at the Lion training camp—a wild burst of inspirational cajolery delivered with evangelical fervor and punctuated with the crash of the various props which were his particular trademark and were used to illustrate his points. To show that life is an "obstacle course," he would hoist up a track hurdle. Or he'd turn on an air hammer to illustrate that life is "full of windbags," or set off a smoke bomb to indicate "a clogged mind." On the tape of the inspirational talk I heard, there was a sudden deafening crash which I was told was a cherry bomb ("Life is full of abrupt changes" had been the cue for it), which he had rolled out behind him and which had blown a big chunk of plaster out of the wall. The Detroit coaches had him around annually for these talks in the hope of perking up the team, and as Joe Schmidt, then the head coach, once said, "Buterakos keeps you not only on the edge of your seat, but usually two or three feet above it."

"What a salesman," Karras once said reverently. "He'll do anything." He described a speech on business administration he had heard Buterakos deliver before forty-five hundred people in Flint, during which he had talked for over an hour and tossed a variety of props into the audience, including live pigs ("There are pigs in the business world"), rubber snakes ("Competition can turn good men into snakes"), and blood-soaked rubber daggers ("At the top there are people waiting to stab you in the back"). He climaxed his talk by bursting through a mock brick wall that had been set up on the stage.

"What did he do that for?" I asked.

"To show that you can overcome anything," Karras said. "For him there's no such thing as an obstacle. When he went through the wall he was wearing a Superman outfit."

Buterakos turned out to be the proprietor of a small golf course near Flint named Shady Acres where the tournament would be held, utilizing the pro-am format of having one local athlete (most of them from the Lions, but a few representatives from the Tigers, the Piston basketball organization, and the Detroit Red Wing hockey team) playing in a foursome with Flint businessmen who would cough up fifty dollars (to benefit cystic fibrosis) for the privilege. A number of outside celebrities were going to come in to play. "A whole mess of astronauts," Karras told me. "And of course Tiny Tim."

"Is Tiny Tim going to play golf?" I asked.

"I'm going to parachute into the middle of the tournament," Karras said, "and Tiny Tim is going to rush out and present me with a bouquet. In the background the Ortonville band is going to play 'Tiptoe Through the Tulips.' That's what's organized for Tiny Tim at the moment. We may have something else for him to do."

There had been a number of meetings in Flint at which details of this sort were planned. Buterakos was very much in evidence. At one meeting he gave a roar and threw a dead fish onto the table—a big red snapper he had bought from the local fish market. "These proceedings are *dead!*" he shouted. "You've got to swim against the current to get anywhere. You've got to have more zest, more pep. Now let's get down to business." Various duties had been assigned. Carl Brettschneider, the former Lion linebacker, was supposed to turn up at the tournament with a large selection of balloons to be passed out to the crowds by a local Flint clown named Upsie-Daisy. "That's all you're expected to do," Brettschneider was told. "Can you pull it off?"

"Sure," he said. "I'm going to devote two nights to blowing them up."

When Brettschneider turned up early on tournament day, Buterakos ran up and asked, "Where the hell are the balloons?"

"Well," said Brettschneider, "I've got some good news for you and some bad news. The good news is that I've decided I'm going to play in the tournament. The bad news is that I haven't got the balloons."

"No balloons!" Buterakos was furious. "What the hell's Upsie-Daisy going to do without balloons to pass out?"

"I've thought about that," said Brettschneider. "Upsie-Daisy can *shake hands* with people. It's more personal. What can you do with a balloon? But to have your hand grabbed and get the big hello from Upsie-Daisy—well, that's something."

Buterakos was not mollified. He took a hard look at Brettschneider and blew a piercing blast on his whistle. "Let's move it," he said. "Let's goddamn move it."

Buterakos's whistle was his personal trademark; he wore it on a white cord around his neck. I heard it for the first time at five-thirty the morning of the tournament. Arriving in Flint late the previous night, I'd had only three hours' sleep in the motel before the whistle shrilled out in the corridor and a sharp rap sounded on the door. He was waiting for me—a big-chested elf, my first impression was, the whistle tucked in a corner of his mouth as he stared at me with peaceful brown eyes that seemed to belie what I'd heard of his energy. I told him that I wasn't expected to tee off until nine o'clock or so, and that I was awfully tired. No, he said, I had to come out to the golf course and see the "whole damn thing unfold—right from the beginning."

I gave in, and we drove out to the golf course. I stood and stomped my feet in the cold. There was no end of activity. Buterakos said it was worth having a tournament just to see so many of his friends up at six A.M. He pointed out a man struggling with a wheelbarrow full of soft drinks. "That's Dave Doherty. He's got an undescended testicle—one ball. Hey, Dave," he shouted. "You're really working your ball off."

Doherty shook his head wearily.

"He takes a lot of kidding," Buterakos said.

He took me over to a table crowded with tape recorders. The man tinkering with them looked up and said, "Hey, Pete. You want to hear the lions?" He flicked a switch which turned on a weird jangle of sound. "The tape's on backwards," the man said, "but that's a fantastic sound—right, Pete?"

Buterakos beamed at me. "The sound effects are going to be

something else." We watched a man going by carrying a small cannon. Buterakos explained that it was to be hidden behind the first tee and shot off from time to time, just at the height of a competitor's backswing. "Wait till you hear that thing," he said. "It'll make the golfers jump into the next county."

Karras arrived. He wore his heavy horn-rimmed glasses and was dressed in a white mesh shirt and yellow golfing trousers. His golf hat bore the JEWISH OPEN decal. "Have the horses gotten here yet?" he asked.

He was assured that they had. At that moment a small cart appeared around the corner of the clubhouse with two ponies in the traces. A man with a guitar walked alongside.

"You know what that guy's going to do?" Karras said to me. "He's going to travel around the golf course in that little cart, with those ponies dragging him, and he's going to stand up with his big Mexican grin and sing 'The Mexican Hat Dance.' He's going to belt out that song all day long, just that *one* song. He said to me, 'But I know a *lot* of songs.' I said, 'No, "The Mexican Hat Dance" is the one we want. It's a big golfing song because it inspires golfers when they're putting.' He didn't know what putting was. So I told him, 'That's when the guys are bending over the ball, trying to put it in the hole, and that's when you should get in real close with those ponies and your cart so you can belt "The Mexican Hat Dance" right at them.' "

Out in the parking lot, the competitors began arriving, getting their golf bags out of car trunks and toting them to the lawn in front of the clubhouse. I recognized some of the Lion players—Nick Eddy and Mel Farr, who played in the offensive backfield, and Mike Lucci and Wayne Walker, two of the starting linebackers. The rest were primarily Flint residents, mostly businessmen, two hundred of whom in the course of three weeks had bought fifty-dollar tickets. Many of them went down to the practice putting green and began working on their putting strokes. They seemed very serious. They wore the latest style in golfing attire, fancy golf shoes with flaps over the laces, and golfing hats with the decal of their home course. Almost all of them had the hunched shoulders and locked knees of the Arnold Palmer putting stance. Their impressions of the tournament must have been reasonably favorable; there were at least some concessions to tradition. A scoreboard. And the caddies had the name of each foursome's leader on the back of their shirts—a fine professional touch, except the letters were stuck on with adhesive that wouldn't hold, and one or two of the letters dropped off and left startling variations of the original name. In no time at all Nick Eddy's name was reduced to ICK EDD. Mel Farr's took on Mideastern simplicity: EL FA.

The first indication of the tournament's special quality was the Mexican guitarist's serenade at the practice putting green. As Karras said later, he must have gone wild seeing all those golfers putting at once. "De *da,* de *da,* de *da,* de da-da-da-da-de-*dah,*" he sang with an enormous grin, his foot tapping, his fingers strumming hard.

The golfers looked up. "Hey, can it, man," I heard one of them say. The foot kept tapping, the guitarist imparting an odd beseeching quality to the song, straining for a therapeutic effect.

If there was any remaining doubt about the tournament's character, it was settled at eight-thirty A.M. when the first foursome went off. Bill Munson, the Detroit Lion quarterback, was the first golfer off the tee. The amplifiers were suddenly turned on full tilt—the sudden scream of tires, the rattle of gunfire—and just at the top of his backswing someone pulled the lanyard of the cannon. The report was deafening. Munson leapt straight up in the air with his legs a-twangle, like a puppet gone awry. A cloud of white smoke drifted down the fairway and Buterakos's whistle began shrilling. "All right, Munson, let's not just stand around. Move it out."

Visibly shaken, Munson addressed the ball and knocked out a drive, then stood by as the three Flint businessmen in his foursome teed off, their faces grim in concentration as around them there blared trumpet calls, cymbal clashings, and the amplified sounds of toilets flushing.

It was difficult to gauge the reaction of the players. When the cannon went off, they started up from their Arnold Palmer stances down on the putting green and looked at each other; they stood around somewhat nervously, resplendent in their togs, like egrets about to take flight, but I didn't see anyone pack up and go home. When their time to drive off came, it was extraordinary to see them in that hurricane of sound on the first tee—Buterakos intoning a windy biography about each of them into a microphone ("That sweet, sweet guy on the first tee is Clint Jones of Flint, out on ten thousand dollars' bail his niece scraped together..."), the amplifiers bellowing their startling variety of sounds, and the golfer himself, poised over the ball, murmuring to himself to let his "left side come through" or whatever mental tip had priority, and actually worrying not about a slice but about the cannon going off. Those who hit straight drives moved off down the fairway with alacrity.

"Look out for the swamps!" Buterakos shouted after them. "Look out for what's going to be coming out of the swamps!"

"What's going to be coming out of the swamps?" I asked him.

"What swamps?" he asked. "No swamps on this course."

My own foursome moved off an hour or so later without incident, but behind us Errol Mann, the Lion placekicker, mishit three drives in a row, one of which went four feet. I heard later that he pleaded with Buterakos to turn off the noise so that he could concentrate, and Buterakos had agreed and then palmed him a trick golf ball that smoked and popped sharply into two pieces when Mann lashed at it.

Storm clouds had been gathering most of the morning, and the first drops began to come down about one o'clock—a heavy abrupt spatter in the trees off the fairway. My own foursome had reached the far corner of the course, and we were out of shot of the tape recorders. The "Mexican Hat Dance" man had materialized on two greens as we were putting out. With the rain, golf umbrellas were hastily put up, and under them nervous discussions went on about the lightning which was ripping around, making us start nervously. No one could agree on the safest place to be. The rain began to come down so hard that the landscape went gray and the raindrops flickered off the fairways like hailstones. One of our group went out and stood in the middle of the fairway under an umbrella. His caddy stayed with us. We were under trees, such a large patch of them that we felt ourselves safe, but the golfer was insistent and said we were wrong and all damn fools. We watched him through the hissing sheets of rain and wondered if there was enough metal in our umbrellas to conduct electricity. The lightning was awesome. Someone muttered that Karras and Buterakos had let their special-effects department get out of hand.

After a half hour of constant downpour we trudged back to the clubhouse. The golf course lay under stretches of water, still being pocked by rain as the thunderheads moved on. Both competitors and onlookers had pushed inside the clubhouse, and the noise was fierce. I could hear Buterakos's whistle going as he desperately tried to keep things stirred up. I saw him trying to lead a group in some squat-kicks that I assumed were variations of a Greek dance. "Faster, faster!" he kept shouting at the band.

"It's a disaster," someone said in my ear. "The band ought to be playing 'Nearer My God to Thee.' "

Across the way a heavyset man was shouting, "Tiny Tim's not coming. He's got halitosis."

"It's laryngitis," I was told. "The weather. He's got to protect his vocal cords. That's what his manager said."

Karras came by carrying a bouquet of blue flowers.

"I hear Tiny Tim's not coming," I said.

"Things were going too smooth. I knew something like this was going to happen. It was so well planned, too."

The rain stopped, and after a while the tournament started up again. We heard the "Mexican Hat Dance" man off in the distance and could see the ponies straining to pull the cart through the mud. There were distant explosions.

My own golf was atrocious. The rain had soaked my golf pants and they had split completely down the seam in the rear without my being aware. A girl had come up and said, "Hey, are those good-luck pants or something?" and I had reached back to find the back of the pants gone. My golf style changed abruptly; I developed a tendency to keep my back to the trees and away from the crowds, and on the putting surface I changed my Arnold Palmer putting crouch to an upright telephone-pole stance, so straight that I could barely reach the ball with the putter.

When we got in from the round, I went back to the motel to change. I returned for the post-tournament golf dinner, which was held under a vast moldy tent, somewhat low-slung and inadequately lit so that one had the sense of eating in a brewery cellar illuminated by lanterns. The noise was deafening. A bagpipe band entered under the flaps at one end of the tent and skirted around for a while, marching up and down between the long wooden tables until someone gave a signal and they sat down at a table for dinner, the instruments propped up on the benches beside them.

Karras had urged me to come to the golf dinner because it would be "different"; the prizes were not what I would expect. In fact, I would not recognize the usual pro-am dinner—with its familiar climax of applause and the day's low-ball team sauntering up to the awards table to receive silver bowls and sets of matched irons—"No, *sir,*" said Karras.

Preceding the awards was an auction which Karras presided over, shouting above the noise. The Flint merchants had donated a number of items, any one of which would have tested the mettle of the most expert of auctioneers. Among other things, there were ten Big Boy flashlights to be got rid of; ten stencil kits; five domino sets; and quite a lot of men's wear. "What do I hear for these socks?" Karras would shout, holding them aloft. "Do I hear a dollar for these socks? They run from size ten to thirty-three. Size thirty-three will cover your entire body!" The last item was a small desk globe. Karras tried to sell it to the man with one testicle. "Dave, you'll want this thing around the house," he called out tenderly.

For the awards ceremony Karras was relieved by Sonny Eliot, the Detroit TV weathercaster. Eliot is an extraordinary phenomenon in the area—a small lively man with a quicksilver approach who has added such a dimension of entertainment to reporting the weather that he is a considerable hometown celebrity, right up there with Gordie Howe, the hockey player, and Al Kaline of the Tigers, and six blocks ahead of the mayor. Detroit people set alarm clocks to be sure they don't miss Sonny Eliot's program, which concludes the eleven P.M. evening news—waking up to see what comic ingenuity he can bring to a weather front bearing down on the Peninsula area.

But even Eliot seemed somewhat shaken by his duties. Taking over the microphone, he held it as if he expected it to explode. Karras and Buterakos stood behind him and prompted him from time to time. The chief awards were for the winning foursome. All day long there had been rumors that each member of the low-ball team was going to win a car. Flint is a big automobile town with many General Motors divisions, particularly Chevrolet, and a number of people lining up birdie putts doubtless sparked their concentration by reminding themselves that a car could be riding on the stroke.

"And now the grand moment!" Sonny Eliot shouted. A silence descended. A group near the "Mexican Hat Dance" man turned around and tried to get him quieted down. "Each member of the winning foursome"—Eliot shouted, and he read off their names—"receives an auto-mo-*bile*"—incredulous cries—"and we got these cars right outside waiting for their new owners!"

One of the winners was sitting down the table from me, and his eyes were bright with excitement. He had bought a Big Boy flashlight set during the auction and he began banging it on the table. "Holy Christ!" he shouted.

Eliot was calling directions to a group of people down at one end of the tent. The flaps were hauled back and we stood up from our benches and craned to see in the semidarkness what turned out to be four wrecks hauled in from a junkyard, victims of head-on collisions, wheelless, jumbles of blue metal, and Sonny Eliot began shouting, "All right, you winners, you'll find the keys above the sun visor. Gentlemen, start your engines and let's get those damn things out of there."

The winner with the Big Boy flashlight began shaking his head. I felt a twinge of sympathy. There must have been some part of him which felt that he really *was* going to get a car, with its new-leather smell, and he was going to slide into the front seat and reach for the keys...

After the ceremony I wandered over and spoke to Karras, who had a cigar stuck dead center in his mouth. He removed it and said that he and Buterakos were already jotting down ideas for next year's Karras Classic. "It's going to be bigger and louder," he said.

Buterakos came by. "We're talking about next year's Karras Classic," I said.

"We're going to shoot Alex out of a cannon," Buterakos said. "Did he tell you about the trumpeters in the trees?"

"Oh yeah," said Karras. "There're going to be these trumpeters in the trees. A lot of them. You'll see them sitting up there, and they'll blow a lot of cavalry charges."

"What about the animals?" Buterakos said. "Tell him about the animals."

"Yeah," said Karras. "These animals are going to rush out onto the fairway from the forest—whole herds of them. We'll ship them in secretly at night and get these kids to drive them out during the tournament. Strange animals, too, like llamas; these Flint golfers will look up from their shot and say, 'What the hell's *that?*' "

"And yaks," Buterakos said. "The bushes part and these yaks stream out."

"Is there an animal called a ginook?" Karras asked abruptly.

"A ginook? I don't think so," I said.

"Well, there ought to be," Karras said. His eyes were fixed. "The bushes part and these ginooks rush out, a whole mess of them.

"Then we're going to have these mysterious professionals playing with some of the foursomes. We'll tell these Flint businessmen that boy, are they lucky. 'You may not have drawn Al Kaline for your celebrity,' we'll tell them, 'but you've got an honest-to-God professional playing with you. You've drawn Bill *Tank*. You're going to break the course record.'

" 'Bill who?' they'll ask.

" 'Why, Bill Tank. The pro. He's out of San Fernando Country Club. Came in third in the Western Open one year.'

"So these Flint guys get all excited," Karras continued, "and they get out early on the course to practice their putting. They bet on themselves. Then, to meet them on the first tee, we get this seedy cat in old britches and he says, 'Tank's the name. I'm your pro partner,' and he steps up and hits the ball about thirty-two feet. He drinks a lot, this guy, out of a stone jug, and on the fourth hole he topples into a sand trap and they can't get him out of there. He's out cold."

"How is the rest of Bill Tank's foursome going to take this?" I asked.

"Take it? Well, the thing is, you keep them off balance so they don't know if they're being taken for a ride or maybe just unlucky. You ride out to see them in a golf cart, somewhere on the back nine, all excited, and you say, 'Gee, for God's sake, where's Bill Tank? You guys must be ripping the course apart.'

"They give you one of these—the cold look—and say that Tank's back in some goddamn sand trap, out colder than ice. 'What a damn shame,' you say, 'what a real damn shame you got him on one of his bad days.' "

"Alex," said Buterakos. "I'm going to stir up the natives." He gave a blast on his whistle. "Get the drinking under way!" he shouted. As he walked off he called back, "You tell him about the midget?"

"Yeah, the midget," said Alex. "Well, we tell this one foursome that they've got a great pro playing with them, this guy called Jim 'Dynamite' Grogan, and they get to the first tee all excited and say, 'Well, where's Grogan?' and the midget steps up and says, '*I'm* Grogan.' He's real nattily dressed in a golf outfit, very correct, and he's got this great hulking caddy, a real monster of a guy, who carries the midget's golf bag tucked under one arm, the way you carry a telescope.

"The midget steps up to tee off. He's got this British ball he's playing with, which is a little smaller than the American, and after he's put it down on the tee, he squints out from under his tiny little golf hat and says in that little helium voice that midgets have, 'Hey, how *long* is this course?' They tell him it's about six thousand yards. 'Six thousand *yards?*' the midget says.

"Well, it turns out that the midget regularly plays these par-three courses, with the more difficult holes marked up to fours and fives, and he gets around in what scratch players do around a regular course—maybe seventy, seventy-two. He's never played a regular course. So he tells these Flint businessmen, 'Gee, you guys, this is quite an experience for me. This is some privilege, playing a regular course.'

"He steps up to the ball and he's got this real perfect grooved swing, sweet as anything, except the arc of it isn't more than three feet. The ball goes out, *click,* real straight for fifty yards down the center of the fairway. The midget watches it, real proud, and the Flint businessmen hear him say to himself, 'Oh, you sweetheart. You really sweethearted *that* one.'"

"How do the Flint businessmen go for this, Alex?" I asked.

"You blame the PGA," Karras said blithely. "You tell the Flint businessmen that the PGA recommended this guy, and how are you going to tell from the guy's name, Jim 'Dynamite' Grogan, that he measures in at a shade over three feet tall?"

"And the caddies?" I asked. "I suppose you'll have a number of them planted to do mischief."

"The caddies!" Karras began to laugh, his hand flying up to his mouth. "Oh my," he said. "The caddies. Oh Christ. We'll get these real wise-guy caddies, these old Scottish people, old and wrinkled, and with these thin mean voices, so that you think they're terribly old *women,* one hundred and fifty years old, but they 'know the course.' And they give these Flint guys this weird advice—like they show the guy an angle off the tee facing a forest that goes all the way to the Canadian border, and they say, 'Clear that tree and you're home free on the dogleg.'

"'Hell, man…'

"'It's the shot, I'm telling you. Hit it right and you drop right down for a wee easy chip. I've been working this course for sixty years.'

"So the guy faces around in this absurd position, just as crazy a shot as hitting off the stern of a boat, and he hits a tremendous drive, probably the best drive of his life, and after a while they can hear the ball rattling around in the tree trunks. So the caddy says, 'What did you hit it in there for? That's a bloody forest.'

" 'You *told* me to,' the guy says.

" 'You were supposed to *fade* the shot,' the caddy says, 'not hit it into the bloody forest,' and he gets all disgusted and stomps around, this furious wizened little man, and the guy from Flint feels all *guilty*."

Buterakos's whistle was shrilling in the distance. "His mind is turning," Karras said. "Hey, you want some golf tomorrow?"

"You must be kidding, Alex."

"I know a good course a hitch down the road," he said. "We'll play early tomorrow morning."

"Will there be trumpeters in the trees?" I asked.

He looked at me. "What are you talking about?"

"Or llamas? The bushes parting and these llamas rushing out?"

"You gone loco?" he asked. "A friendly game of golf—that's all I had in mind."

"I wasn't sure," I said. "I just thought I'd ask."

# CHAPTER 8

They came in the morning. Both seemed in good spirits, though the night before we had been on the town with a group of people and everybody had got home, Karras and Gordy to their hotel, about three in the morning. One of the girls out with us that evening was Wendy Vanderbilt, the daughter of Alfred Gwynne Vanderbilt, who owns a great stable of racehorses—a very pretty girl whose date, a young man wearing a black suit of expensive cut, sat brooding at the little nightclub table around which we were crushed. He kept looking across at her, half listening to the rest of us.

Karras was talking about him that morning. He referred to him as Vanderbilt's "sidekick." "Hey, do you know what the sidekick said to me last night?"

"What?"

"He said to me that he enjoyed boxing. I said, 'That's wonderful.' He said, 'I think I could knock you out.' I said, 'Well, you might be able to knock me out, but before you did, I would probably beat the crap out of you!' He looked at me, and then he said, 'You might have a point there.' Isn't that great? 'You might have a point there.'" He leaned back and roared with laughter.

An evening out with Karras and Gordy always seemed to attract its dramas, as if some quality in them courted a Punchinello mood. I remember having dinner with Karras one night in a small uptown

Italian restaurant, years back, when I first knew him, and he was carrying a little case which he opened up on the table and showed me. Inside was an electric vibrator machine, a hand model, with a long electric cord, and various interchangeable implements that could be attached to it. These accessories lay in shaped indentations in the box, like instruments in a surgical kit, and Karras picked out a few of them to demonstrate. "These fit on the vibrator itself, which is called the Picomaster," he told me. "I'm into big, big business with the Picomasters. I'm the Midwest distributor. I should tell you that these vibrators are the best of their kind—known in the trade as the 'Cadillac' of vibrators."

"Very grand," I said.

"Right. Now here are some of the accessory attachments for the Picomaster. This rubber suction cup is for the female pectoral region," he said in a voice heavy with sincerity. "This attachment," he said, taking another accessory out and clicking it onto the vibrator, "is for general massage purposes."

He looked around.

"Ah."

Behind him, at a neighboring table with her back to us, was a woman in a dress cut just below the shoulder blades. She was bending over her soup. Karras leaned down, found a socket in the wall next to our table, and plugged the cord in. A low hum rose from the vibrator. "The Picomaster lives," he said.

He turned in his chair and applied the "general massage" unit to the woman's back. She stiffened abruptly, and her escort, sitting across from her, looked up in alarm. "Hey, what the hell?"

"Don't worry," said Karras. "It's the Picomaster! Hold steady there, ma'am."

She had half turned and was staring into Karras's big pale face; her spoon remained poised an inch above the soup.

"That's better," Karras said soothingly. "The brushes on this massage unit are *sisal*—the very best sisal and just the thing to soothe jangled nerve ends."

The woman's back was beginning to glow a vaguely mottled red under the vibrator brushes. I kept watching her escort, expecting a violent reaction. He had a tentative, somewhat worried expression; perhaps he recognized Karras, or had been intimidated by his size.

"Helen?" he asked, as if her reaction would determine what he was going to do. There was no answer.

"I wonder if you would tell me how it feels, ma'am," Karras said solemnly.

"Well, it feels sort of *rubbery,*" she said after a while.

"Exactly," said Karras. He removed the vibrator from the woman's back and turned in his chair. He looked directly at me, but his eyes were not focused; he was fantasizing again, this time speaking a commercial into the lens of a television camera. He intoned: "And *that's* the Picomaster, the Cadillac of hand vibrators, the only sure-fire cure for what ails you, and you've seen it *live*—a Picomaster at work on the back of this lovely young woman picked at random. Now watch how this woman, newly massaged by the Picomaster, digs into her soup with renewed vigor."

His eyes focusing again, he said, "What I need is a long extension cord. I could give a demonstration to everyone in the restaurant."

The woman tapped him on the shoulder. "Are you *taping* this, or something? Is there a camera somewhere? Don't I have to sign a release or something?"

"No, ma'am," said Karras. "It's a personal survey. We're just spreading the word."

I had asked Karras and Gordy to my apartment that morning in the hope that they would talk about football players and their business ventures, such as the involvement with the Picomaster vibrator. Business was always a constant topic with players. Invariably, there was a frantic, naive quality to such discussions—wild-eyed excitement as they described oil fields, mutual funds, land values, food franchises, speculations in timber, duck farms, fortunes to be made by investing in locomotives, boxcars, or penny stocks. One could scarcely get through a day at training camp without hearing a big tackle clear his throat and remark, "Nice yield on that Caroline-Sidney preferred." There was only one Lion player who ever admitted to me that business matters were beyond his ken. "Hell," Dick LeBeau, the cornerback, told me, "I couldn't sell ass on a troopship."

I began by asking Karras about the Picomaster. Had that been a success? Both he and Gordy groaned. From the first, I was informed, the Picomaster venture had been a painful business. It was a distribution deal, arranged with a German manufacturer's representative, and they found themselves overwhelmed with enormous stocks of vibrators they could not seem to unload.

"They arrived in enormous cartons higher than a man's head," Gordy said.

"Remember the time we took the Picomasters out to the racetrack?" Karras said. "We were desperate, trying to sell them. Pete Larco and I went out. Larco," he explained to me, "was a partner in the Picomaster deal. He runs a restaurant, Larco's, where all the Lions go after a home game. Well, we went out to the racetrack at six o'clock in the morning, just after the horses had been exercised. We went in and talked to this guy, one of the top trainers in the country, who said, 'You know, I don't think anyone in the horse business has ever *thought* of rubbing horses down with a vibrator. But why not? Let's try it on the most temperamental horse we have.'

"Well, we were all real excited. We went down to the stables where there was this one horse, absolutely mammoth, a real Thoroughbred, you could tell, who was just *tense,* man. The trainer said, 'Calm, baby. Calm, baby.' He turned the vibrator on, *b-z-z-z-z,* and put it on the horse's neck. God's truth, I'm not lying. The horse went *b-b-l-l-a-a-h-h-h*... just completely relaxed. Like a lamb. Damn near went to sleep on us right there in the stall. The trainer really flipped. 'It's the first time this horse has ever relaxed,' he said. 'This vibrator of yours will revolutionize horse racing!' We thought we were saved. A Picomaster for every Thoroughbred."

"Of course that horse never ran a good race again," said Gordy.

"That's right," Karras said. "Larco and I went out to the track the next time he ran. We put a fin on him, a 'sure thing' we thought, because of the Picomaster, but I don't recall that he ever came out of the starting gate. At least, that's what we decided—that the horse had put his head out of the gate at the starting bell to see what all the commotion was about and then had gone back in there to *sleep.* But at the time the trainer thought the vibrator had great therapeutic value. He bought his for cash right there in the stall."

"John," I asked Gordy, "how were you involved in the Picomaster project?"

He clasped his head. "Oh my," he said. "I was one of the pitchmen. I worked in Montgomery Ward's. I was there from eight o'clock in the morning to six o'clock at night. I never talked so much in my life. I stood up on a little platform. 'All right, all right. Gather round. We're going to have a demonstration of the amazing new revolutionary Picomaster.' "

"We had these plants in the audience," Karras explained. "We'd pay them to stand out there—crumpled over, with one arm twitching like the guy had the palsy—and John would call out, 'You, sir. You with the arm! Come up! You look like you need...' And this guy would *crawl* up on the stage, all bent over like a hunchback, and John would say, 'All right, sir, we'll just kind of rub you down with this vibrator, we'll just kind of rub this thing here, this *hump*...' and the guy would straighten up like an arrow. 'It does feel better. Yessir, it does.' Oh, it was terrible."

"All day long I did it," Gordy said. " 'Gather round, gather round!' " He was laughing so hard he could barely stay in his chair.

"Remember the *arthritis?*" Karras shouted.

"Oh Christ!"

"John would run the vibrator over this guy's *fingers.* 'Can you feel it, sir? Can you feel any change?' 'Why, I do believe I can! My fingers are better! My fingers are better!' 'That's right, sir, your fingers *are* better.' "

Gordy shouted, "Then I'd say to the crowd, 'Did everybody hear this amazing statement, right from the lips of a man who's had arthritis since he was nineteen? Speak right up, sir.' 'My fingers are better. My fingers are better.' "

"It's a wonder the Food and Drug authorities didn't lock us up for a hundred and ten years," Karras said.

It took a while for the two of them to calm down and I was able to ask them if they could generalize about business and football. "*Can* a player become involved in another profession?" I asked.

"It's impossible," said Gordy. "The frightening thing about playing professional football is that it gives you a false sense of security. The trouble is that a player enters football when he's about twenty-one. Barring an injury which obviously will put him out earlier, he has a career of ten to fifteen years during which he advances his education only in football. He has time for little else. But the guy up in the stands who comes to watch him play, who envies him, who daydreams of doing great things out there on the field—well, all that time *he's* pecking along in his own profession, day by day, learning, until finally at thirty-five he's a vice president or a manager, and he's got all that practical experience behind him. On the other hand, the football player, when he leaves his profession to try another—hell, he's just *starting*."

"He's been dormant for fifteen years," Karras said. "So he goes in there for his first job interview and says, 'My name is Alex Karras. I played football for the Detroit Lions.' And these cats look up from their big wide desks, and they rattle some papers, and they say, 'Hey, Al, how's the team going to do on Sunday?' "

"Does this make you feel sorry for yourselves?" I asked. "I mean that you picked football?"

"No, no," Karras said. "I've accepted it. There's a good pension plan."

"It's just being realistic," said Gordy.

"Besides," Karras went on, "what I've done since I've started pro ball is to scrimp and save, so that when I finally leave football I'll have enough to invest in something that will give me a comfortable annual income."

"And how much money do you think you'll have to invest, Mister Karras?" asked Gordy, playing the straight man.

"I feel," said Karras, "that twenty-seven dollars and fifty cents will take me to great heights."

"Christ, that's the truth, man," Gordy said.

I asked if it wasn't possible to apprentice at a job while playing football, but both Karras and Gordy said that playing professional football and being in business at the same time was an impossible combination, and that a player's ability at both suffered if he tried them simultaneously. "It's like someone being a doctor," Karras said, "and turning around early in the morning and being a milkman. I mean, you've either got to be one or the other. A guy can't honestly concentrate on the game of football and be in business at the same time."

"What about during the off-season?"

"The off-season isn't that long," Karras said. "By the time you're wrapped up in some business arrangement, you get that call again, you put the jockstrap back on, and out you go."

"Besides," Gordy said, "if you've got to be in training camp by July tenth, you should be working out in June, and if you're an older player, you probably should start getting ready in April. And in the off-season many of us should be in the training room lifting weights. That sounds like a dumb thing for a man to be doing on a winter morning, but I'm worried about a pinched nerve, and my shoulder problem, and the tendinitis in my arm, and the operation on my knee, and the twisted Achilles tendon—all that *junk*. I have to do it. If I can build up a certain muscle tone around the nerves of my neck by lifting weights, then I'm less likely to have that pinched nerve in training camp, and I'm likely to have a better year as a result.

"And hell, in the evening, when maybe I could be working at another job, it's better if I watch football movies every now and then to keep myself thinking about my stance, about pulling, about my footwork, about watching my opponents, about—well, how the hell can you think about putting together conglomerates when you've got all *that* tugging at you? You've got a very limited time left to think about other things."

"That's true," Karras said. "Besides, most employers don't want to hire a guy for five or six months who's got his mind half on something else. Consequently, about the only job a football player can get is selling things door-to-door, and the simpler the object—like a screwdriver—the better. It's important to get your foot in the door, and that's the one advantage the football player has. He knocks on the door and he says, 'Hello, my name is Alex Karras. I play with the Detroit Lions.' 'Oh yes,' the guy says, and if he's a football fan he lets you in. That's it—just an entrée. Beyond that, it's tough, especially if what you're trying to sell him is anything complicated. No one has the time to teach you the business properly. So this guy asks, 'How does the three-inch channel distributor compare to this *five*-inch baby?' What am I to do? I look at my shoes and I repeat, like a robot, 'My name is Alex Karras. I play with the Detroit Lions.' "

Actually, Karras was demeaning his abilities as a door-to-door salesman. Joe Schmidt once gave me a description of Karras selling Bibles door-to-door—one of his jobs, along with professional wrestling, during the year of his banishment from the NFL for gambling. Karras had met a Bible distributor, a very sharp cat, who had said, "Karras, the Bible is the only item in the world that people are ashamed *not* to buy. There can only be one hitch." "What's that?" Karras had asked. "That's if the people say, 'Sorry, we're Jewish.' Well, we have an *answer* to that," the distributor said, rummaging in his suitcase. "We have these Bibles made in Germany by Jewish craftsmen. Right? So if they come up with 'I'm Jewish,' you just throw the Bible at them and tell them it was made by Jews. Karras was naturally skeptical, but he felt he could make at least one sale—to Joe Schmidt, who, besides being a close friend back then, was a God-fearing man and a regular churchgoer, to say nothing of being of German heritage. So Karras tucked a couple of Bibles under his arm and went to call on Schmidt.

The exchange was difficult from the beginning. When he opened the door, Schmidt was delighted to see Karras, but when he discovered the purpose of the visit, he said firmly, "No, Al, I've already got a good family Bible in the parlor. I don't need another."

"Well, you'll need a reserve," Karras said crisply.

"What would I want a reserve Bible for?"

"In case something happens to the one you've got now," Karras said impatiently. "Christ Almighty. Suppose the mice got at it."

"The mice?"

"Right, man. The mice. Or maybe termites, Joe. I mean, suppose you open up the big family Bible at some great occasion, the christening of a baby, with everyone standing around all *pious,* and it turns out that Revelations has been eaten away."

"What the hell are you talking about?"

"That's when you can wheel out the reserve, Joe. You look at all the worried people standing around there in your parlor, the baby beginning to whimper, and you give them the quiet, superior smile and say, 'Fear not, folks, I've got a reserve Bible for just this sort of emergency.' "

Schmidt grunted sourly, and Karras, sensing umbrage being taken at the suggestion that the Schmidt house harbored enough mice and termites to threaten the family Bible, shifted his tactics abruptly. "Joe?"

"What?"

"Joe, this Bible I'm trying to sell you, it's different—it's a *German* Bible, for one thing. Joe, wasn't your pappy a kraut?"

"For Chrissakes, Al, what the hell difference does it make if it's a German Bible?"

"It's been made by Jewish craftsmen."

"Listen, Al, I've got things to do. I'm not really in the market for a Bible," Schmidt said, not unkindly. "Why don't you try someone else? What about Night Train Lane? Try him."

"Joe," said Karras, groping desperately. "There's one big difference in the German edition."

"What's that?"

"They've... they've changed it. They've fooled around with the ending."

"They've *what?*"

"That's right," Karras said. "The whole ending's different. It *comes out* different."

"What are you *talking* about?"

"You remember all that business about the Resurrection and Christ rising up from the dead and sitting on the right hand of God?"

"Yeah?"

"And how they rolled away the stone from the front of the cave and He wasn't there?"

"Yeah?"

"Well, that's not the way this German Bible has it. They roll away the stone and guess who's sitting in there looking out, smart as brass."

"Oh, damn, Al. I don't know."

"Guess."

"What?"

"Take a guess."

"Oh, I don't know. Was it Christ?"

"Christ? Hell, no. Much more interesting than that. Try again."

"Mary Magdalene? Pontius Pilate? Damn it, Al, I don't know *who* was sitting in the cave. Why don't you just tell me and let's get it over with."

"Joe," Karras said, holding up a Bible seductively, "it'll cost you exactly fifteen dollars and six cents, which includes the sales tax, to find out..."

That was enough for Schmidt. He closed the door, and went down to the basement of his house so he wouldn't hear the knocking and the doorknob rattling.

That morning I asked Karras and Gordy if the Lions had ever got together on a *joint* business venture. Wouldn't a cooperative attempt—? Gordy interrupted with a burst of laughter. "Al," he said, "do you remember the phonograph record we thought was going to make us all billionaires?"

Karras doubled up in his chair.

Gordy could hardly speak. "I got this idea that some of the Lion players would get together as a singing group and cut a record. Everyone in town would buy it. Dick LeBeau and Joe Schmidt were the vocalists. Bruce Maher would play the guitar. I was the producer. So I got the players together and we rehearsed. Then I hired a band, and we actually physically cut a record and had ten thousand copies made. One side was 'The Grapes of Wrath' featuring Dick LeBeau; the other was 'Cry Out, Freedom' by John Philip Sousa. The day we finished was the day John F. Kennedy was assassinated. Can you imagine coming out with a record called 'Cry Out, Freedom' right after that?"

"The timing was bad," Karras agreed, "but that's not the reason you only sold ten records. I bought one of those records, put it on the jukebox at the Lindell A.C. bar, and played it every three minutes. 'The Grapes of Wrath.' The guys would be leaning along the bar, a whole line of them, drunk, barely able to stand, and when that song 'The Grapes of Wrath' came on they'd get *sober*. They'd say, 'What the hell was *that?*' "

"You're right," Gordy said. "It was the *worst* song. Once we had a disc jockey party to introduce them all to the record. We gave them each a copy and sent them back to their turntables. We never heard it played. We called around: 'I'll send you another copy if you've lost the one we gave you.' I felt like telling them that if they really liked it I knew where I could get my hands on ninety-five hundred copies."

"Do you remember the Four Coins?" Karras asked. "A singing group. They sang 'Shangri-La'—Greek kids from Pittsburgh. One day the Coins were in Detroit and they came down to the bar. I thought maybe I could convince them to do something about 'The Grapes of Wrath,' so I gave them free drinks. I never gave *anyone* free drinks. I asked these guys, 'When was the last time you had a real hit record?' They said, 'Nineteen thirty-three,' or whenever the hell it was. I said, 'Well, I've got something for you; it's going to be your *next* hit. We'll fix up a royalty deal, but you got to give five percent to the guys who did it originally.' They said, 'Sure, why not?'

"You know something? I really thought they'd like it. I was beginning to think 'The Grapes of Wrath' was pretty good, maybe because I'd heard it five thousand times on the jukebox and it had got to me. So I turned it on. The Four Coins sat there without any expression. When it was over, I was real excited. 'How did you like it?' One of the Coins looked like he was going to vomit on himself. He said, 'That's the worst song I've ever heard.' "

"Who sang the 'Cry Out, Freedom' song?" I asked.

"Joe Schmidt," Karras answered. "Joe's got a bathroom voice; sounds good in bathrooms."

"He's very embarrassed about that record," Gordy said. "When he was made head coach of the Lions, some guy called up and said they were going to hawk 'Cry Out, Freedom' outside the stadium on opening day. Joe called the mayor and got him to refuse to issue these guys a peddler's permit."

"I think that's why he traded away Bruce Maher to the Giants," Karras said. "I told Joe, 'Now there's only LeBeau left to remind you.' "

"I suppose in these fly-by-night schemes—well, you can take a helluva bath," I said.

"In my case," said Gordy, "it was a chain of hamburger joints. 'Gordy's Lionburgers.' " He shook his head and Karras snickered.

"These business guys came to me and said that since I was a football player with a name, they would agree to accept me—and my money—in the restaurant business. It all seemed very glamorous—my name up in lights on this big sign: GORDY'S LIONBURGERS. And easy: they would keep the books and records and run the place. No problem at all!

"Two years later, I couldn't find those people. Or the books or the records. Or the money. I was ruined—literally—and I had to declare bankruptcy. The whole thing was a disaster. We did have two Gordy's Lionburgers stands physically up and running, but they were failing badly. My name wasn't as big as I thought it was. I should have known that offensive guards haven't got selling names. Besides, people didn't associate 'Lionburger' with the Detroit football team. Maybe they thought we were offering them exotic cuts from big cats. I don't know. I do know that a lot of people came in and ordered *loin*burgers. I'm telling you, I got a good business degree out of that experience—the Lionburger Hard Knocks School."

"Is that typical? Do a lot of football players go through experiences like that?"

"They certainly get the opportunity," Gordy said.

"That's right," Karras said, shifting in his chair. "Like oil strikes. Always! Ever since I've been in the league there have been oil strikes. A football player runs into the room and shouts, 'Man, I've got a deal on oil. The gusher's coming in! The oil is one *inch* under the ground. All they've got to do is put a little finger in there and the oil just pops up.'"

"That's right," Gordy said. "The oil is just offshore, and as soon as the tide goes out all they've got to do is walk out and fetch it in."

"What sort of person gets players involved in propositions of that sort?"

"Almost everyone," said Gordy.

"It's usually a guy from New York," Karras added, "with a slick, shiny suit, and a nice tie, and a gigantic jeweled diamond for a tie clasp. Now someone like that, you *know* he's got to be making money, right? See, I'm sitting there in the bar with my hand around a small beer, and I've got my T-shirt and Levis on, and this guy, all shiny, steps up and says he needs five hundred dollars of *my* money and he'll make me a rich man."

"Why do players fall for this sort of thing?" I asked.

"One of the reasons," Karras replied, "is that football players are gullible because they've been surrounded and protected by such nice people. In high school, the coaches are nice because they want you to do the job. So are the teachers, because being on the football team you represent the school. It's the same at college. So you've hung around with nice people all the time, and you tend to think that *all* people are nice, including the guys in the shiny suits."

Gordy nodded. "Then you find that they have the ax out."

Karras said, "They're sharks. Most of the time you find them in the bars. They always begin by coming up and saying, 'How ya doing?' One time we were just getting ready to close the old Lindell A.C. bar and move into the new place. It was the year I was suspended. I was in the new place, polishing the bar and looking out at the empty bar stools, when all of a sudden in comes this guy from New York with a shiny suit and a gigantic stickpin and a ring on his finger so big that he had difficulty lifting his hand, which had in its fingers a glossy calling card that read: MAX EINSTEIN. 'How ya doing?' he said. He sat down on one of the bar stools. 'I've got a real jewel for you.'

" 'Okay,' I said. 'What is it?'

" 'You know how much salmon comes out of Alaska per month?'

"I'm always being asked goddamn questions like that—those real impossible questions which are used to start a long boring speech. I'd give anything to know the answer. Like if one of those guys asked me, 'Hey, buddy, you know how much orange juice the American public drinks per day?' and I was able to answer real quick, 'Sure, four thousand three hundred and seventy-two tons. What of it?' Well, that would throw him. Something would go wrong in his eye.

"Anyway, I always try to answer questions like that in the hope that just once I'll stumble on the right answer. So when he asked how much salmon came out of Alaska, I said, after thinking awhile, 'Thirty-five tons.'

"He didn't even answer me. He asked, 'You know how many salmon canneries there are in Alaska?'

" 'Two?'

" 'Five,' he says. 'There's a cannery in Alaska that's going under. You can get it for a song—twenty-five thousand dollars.'

" 'What's the deal?' I asked.

" 'I've got these fishing vessels,' he said—Max Einstein from New York with his big stickpin and he's got *fishing* vessels. *Fifteen* of them. 'Not only have I got fifteen boats,' he went on, 'but I've found virgin waters. I'm telling you, no one has ever taken salmon out of these waters. They are *virgin*.'

"I said, 'That sounds pretty good. What's the picture?'

"He said, 'I need twenty-five thousand to get the cannery started properly.'

"I asked him if he had a lawyer in Detroit.

" 'No,' he said, 'but we can fix up the papers between ourselves.'

"I told him that I thought I could get a lot of the other Lion players involved.

" 'That's great,' he said. He was getting very excited. 'We want you to get as many of the guys as possible. If you can get enough other guys, you won't have to pay your share. We'll *waive* it.'

" 'What are we going to call this cannery?' I asked.

" 'Virgin Waters Cannery!'

"Man, I'll never forget that: Virgin Waters Cannery. But by that time I was experienced enough not to bite on such proposals. Two years before, he'd have caught me, *easy*. I'd have been in for five big ones, and I probably would have persuaded some of the other players to come in with me. At training camp I would have gone into their rooms. 'Hey, do you know how much salmon comes out of Alaska?' And I'd start my pitch."

"You would have gotten me," said Gordy.

"You know how I would have ended up?" asked Karras. "I'd have had fifty thousand cans of salmon in the basement of my house! My kids would have been eating salmon until it came out their ears. Virgin Waters Cannery!"

"What else have you got down there in the cellar?" Gordy asked.

"Are those phonograph records down there?" Karras wondered in alarm. "Are 'The Grapes of Wrath' and 'Cry Out, Freedom' in my cellar? Jesus Christ, they could be! It's awful crowded down there. I know there are some Picomasters down there—four or five big crates."

"My cellar's pretty crowded, too," Gordy admitted.

"You got a lot of old Lionburgers down there?" Karras asked. "I always thought you were lucky because at least your stuff was *perishable*."

The two of them sat quietly, considering the state of their respective cellars.

Karras stirred. "Sometimes it's a guy with an invention who traps the football player. Inventions are big. One time a guy called me and said over the phone, 'How ya doing?' He told me that he had a real jewel for me—an inventor who'd come up with a great new health machine. So I said, 'That sounds great.' "

"What's so great about a health machine?" Gordy asked.

"Well, I was *curious,*" Karras said. "The inventor might have been a guy with a billion-dollar idea. You never can be sure. So I asked the guy to tell me more."

" 'This thing is sensational,' the guy said, 'but I can't explain it to you over the phone.'

" 'It must be quite something,' I said.

"He said, 'Come on down and you can look at it and see whether or not you would care to invest in it. Why don't you bring a business partner with you—maybe another football player?'

"So I called up Pete Larco, who had been partners with me in the Picomaster venture. I said, 'Hey, Pete, how ya doing?' I told him we might have another venture, with almost as much potential as the vibrators. This was when we were just starting with vibrators and before the crash. He said, 'You're kidding! But I'm not through with the vibrators yet.' Even *then* he was sick of vibrators. He was up to his ass in them. He had to move vibrators to get to his telephone."

"I remember that," said Gordy. "He had this nice little apartment downstairs in his restaurant, and it was *stocked* with vibrators. They were coming out of the wall."

"There was about this much space left," Karras said, indicating with his hands, "where you could walk in between to get to the bathroom. A wall of Picomasters."

"Yeah," Gordy said. " 'Where's the toilet paper, Pete?' 'Under the vibrators.' "

"But Pete's like me," Karras said. "When I told him about the inventor and his health machine, he got curious. 'It sounds sensational,' he said. 'I'll be right down.'

"So this guy who had telephoned me took us into the old part of Detroit where this inventor had his workshop. It was actually a little auto repair shop, and the workshop was up these wooden stairs in an attic. We walked into the shop, and it was hot. It must have been a hundred and ten degrees—just *stifling* hot. Pete still had on his white apron. He was so excited that he'd just come rushing over from butchering something for his restaurant, and he was covered with blood and spaghetti sauce. My business partner!

"So this guy introduced us to the inventor, who was about a hundred and ninety years old. You knew immediately that he was a health nut because his face looked halfway decent, but his body was shot! I didn't really know how old he was until his wife—who was just rusting away—came easing in, and she must have been two hundred years old, if a day.

"Well, this guy told us in this high creaking voice that he thought that we would be just the people to distribute this item of his in the United States. 'I'm primarily an inventor,' he said. 'I don't have time to distribute. If you like the invention, we can work out a price where you can take the whole thing over.'

"We said that was fine. We were in the vibrator business, and we were kind of cocky. 'You came to the right people,' I told him. 'We're in the health business ourselves. Sure, we'd be interested.'

"He said, 'It's upstairs in the attic. That's my workshop.' So we went up these real creaky wooden stairs. Man, miles up! At every step it got hotter—the sweat just pouring off, especially from Pete, who's short, and sort of squat; he was just sweating his ass off. So we walked in and the inventor said, 'Well, there it is.'

"It was a sort of revolving hospital examining table, like one of those Frankenstein movie tables the monster lies on. It was built up on a scaffold of little pipes, and it had leather Frankenstein straps that came down over the arms and legs.

" 'It looks sensational,' I said. 'What does it do?'

"The inventor said, 'Are you familiar with yoga?' From the way he pronounced it, I thought he was referring to Yogi Berra, the baseball player. But then he said, 'Well, the secret of yoga is the redistribution of the parts of your body. In other words, people stand on their heads so that the kidneys can rest at a different angle for a while. In this way, the blood that flows within the capillaries is replenished.'

"Pete Larco said, 'Of course. We know about that; we're in the massage business.'

"The inventor looked at him and said, 'What we do is put a guy on this slab and strap him in so that he can't fall off. Then we turn on the motor and gradually elevate him, head down, so that the blood begins to flow down from his toes and through his sinews to his head, and as he revolves he gets this splendid *flow,* back and forth.'

"I said, 'In other words, you slowly flip him over, like something on a spit.'

" 'That's the principle,' he said.

" 'Pete,' I said. 'Get up on the thing. Try it out. Let's see how it works.'

"Pete shook his head, but finally he agreed. He climbed up on the slab and we strapped him down. The inventor talked at him like a hospital nurse. 'How are we feeling?' he asked Pete. 'Are we feeling good and secure?' Then he stepped back and pushed the button. A motor began whining and the table slowly tilted up. Pete's eyes opened wide; the blood was beginning to flow out of his feet. Meanwhile, while he was tilting slowly in front of us, the inventor and I began to discuss details. 'How many can you build in a month?' I asked. He said, 'Well, that depends on production orders.'

"I waited until Pete was absolutely upside down, his feet at eye level, his head just off the floor, and then I said, 'Hold it a minute right there.' The old guy pressed the buzzer and the machine stopped—with Pete hanging there, his face just *glowing* red, his veins popping—and I said to the old guy, 'Well, my projection of sales is that they will be higher in winter, especially in Northern cities like Buffalo, because people don't get enough exercise in the cold to get that proper *flow*' . . . just gabbing on like that, this old geezer nodding and saying, 'Yes, yes,' and all the time Pete is hanging upside down. I said, 'Why don't we go down to your office to work out the details?' We started down the wooden stairs, and behind us Pete began to shout, 'Hey, you bastards, get me out of this goddamn thing.' He could barely speak, his head was so congested.

He sounded like he had a handkerchief in his mouth. He might have died there. So we went back and the inventor pressed the button to get him back on an even keel again. Man, Pete was as red as a lobster. The veins in his neck were just banging away, and his feet were pale white, just *ghostly.* When we got him unstrapped he could hardly stand. 'I'm going to have a stroke,' he said. 'In fact, I think I *had* a stroke.' We practically had to carry him down the wooden stairs."

"Did you end up investing in the machine?" I asked.

"The old guy gave some fantastic figure for the prototype," Karras said. "Twenty-five thousand. I told him that Larco and I would give it a lot of thought and talk it over with our accountant. Poor old Pete almost had another stroke right on the stairs there, when the old man said twenty-five thousand. He gave a little moan."

"Poor Pete," said Gordy. "He had enough to worry about with the Picomasters. His restaurant was jammed to the rafters with vibrators. His employees were always falling over them — the waiters, the cooks. 'The phone's ringing. Where is it? Where's the phone?' 'It's in that pile of vibrators. Just dig around in there. You'll find it.' Poor Pete, he did everything he could to clear himself of all that stock. He went everywhere with samples. He'd be out in the back of the kitchen, shoveling out spaghetti, and he'd ask the waiter, 'Who's buying this order?' If it was someone he knew, he'd go right out into the dining room with a plate of spaghetti in one hand and a Picomaster in the other. He'd give a demonstration right on the spot."

"What was our national slogan?" Karras asked.

"TRY IT AND YOU'LL BUY IT."

"Jesus, I'm sick," Karras said. He was laughing so hard he could hardly speak. "We went everywhere with them. We hung them around our necks. We'd be playing golf with friends and they'd say, 'What's that?' We'd say, 'I'm glad you asked. Funny you should notice!' I used to walk into barbershops — we thought that was the big potential market for our vibrators — and I'd say, 'Hello, hello, I'm Al Karras. How ya doin'?' The barber would say, 'How you doin', Al? You want a haircut?' 'No.' 'What you got there in your hand?' 'Funny you should ask . . .' "

"I know what you said then," Gordy said. He was slumped hopelessly in his chair. "You said, 'Here it is. The Picomaster. It's the *Cadillac of its field.*' "

"Absolutely right," Karras replied. "One time this barber asked me what would happen if the vibrator broke down. 'This machine is German, isn't it?' he asked. 'Do I have to send it to Munich, Germany?'

" 'No, no,' I said. I had so many Picomasters that I was panicky. 'If it breaks down,' I told this guy, 'we'll give it instant repair.' The barber said, 'What do you mean by "instant repair"?' So I said, 'I'll give you another one to replace it.'

"Everywhere I went, I had one in my hand. Oh Christ, I'm sick. We thought it was going to *work.* We thought we were going to be *billionaires.* People *fought* over the franchises. 'I can give you Idaho and North Dakota.' 'Gee, thanks.' 'Texas ain't gone yet.' 'What? Oh Christ, can I have Texas too?' Dave DeBusschere, who was playing basketball for the Detroit Pistons then, got the Pennsylvania franchise. *Man,* he wanted it. When things went sour, he didn't talk to me for a year. I knew he was mad because he wouldn't put me on his summer softball team."

"What's happened since?" I asked. "Where are all the vibrators now?"

Karras said, "My father-in-law out in Clinton, Iowa, has five thousand down in the basement—down in his recreation room. He had to move the Ping-Pong table out. He can't have any parties in there; he doesn't have any room. He might be able to get three people in there, but no more."

"Damn," said Gordy. "I wish I'd known about your father-in-law's recreation room. Maybe I could have stored some of the 'Cry Out, Freedom' records down there."

The two of them were out of their chairs now, stalking stiff-legged around the room, bawling with laughter. It seemed as good a point as any to bring the discussion on "business" to a close. I got them quieted down, and we went out somewhere and had some lunch. I paid the check. The fact was that both of them were much better at money matters than they ever let on.

# CHAPTER 9

How often do Karras and Gordy come and see you?" a friend asked.

"Oh, every once in a while."

"Jesus, it must be great to sit there and listen in on those people talking about football. Jesus!" He was a tremendous fan. "You must be getting all this great stuff."

"The best thing is how funny they are," I said.

"Funny?"

He looked at me in surprise, as if the word were inappropriate. He seemed miffed.

Humor has always been a major and somewhat neglected constant in professional sports—perhaps not a particularly high quality of humor, but pervasive, though not much discussed or written about since the popular view of professional football is that it is what my friend imagines—largely a grim, dedicated business.

Yet the humor *was* everywhere—in the good stories one heard, in the quick ripostes and the one-liners, the constant joshing and put-downs, invariably bawdy and raucous—all of it a hedge against the boredom and regimen. True, the most elaborate level of the humor was often the practical joke, considered a lowly form in most societies.

Authorities consider the Americans the world's greatest experts at the practical joke, with the English a close second, the French a distant third, and no one else at all in the running. Latins are psychologically ill-equipped to perpetuate practical jokes, though they are splendid victims since an essential ingredient is the ability to *imagine* rather than witness the joke's denouement. The American sense of detachment is more constituted to this. For example, an American can crate up a large barber chair and send it to a family in Malaya, say, with no return address or sender's card—and sit back in his bath and bask in imagining the puzzlement of the family halfway around the world as the barber chair emerges slowly from its wrappings. The Latin, on the other hand, is too impatient to let his imagination satisfy him. He wants to be on hand to witness what is going on, and if he could, he would surely fly to Malaya to caper around in the flower beds outside the house, chinning himself so he can peer in over the windowsill to watch the chair being unpacked and to check the reactions of the bewildered family.

Of course the foremost perpetrator of practical jokes on the Lions was Alex Karras. But the odd quality of his tomfoolery was that it was marked by a strong Latin flavor. He was intensely curious about the effect of the joke on his victims, and also, I think, he was self-centered enough to wish to indicate publicly that he was the joke's author, which is not at all in the spirit of the true American prank.

For example, I remember Karras at the motel where Detroit stayed when they came to San Francisco to play the 49ers—lying prostrate on the bed yawning, and then reaching for the phone and asking for John North's room. North was the offensive end coach, a dedicated man with an abbreviated sense of suspicion, a fine dupe for someone of Karras's deviousness.

"John," Karras said. "The photographer from the *Chronicle* is up here. He wants a picture of you and all your receivers, a formal picture with blazers and ties. You better call them together. Where? Down by the swimming pool. He'll meet you there in ten minutes."

By and by, Karras swung his legs off the bed and pulled the window curtains of his room slightly ajar to peek out. "Hey, look at this."

Those of us in the room peered out on an Antonioni-like scene of seven or eight men, all with coats and ties, moving around the motel swimming pool, which was empty, in a San Francisco fog heavy enough to be classified as a drizzle.

At the window Karras's shoulders heaved as he giggled. "They've been down there for twenty minutes," he said.

We watched as one by one they drifted back to their rooms. The last to leave was a first-year man short on personal publicity, craving "ink," dragging his feet as he left the desolate fog-swept scene with its empty pool, looking back over his shoulder one last time for the photographer from the *Chronicle* as he swung the motel door shut behind him.

At this point in one of his jokes, Karras, never letting well enough alone, would begin to fidget. At the team dinner that night he would suddenly ask in a voice loud enough to be heard in most sections of the room, "Hey, what were you guys all standing around this afternoon in the rain for—in your blazers and ties and everything? That's pretty quirky. That's weird."

Those players who did not already know that Karras was responsible could tell by the cast of his voice, loud and merry and supercilious, that he was behind the joke, and they would look down at the remains of their steaks and potatoes, eyes narrowed, wondering at their gullibility in being tricked yet again.

It always seemed to me that Karras was putting his life on the line with such capers, because his dupes were invariably large people with quick tempers, and certainly possessing the physical wherewithal to dish out retributory punishment. Of course, Karras himself was large, and unbelievably powerful; perhaps this was a canceling factor.

The most dangerous of Karras's stunts, with the most chance of severe physical retribution, was a ritual he occasionally put a few of the rookies through when he was still the proprietor of the old Lindell A.C., a somewhat seedy bar which he was forced to divest himself of to get back into the good graces of the commissioner during the year of his banishment from football. The bar was on the first floor of a run-down hotel with about forty rooms, many of them occupied by skid-row bums and people barely scraping along. Room 232 had a two-way mirror set in the wall, so that eight or ten people could pack into room 233 and watch what was going on next door without its occupants being aware.

The voyeuristic entertainment would be initiated by Karras sidling up to a Detroit Lion rookie visiting the bar for the first time and saying, "See that girl over there?"

"Who?"

"That girl over there wearing the blue thing—hell, man, the only girl in the place."

"Oh, her. Yeah, I see her."

"Well, she can hardly sit still, she has such eyes for you."

"Wha'?"

"That's right. In fact, she wants to meet you upstairs—in room 232."

"No kidding."

So after four or five quick beers, the rookie would go up to the room to see the girl—who was in on the gag, of course, and knew that in the next room Karras and four or five others, trying to keep their voices down, were sitting in hard-backed chairs and looking through the trick mirror. Occasionally, she would make faces at the mirror over the rookie's shoulder.

Karras said that often it was hard to keep from falling off the chair from trying to contain one's laughter. The best to watch were the country boys who came in shy and awkward, and huge if they were tackles or guards, not knowing whether to sit on the bed, which was the only piece of furniture in the room, or to stand, and getting one shoe off finally and maybe another, and often forgetting to get out of their shirts and ties.

When the rookie came back down to the bar, Karras would be there waiting.

"How was it?"

"Great."

"Hey, tell me something. You always wear your socks?"

"Wha'?"

"And where'd you get that tattoo on your butt? The one with the little red heart that says 'Jody'? D'ja get that in Shanghai?"

The rookie's jaw would drop and he would hope desperately that the tattoo, which had been done in Duluth on the night of his high school graduation and was the bane of his life, was something Karras had noticed in the showers at training camp. But the divulgence about the socks was devastating, and he knew then that somehow he had been spied upon and the anger would begin to churn. It always seemed to me lucky that no one ever threw a punch at Karras at that moment, but no one ever did.

The old Lindell A.C. was finally condemned and the hotel, along with room 232, was torn down, which left the rookies with one less possibility of indignity to suffer through their first year.

Invariably, however, all of them were taken in by a far more wholesome practical joke, which was referred to as the Annual Turkey Caper. This involved making the rookie believe that it was a Thanksgiving tradition to receive free turkeys from a market proprietor named Milt Harris, a Detroit football fan of such intensity, they were told, that annually he gave the Lions these substantial tokens of his support and gratitude.

The trap was always set two weeks before Thanksgiving. Friday Macklem, the equipment manager, would write on the blackboard in the Tiger Stadium locker room: "Next Tuesday has been set as the day to pick up your free turkey at Milt Harris's store at Eastern Market. Specify weight, type of bird, if it is to be dressed, not cooked, or precooked."

A pad was hung by a string from the board, and the veterans and coaches—all in cahoots, of course—would dutifully sign up, specifying such detailed orders as "Twenty-pound bird, with dressing, please include gizzard, and tail feathers for decoration."

The rookies would watch this activity with interest, and finally one of them would ask, "Hey, do we get in on this, too?"

"Hell yes. Why not?"

So the word would sweep through the contingent of rookies, and they would hurry to sign up. The talk around the locker room, and waiting for team meetings, and down along the sidelines during practice, began to feature the Thanksgiving meal. One rookie would ask another, "What kind of turkey did you ask for?"

"Well, I wasn't going to have anyone for dinner. I was going to have a turkey sandwich or something, down at the corner, and take in a flick that night. Hell, my folks are all down in St. Louis. But now, because of that turkey, I got them coming up for the game on Thanksgiving Day and afterward I got some company coming in to meet them, and so I asked for a twenty-five-pounder with dressing. My mother's going to bring up this special cranberry sauce in a jar in her suitcase."

Then the other rookie would talk about the turkey *he* was getting, and who was coming to *his* party, and George Wilson, who was the coach then, got to hate the whole business because no one's mind was on football, though of course he played along with the veterans by signing up himself. The rookies thought of little else. Joe Robb, one of the veteran defensive linemen, once asked a rookie what sort of turkey he was asking for, and the rookie said he had put in his order for a thirty-pounder, because he had a lot of people coming to his place and he needed a big one. Robb said that he was having a big party too, but he was going to get two fifteen-pounders because they cooked faster and were easier to handle in the kitchen.

"Well, of course," the rookie said. "Why didn't I think of that? That's a great idea. I'm gonna do that too."

Karras told me that once a rookie had asked him the weight of the biggest available turkey at Milt Harris's store.

"The biggest?"

"Yeah."

Karras thought for a while and then told the rookie that he had heard that Harris had a special corn-fed, double-breasted cackle-bird tom that dressed out at sixty-five pounds.

"Sixty-five *pounds,*" the rookie said. "That's a big mother. Well, man, that's the one *I* want."

"How many people you got coming to dinner?" Karras asked.

"I ain't got nobody coming for dinner. I don't know nobody yet in this town," the rookie said.

"Well, what're you gonna to do with that sixty-five-pound turkey?"

"I'm gonna set that mother right in the refrig'tor. All cooked, man. Then when I feels like it, I can swing open the do' and there that baby is..."

"Do you think you can fit a sixty-five-pound turkey in your refrigerator?" Karras asked.

"I ain't got nothin' else in there, except maybe two cans of beer."

This disarming admission suggesting the lonely state of a rookie, perhaps from a small southwestern college spending his first season in the big city, might have touched the sympathies of a lesser man than Karras.

"You may have to squeeze that big ol' tom to get him in," he said.

The rookie thought. "How long is a sixty-five-pound turkey?" he asked finally.

Karras brooded. "A sixty-five-pound turkey has got to be pushing four feet long."

"Four *feet.* Christ, man. What I can do is take out all the shelves and tilt that mother up on its end," the rookie said.

"That's a real good idea."

"Besides, I'm gonna eat a lot of the turkey, so she'll be thinning down right smart..."

On the day or so before the Tuesday pickup, Friday Macklem would post the rather complicated directions to the Eastern Market, which was on the far side of Detroit, and the veterans would groan and tell the rookies that there was no point in all forty members of the squad going out to Harris's place for the turkeys. Why wouldn't it be simpler if the rookies picked up all of them? Since traditionally they were sent on errands for the veterans, the rookies agreed, if somewhat sulkily, especially the one who expected to be wrestling with the sixty-five-pound turkey. He said that if he was going to have to worry about *other* players' turkeys he would have to hire himself a bus.

Karras said that it always took an enormous amount of willpower to keep from driving out to the Eastern Market to hide behind the meat counter and bob up and peer over the top to watch what went on when a rookie, standing there with a long list in his hand, realized that he was involved in a hoax. Milt Harris was a no-nonsense party to it all, and when a player turned up in his store he would stare at him in feigned disbelief: "A free turkey? What are you talking about? You crazy or something? You got a *screw* loose? A sixty-five-*pound* turkey? You got to be thinking of an *ostrich!*"

Sometimes it took a lot of persuading before the rookie would accept the idea that he was being duped. "Listen," the rookie would say. "I don't care about *my* turkey. Forget that. But I'm supposed to bring back Coach Wilson's turkey. If I don't bring back his turkey, I'm going to be searching around for an assistant high school coaching job. Please. Now according to my list, he ordered a twenty-pounder, not precooked, a chestnut dressing, and the giblets in a separate bag."

"Can't you get it through your head that you've been had?" Harris would shout. "There's no free turkeys here."

The rookies did not necessarily take the hoax with resignation. Bruce Maher, the peppery safetyman, was so fixed on picking up a turkey that he threatened to take Milt Harris's store apart if he didn't get one. Harris saw the look in his eye, and felt the rage boiling in him, and said, "Okay, okay, but for Chrissakes don't let on," and he went and got a turkey out of the freezer.

Another player, Roger LaLonde, a rookie nicknamed "Jug" because of his wide hips, was incensed enough to buy a live turkey, and on the Saturday after Thanksgiving he shut it up in Karras's locker, whom he considered the chief instigator, in among his spare T-shirts and a fine pair of knit golf trousers. Karras came in that day, thinking about the offensive guard he would be facing the next weekend, and when he looked in his locker, reaching in to get a sweatband, the big turkey sprang at him and scared him almost across the room. Karras said later that the turkey had all the moves required of a good offensive lineman:

"speed, surprise, great lateral agility, and quick off the snap. Jerry Kramer of the Packers is a goddamn *wren* compared to that turkey of Jug's."

Karras bore no grudge against LaLonde. It was in the best spirit of the practical joke to suffer a reprisal gladly. Usually, though, he got away with whatever impertinences he wrought, largely because, unlike LaLonde, his victims had no idea how to retaliate. Since a consistent element in Alex's humor was to *startle* people, my own experience was that it was best to edge away at these times and let whatever he was doing take its course. Once I was sitting with him in a rather fancy restaurant and looked up to see that he was jabbing a fork loaded with lettuce into the center of his forehead. He was quite persistent, and eventually, from the force of the jabbing, a piece of lettuce fell off the fork, glanced off his nose, and dropped onto the tablecloth. It was such a surprising sight that I was speechless. He noticed that I was staring at him. He put the fork down on his plate and asked, "Well, why does the mouth always have to get all the food? I mean, why can't it be passed around to other parts of the face?"

I could not think of much to say.

"It's unfair," he said. A piece of lettuce was still stuck to the middle of his forehead.

I managed to say, "Well, I would think that an ear or a nose might *work* better. At least there you have an aperture."

"The forehead has been neglected," Karras said, with a finality that put an end to the discussion, and we went on to something else. Throughout the evening the lettuce remained stuck to the middle of his brow, until just before we left the restaurant it dropped off as the waiter was bringing the change from the bill.

Karras stared at the leaf as if he had never seen it before. "Who's been throwing their salad at me?" he asked the waiter.

"I beg your pardon?"

"Someone in this café is throwing their salad. Look at this. It just dropped off my forehead. Someone hit me smack-dab in the middle of the head with their salad. What sort of a joint are you running here?"

"I beg your pardon?"

Karras motioned the captain over.

"Yes, sir?"

"You've got someone in this restaurant who is throwing food."

"Sir?"

"Look at the middle of my forehead." The captain squinted at the faint spot still glistening slightly from salad oil, where the lettuce had stuck.

"Someone hit me right there with some salad," Karras said, pointing. "Maybe it's someone at that table over there." All of us wheeled and stared at an elderly couple sitting opposite each other along the side wall. They noticed us staring at them; their jaws stopped moving.

"They are eating the fish dish," the captain pointed out. "The sole meunière. They are not eating salad."

"Maybe it's the fish dish they threw," Karras said. "Or the lemon maybe. Whatever it was, it came from their direction. Did you throw your fish dish at me?" he called out. "Or the lemon?"

"Sir, sir," the captain was hissing. "You are disturbing the patrons. I must ask you to leave the premises. Please."

"Well, okay," Karras said huffily. "Do you think I have any interest in hanging around in a dump where the customers get peppered with food?"

"Christ, what a place," Karras said when we were out in the street. We strode a few yards, and then he said, "Hey, *you* didn't throw the salad at me, did you?"

"What?" I looked at him. "What are you talking about? You did that yourself."

"I did *what* myself?" He blinked convincingly behind his spectacles. "You mean I threw salad at my own head? What would I want to do a thing like that for?"

"Come on, Alex," I said. "You said that the mouth was getting all the attention and you felt the forehead had been neglected. You tried to get it to eat the salad, and you jabbed your fork into it."

"I jabbed my fork into my own *brow?*" Karras said. We walked along in silence. "You got to be kidding."

I took three or four steps and then said, "Well, I *am* kidding. I don't know what possessed me. In fact, I think it *was* the old geezer at that side table."

"'Course it was," Karras said. "The guy had a hell of an arm..."

# CHAPTER 10

When I stepped out of the plane at the Flint airport, awkwardly because it was a small four-seat, low-winged Cessna from which one clambered first onto the wing, then down to the ground, a representative from the airport staff told me that someone was waiting for me out front in a limousine. He said "someone" in a somewhat inconclusive manner, as if he were not at all sure of himself.

The only car in front of the terminal was a Cadillac of the "stretched" variety for use in funerals or weddings where it is provident to keep a family unit, however numerous, in one vehicle. At first I could see no one sitting in the cavernous rear section, but a chauffeur stepped smartly up and after relieving me of my golf clubs opened the door with a flourish, and I saw that perched in a far corner of the backseat, his feet sticking directly out in front of him, was a midget. He wore a gray fedora of the type cultivated by Chicago gangsters, and his face was largely obscured by an enormous cigar. I got in beside him, nodding politely, and the door shut behind me.

I said that it was very kind of him to meet me. He did not reply. Though his cigar was going satisfactorily, he produced a kitchen match, struck it on the heel of his shoe, and sucked in on the flame. Clouds of smoke began to thicken in the car, and the cigar tip glowed sullenly. I cleared my throat and discreetly lowered the window on my side. The car began to move. Where were we going, I asked. No reply. The midget stared straight ahead. Up in front the chauffeur tended to his driving. We began to move through the outskirts of Flint. I tried again. How were the preparations for the Karras golf tournament the next day coming along? More thick smoke. I gave up and looked out at the scenery.

The midget's appearance at the airport, and his silence, had obviously been cooked up by Karras and Buterakos to put me in the proper frame of mind for the second of Karras's weird golf tournaments held to benefit the National Cystic Fibrosis Campaign. For a month Buterakos had been calling me and telling me that the tournament was going to eclipse its predecessor both in scope and lunacy.

"Big Man!" Buterakos would shout over the phone. "The tournament's going to be the biggest thing in the country. We got a new slogan this year. 'The benefit is one giant step forward for mankind and one giant step backwards for golf.' Guess who's coming?"

"Who?"

"Johnny Weissmuller!"

"Johnny who?"

"Weissmuller, goddamn it. The original Tarzan. He's coming with his chimp. He's got this chimpanzee he runs with. The two of them can't live apart. The chimp picks up his hat and hands it to him. He fetches the paper. I'm telling you, those two are going to set the tournament on its ear."

"What are they going to do?"

"Tarzan is going to yell," Buterakos said. "From time to time he's going to really *scream*—just as a competitor is at the top of his backswing. You know what else he's going to do? He's going to *swim*. The golf course has one water hole, and he's going to plunge in and emerge at the other end, dripping wet, and creep up on this poor guy playing out of the rough, and he'll say 'Ahem,' and this guy, this poor sucker who's coughed up fifty bucks to play in the tournament, is going to turn around and see *Tarzan,* soaking wet in his leopard skins, maybe holding the chimp by the hand, and man, it's going to blow the guy's *mind!*"

"I should think so," I said.

"That's right, Big Man. The tournament this year is going to be *big.* We got the biggest celebrities in the country coming. Joe O'Higgins, the sheriff who does those Dodge car commercials—*he's* coming. Not only that, but we got twelve midgets in from Chicago..."

I could not remember the other celebrities and events that Buterakos and Karras planned, but there were a raft of them. Once again I turned to the midget sitting next to me. "I hear there are eleven more of you," I said. The sentence seemed awkwardly put, and I was glad that he chose to answer it by once again striking a match to his cigar. We sat in silence. Up in front the chauffeur's shoulders were heaving—either from suppressed laughter or from the thick cigar smoke.

The limousine swept through downtown Flint and pulled up in front of the Durant Hotel. As the chauffeur hopped out and opened the back door, two men standing on the sidewalk leaned forward to see who was within. The midget stepped out briskly and spoke his first words. "Clear the way," he said. He was carrying a small cane about two feet long. He swept it back and forth. "We've got important business to conduct." His voice was astonishingly deep and husky. I stepped out behind him and we hurried into the hotel.

I followed him to the elevator, and the operator said, "Floor?"

"The Presidential Suite," the midget said. "Let's get this crate moving." He made another impatient move with his stick, and the operator swung the doors shut. He seemed annoyed. To make conversation I asked, "Has the Presidential Suite ever been used by the president?"

"Nah," the operator said. "But we had the president of San Salvador in here once. Stayed for three days."

We reached the top floor, and the midget led the way briskly down the corridor. The door to the Presidential Suite had a presidential seal set in the wood. The midget swung it ajar. Inside, a big galvanized tub of ice and beer had been placed in the middle of the room, and around it, lolling back in armchairs, were a number of men, some of them wearing golfing hats, whom I presumed were tournament officials. As soon as the midget and I came in they started guffawing; apparently they were privy to my odd greeting at the airport. Having done his duty, the midget turned with a big grin on his face. "The name's Gus," he said, putting out his hand. I shook it solemnly.

The others all wanted to know what had happened. "Did Gus pick you up at the airport? What'ja make of that, huh? Did he blow the cigar smoke at you?"

"Yeah," I said.

"What'ja think?"

"I didn't know what to think. I guess it was a helluva idea."

They roared with laughter, then turned and asked the midget what *he* thought. "Tell us, Gus!"

"Well, I damn near got sick puffing on those cigars." He had a big grin on his face. "Puffed so hard I smoked my way through *three* of them."

They rocked back and forth in their chairs, snorting with laughter. "*Christ,* what a gas."

Buterakos came bustling in. "Hey, Big Man!" he shouted. "What'ja think of that, hey?"

"Well, I—"

"Did Gus meet you okay out there at the airport? Hey, Gus, did you meet him out at the airport? Did you give him the cold-shoulder treatment and all that stuff?"

Buterakos is one of those ebullient people who cannot wait for an answer to a question before hurrying on to another. "Hey, were you surprised?"

"Well, I—"

"What'ja think when you looked in the car and Gus was in there?"

"I didn't—"

"D'ja know where he was taking you?"

"No, but I—"

"What'ja think when he didn't say anything? Hey, Gus, you didn't say anything, did you? That was Alex's idea—for Gus just to sit there and puff smoke."

"Yes, I—"

"What'ja think when he puffed all that smoke at you? Huh?"

"I didn't know—"

"Blew your mind, didn't it? Hey, Gus, did you blow that smoke right in his face? Hey, what'ja think when he kept lighting his cigar when the cigar was already *lit?*"

"Well, I didn't really—"

"Did he tell those two guys in front of the hotel to clear out of the way? Did he swing his cane at them? That was all planned. What'ja think?"

"I didn't know—"

"D'ja bring your golf clubs? You're going to be playing in the biggest tournament that ever hit this state!"

By and by Buterakos calmed down and I was able to ask him if Karras was in the hotel. He told me that Alex was out at the golf course talking to the animal trainer. "We got a whole *zoo* coming tomorrow. That golf course is going to be *stiff* with animals. We got a goddamn llama coming. Not only that"—he gestured extravagantly at the ceiling—"the *sky* is going to be full—airplanes, balloons, parachutists..."

A tall man touched Buterakos on the shoulder. "Tarzan!" Buterakos shouted. He wheeled him toward me. "Big Man," he said solemnly, "this is Johnny Weissmuller."

We shook hands. "Howdy," he said. He was a silver-haired man with a florid, somewhat pocked face, and his voice was surprisingly high and squeaky. Though we were indoors, he was wearing a wide-brimmed safari hat with a leopard-skin band.

"How's the chimpanzee?" I asked, looking around, half expecting to see one lolling in an armchair wearing the usual circus ensemble of a little paper hat and a high-riding jumpsuit.

Weissmuller's face fell. "The tyke's sick," he said. "Ate something. When a chimp is sick, he sulks around. Can't do anything with them. Not much fun to have around. Give me a sick parrot anytime."

"That's too bad."

We fell silent. Buterakos was in the far corner of the room. To make conversation, I said, "I wonder how your chimp would get along with the midgets—I mean how he'd react. There are eleven or twelve of them in from Chicago. Has your chimp ever met a midget?"

"Most of these guys from Chicago are not midgets," Weissmuller said. "They're dwarfs. Actually they all like to be called 'little people.'" He leaned closer to speak confidentially. "Midgets are perfectly formed tiny people. They have high little voices, like they'd been breathing helium. Now dwarfs, they have near normal-sized heads and bodies, but they got these very small extremities, which are the arms and legs. The guy that come out to meet you at the airport was a dwarf. That's Gus. They tell me he's a family man—got a couple of kids."

"Oh," I said. "I didn't mean to be disrespectful of them, but I wondered what a chimp's reaction to them would be."

Weissmuller looked into the palms of his hands. "I'm no midget... er... *dwarf.* I'm no chimp, either." He laughed sharply. "But what I think is this: that a chimp can take them or leave them."

"I see," I said.

Buterakos drifted by to say that we all had to drive out with him to the golf course to see the arrangements for the tournament the next day. He wanted to show us the big tent they had put up for the golf dinner; also, there was going to be a practice balloon ascent.

"Balloons?" Weissmuller asked.

"That's right. Isn't that right, Gus?"

Gus, standing beside him, did not seem very happy. His cigar was unlit.

"We're sending Gus up tonight," Buterakos explained. "He's going to be the first midget balloonist. Right, Gus?"

Some asked what sort of a balloon it was.

"It's a great big mother," Buterakos said. "With a basket. A hot-air machine pumps the son of a bitch with hot air and up she goes. We got the greatest balloon man in the world—Captain Phineas Phog, he calls himself—to come to town with his balloons. Tomorrow Karras is going to open the festivities by sweeping across the tops of the trees in the big balloon and throwing out the first golf ball. Isn't that a great idea? I'm telling you, this is going to be the biggest golf tournament this state has ever heard of. We got this *elephant* turning up. D'ja know that? The biggest elephant in Michigan."

A group of us agreed to go out to the golf course to watch Gus make his balloon ascent. He said he thought he ought to take along a sweater, so I went down with him to his room. The place was packed with some of the other "little people," and he introduced me to them. There were about six of them staying in the room, and cots had been set up. They were very excited, not about Gus making his evening balloon flight but because a few minutes before they had recognized Dick Butkus, the great Chicago middle linebacker, walking down the hotel corridor to his room with his golf bag on his shoulder. They had all followed him, turning a corner, and then one of them had shouted, "Hey, Butkus, where's your ball and chain?" He had wheeled around, the clubs clinking in his bag, and had stared at them briefly, the group of them poised like prairie dogs, one or two of them just peering around the corner, and then one of them from the back called out, "Hey, Butkus, where's your cage?" Their temerity had scared them, and as soon as the question was asked they ran pop-pop-pop-pop, swaying back and forth on their dwarf legs in their haste, giggling, until they reached the sanctuary of Gus's room. They had closed the door and bolted it, reaching up to do so. They told Gus three times what they had done: "You should've heard Jake. Jake sings out, 'Hey, Butkus, where's your *cage?*' Gus, it was grand. Oh, Gus."

"I wish I'd seen it," said Gus. He walked over to his suitcase and pulled out a sweater. The others wanted to tell him again. "Hey, Gus. Gus!"

"I got to go." He looked at them. "I'm going up in a balloon," he said mournfully.

On the way out to the golf course, Buterakos talked nonstop. Gus was sitting beside him in the front seat. I was sitting in the back with Weissmuller. I could just see the top of Gus's head. "Gus," Buterakos was saying, "you're going to be the first of the little people to fly in a big balloon. It's going to make headlines! History! You're going to make history, Gus. You know something? You got to have a *uniform,* Gus. I should have had an air marshal's uniform made for you. I should have thought of that, but it's too late. You got to go up in your civvies. But you can salute, Gus, and act like an air marshal. Hell, Gus, you can *bomb* somebody. Why didn't I think of that before? Gus can drift over some dude working in his garden, humming to himself and planting some goddamn little shrub, and Gus can *bomb* him... just drifting over this guy's garden, quiet as smoke, and Gus can call something down, very quiet, and the guy will look up and see this tiny face looking over the edge of the basket of this big mothering balloon, and he's holding this bomb, maybe a paper bag full of water, and it comes down *blam!* and hits this guy right in the kisser. Blow his *mind,* right?"

It was evening when we reached the golf course. An occasional warm puff of air turned the leaves backside to, and they showed silver. Swallows in their swift sweeps for insects were flying close to the ground. The air had that tremulous quality that comes before a storm.

"Hey, Gus. You oughtn't to go up," I said as we got out of the car. "There must be thunderheads around."

"Oh, I don't think anybody's serious," he said.

I was not so sure. Buterakos was striding ahead of us across the golf course toward a group of people on a level fairway beyond the eighteenth green. I could see Karras among them, his head tilted back, drinking a beer. The fabric of a balloon was spread out on the grass. "Captain Phog!" Buterakos was yelling. "What's going on? You're behind schedule. Haven't you got the balloon pumped up yet?"

A thin, fragile-looking man wearing a yachtsman's cap with braid at the brim detached himself from the group and hurried over. He looked harried. "We're just getting things ready," he said.

"Well, I should hope so," Buterakos said. "Gus here is pining to get aloft. He's got itchy feet. He wants to fly—isn't that right, Gus? How much longer do you think it's going to be?"

"Maybe fifteen, twenty minutes," Captain Phog said.

When the balloon had enough hot air inside to lift the canopy, we walked through the opening at the base and prowled inside, stepping carefully on the nylon fabric. Captain Phog did not seem worried about the conditions outside. He bustled here and there inside the balloon, its interior lit by electric lamps, bellying out the canopy with the palms of his hands so that it would rise properly. Above the roar of the motor producing the hot air, the distant thunder murmured. "It won't be a free flight," Captain Phog was explaining. "We'll send him up but keep him anchored, and then we'll bring him down."

I went outside. A few feet from the expanding canopy was the balloon's basket in which Gus would ride, the hot-air device attached to the overhead framework. On the ground next to the basket were six coffee containers. "Just got them. They're filled with water," Gus told me. "Those are my bombs."

"I suppose Buterakos prepared them."

"Sure," he said. He looked unhappy.

The half-inflated balloon suddenly rose in a slow heave, stirred by a puff of the warm fitful air, and then subsided to the ground. But it was awake now, and the hot air roaring from the blowers moved it anew, sending shivers across its plastic skin. It heaved again. "Won't be long now!" Captain Phog shouted. The scene took on a bizarre atmosphere of emergency, as if the balloon were on hand to evacuate personnel from a siege—the flashlight flickering on the gasbag as it expanded, the shrill cries of Captain Phog to his crew, and across the fields the ominous flickering of lightning, like artillery flashes.

The thunder rumbled. The entire stretch of horizon to the west was dark with line squalls. Buterakos's shouting lent an additional sense of urgency: "Phog, go to it! You're going to be the first balloon man to get one of the little people up into the air. You're going to be famous, Phog! You're going to get that son of a bitch full of hot air and *up*, Phog!"

"Look at that!" someone shouted.

A quarter of a mile away a solid bank of rain emerged from a background of black clouds and began moving swiftly toward us across the golf course. Shrubs alongside a distant fairway bent double, their branches lashing.

"My God," Captain Phog shouted. "Line squalls! Get her down!" He rushed for a rope. "Pull the safety panel!" he shouted. "Get the air out of her!"

His people rushed around, but it was too late. Drumming hard across the turf, the rain squall reached us and took a hand—the wind picking up the balloon and shaking it violently, lifting it off the ground with a series of loud canvas-like flaps, and the canopy opened a rip which soared up the surface like a flame. The guy ropes ripped and slashed. We did what we could to help the frantic captain, but the wind had shredded the canopy, so that we were like a crew at sea trying to retrieve a vast spinnaker split and trailing to leeward like a streamer.

"I can't believe it," I heard Captain Phog berating himself. "What the hell was I doing?" He seemed utterly puzzled.

In the jumbled roar of the storm I could hear Buterakos crying in the wind like some mad Ahab: "Phog! What's going on? Can't you get that balloon up? Gus is waiting. We can't let him down. Let's proceed with the launch, goddamn it!"

I went over. He was grinning enormously, almost beside himself at his own powers of persuasion. "My God," he said. "Did you see me *motivate* that man! Captain Phog? Did I not pump him up? He was being motivated so hard, he didn't know what he was doing."

"You lost him a balloon," I said.

"He can sew it together again," Buterakos said blithely. "Besides, he's got another one."

I felt relieved for Gus. I strayed over. He was standing in the shelter of the circus tent looking out at Captain Phog, whose black slicker glistened and flapped in rain-strewn gusts of wind. He was still trying to collect what gear was left of his number one balloon. "Man, you're lucky, Gus," I said.

He did not reply for a second or so, and when I looked down I saw that he had a wistful look on his strong farmer's face. "I love a good time better than anyone," he said in his solemn voice. "I'd have gone up in the balloon, I think. That would have been something to remember, eh? You know something? I was sort of sorry when it blew away."

"Damn, Gus, you could have disappeared forever. You could have been blown clear to Iowa. That was a damn powerful line squall."

"Sure," he said. "Still, it's too bad. Buterakos really tried."

"That's for sure," I said. "Buterakos has a tendency to overdo things, doesn't he?"

The two of us got a lift back to Flint, and on the way Gus told me how Buterakos had come to a convention of little people in Chicago and given one of his inspirational talks. He had thrown out a lot of props, and yelled at them, and told them they were the "biggest" men around, and they stood up and cheered for him for ten minutes. "He really made us feel good. I'd have gone up if he told me to," Gus said. The rain had stopped. The headlights glistened on the wet macadam. He stirred in his seat. "Of course, I don't really understand what this golf tournament is all about."

I told him that my own theory was that both Karras and Buterakos played such atrocious golf themselves that, perhaps subconsciously, they were taking their revenge on the game and against the solemnity of those who swore by it. Someone had described the tournament as the "Black Mass" of golf, I said.

"I can see why," he said.

I asked him what had been planned for him the next day. He told me that Buterakos had somehow managed to persuade the local National Guard commander to loan the tournament a small military unit. "He's put me in command," he said. "He's got me a uniform and a pearl-handled revolver. I'm riding in the lead vehicle, which I think is a General Patton tank."

"Is this for some sort of parade?" I asked.

"God, no," he said. "We're supposed to dart out of the forest onto the golf course with this unit and surprise people. Buterakos told me,

'Try to emerge'—that was the word he used: 'emerge'—'from the forest at the top of the guy's backswing. That's the best time.'"

When I saw Gus later that evening, I asked him how the little people had reacted to the news that he had not made his balloon ascent. "They weren't interested one way or the other," he said. "They were into something else. They were all carrying on and planning to knock on Dick Butkus's door at midnight, and when he answered it they were going to gang-tackle him, just for the hell of it—all eleven of them."

The thought of this plan stayed with me through a night's fitful rest, and the next morning when I saw Butkus out in front of the hotel, a golf bag over his shoulder, I was tempted to ask him if the midgets had attacked him the night before. But it was such an odd question to put to someone so intimidating. One had to assume that the midgets had thought better of it.

The tournament started at ten o'clock. Captain Phineas Phog's reserve balloon floated serenely in the summer sky. Already a large crowd had collected. Many had come because they had heard of the hijinks the preceding year, expecting better this time; others because of the celebrities, again most of them from the Detroit professional teams—the Pistons, the Redwings, and the Lions. Many of the children had autograph books. I saw Johnny Weissmuller, outfitted for his golf game in his safari clothes and hunter's hat, and we waved at each other.

About fifteen minutes after the tournament started, Gus put in his appearance. We could hear the motors of his military unit, and the crackling of branches and small trees going down as he approached. His lead vehicle, it turned out, was not a Patton tank but a huge amphibian, heading a procession which included two jeeps and a number of one-and-a-half-ton trucks, one of them a fuel carrier. Gus rode in the prow of the amphibian. He had indeed been provided with a uniform, a weird General Patton outfit; he was top-heavy in a helmet, tank-driver goggles, and a chestful of medals. He brandished a riding crop. Throughout the day, his unit turned up at the most unexpected times and places, bursting through the underbrush that flanked the fairways, with Gus yelling in his startling low voice that boomed above the roar of the motors, "Clear the hell out of the way! The Eleventh Armored is coming through!" From time to time he hit the side of the amphibian with his riding crop. Some of the golfers felt that it was the single most surprising sight of the day—to hear the approaching rumble of motors, the crackling of bushes, and then to see the nose of the amphibian poking through, the tiny goggled figure perched atop the huge machine, waving his riding crop.

I was pleased to note that many of the traditions established in the tournament's first year were continued: each golfer teed off for the first hole in a wail of amplified sound from a loudspeaker system—animal roars, machine-gun fire, steamboat whistles, and the like; the single-minded man in the sombrero was back, who moved across the fairways to the greens to sing "The Mexican Hat Dance" and inspire the golfers' putting. Other music-makers had been hired, or more likely persuaded, perhaps even *motivated* to join the festivities—including a jazz band on a cart that was pulled around by a tractor. But the musicians I would truly remember were the soloists who wandered around the golf course: a lovely girl in a hippie gown, who stood by a sand trap singing ballads in a gentle voice that carried barely six feet; an old man in a bowler hat far too small for his head, who played a vague *plinkety-plank* banjo out on the far reaches of the course. One came across them and their music suddenly, around a tree, like figures in a Fellini landscape.

Karras was beside himself with delight. Later that morning he took me on a tour of the course. He was dressed in white coveralls, with his name in big red letters on the back. He took big puffs on his cigar. "We've really doctored the course, much more than last time," he said. He showed me a green which had been pocked with six cups and flags. The flags, red cloth, snapped in the wind from their thin bamboo poles. "A golfer's delight, this hole," he said.

"Yes," I said. "Does the player have his choice here?"

"He does," Karras said. "Any cup. It's an easy hole because of all those options. In fact, it's the low-handicap hole of the tournament. No one gets a stroke here—not even the highest scoring of the midgets." He puffed enormously on his cigar.

There was another green he wanted to show me, and we set out across the fairways.

"Look at that!" he exclaimed, pointing at what I thought was a large boulder. "That's a three-hundred-pound turtle."

We stood and stared at it. It moved its beaked head, inspecting us with ancient eyes, then, uninterested, resumed its nibbling on the fairway grass.

"You can hear it eating," Karras said. "Swear to God. If you kneel down there and put your ear up close, you can hear that grass getting *chomped.* He's moved about ten yards since he was set down there an hour ago. We expect him to have a hundred-yard day. He's one of our what we call 'movable hazards.' Of course, he's one of our slower movers."

"What are some of the faster movers?"

"Well, you remember last time I was hoping to get some llamas," Karras said. "Well damn, we *did* get one. Not only that; he's a nervous llama. He hasn't stopped running since he got here, and he goes through foursomes like he imagines he's a stampede. He's the fastest mover we got.

"We had hopes for our zebra. Actually, he's really a Shetland pony painted with white stripes. It didn't come out right; he just looks like a painted Shetland pony. He's not much of a mover. Neither is the Indian elephant, which is named Wanda. Big eater, though. Then we got a goat, a cow, and a couple of donkeys out on the course. But they are not your fast movers; they're not worth a damn as fast movers. Neither are the chickens, which are all hanging around the eighteenth green. But the llama has been making up for all of them. Have you seen him run? He's got this strange rocking-horse gait, with this tiny head on a long thin neck which sticks straight up like a woolly sort of periscope, and I swear to God he *materializes*—he's just everywhere. I heard that this one guy was so startled seeing him that he toppled backwards and broke his golf club in half. The llama's doing fine. Of course, he's got a long day in front of him."

"Who provided all this stuff?" I asked.

"An animal keeper. He's around here somewhere. He's got his hands full today. Over on the eleventh fairway he's got a pen with a couple of baby wolves in it, and a leopard and a little tiger cub. The pen was supposed to be a hazard in front of the green there, but the children packed in so tight wanting to pet the babies that he had to move the whole works off to one side. The keeper will get you just about any animal you're looking for. I wanted a crocodile, a big mother, for the water hole, but he finally balked at that. Wouldn't do it. So we got a corpse in there."

"A corpse?"

"It's a storefront mannequin dressed up in old clothes and wearing a wide-brimmed gangster's hat. It floats on its stomach in there amongst the cattails. Gives you a big turn when you spot it. It looks like it had been dumped in there a month ago by the Luchinni brothers and has just floated to the surface."

As we reached the sixteenth green, Karras lowered his voice. "Now we've done a job on this green, a *real* job. There's no flagstick here, because if the caddy took it out of the cup, it would be about fourteen feet long. The cup goes down *eight* feet. Damn right. They dug it out last night and put it back together again, and you can't hardly tell. So what happens is that the player rolls in a long putt, maybe a thirty- or forty-footer, and he strides up with this big grin, reaches into the cup to get his ball back, and in he tumbles, his arm right up to the shoulder in the ground. Helluva sight."

A foursome was toiling up to the green. "Look at them," Karras whispered. We watched them make their approach shots. One of the golfers had to make his from an enclosure immediately in front of the green, with a low fence around it, which included, besides his ball, six ducks. "Robert Trent Jones couldn't have placed a hazard better," Karras whispered. "People have been knocking their shots in there all day long." At the golfer's backswing, the ducks tilted back on their feet, spread their wings, and chattered noisily as the shot glanced weakly off the club face. The golfer swore and climbed over the fence.

"You know, Alex," I said. "Some of these golfers don't look especially happy."

It was true. This foursome looked particularly grim. "Hey, Alex," one of them called over. "Does that llama bite?"

"No, but it sure kicks," Karras said.

The foursome reached the green. The first putt rolled toward the cup, stopping within an inch or so of the lip. Karras tensed. "Damn," he whispered. "The guy may notice." The golfer stepped up to tap his putt in, and then stopped short, peering down the hole.

"Hey!" he called. He motioned the others over. "Jesus Christ! How far down does that son of a bitch go?" one of them asked. They stood in a tight group, looking down. "What's in there?" another asked. The others looked at him. "Damned if I'm putting my hand in to find out," the first man said. "He's probably got a mess of snakes down there." The four looked over, aggrieved. "Goddamn it, Karras," one of them called. "Whatcha trying to do—steal our golf balls?"

"I'm telling you, Alex," I whispered. "Those guys are huffy. They are not amused."

"Yeah," said Karras, turning away. "Who are they, anyway? Who invited them to my tournament?"

One astonishing aspect of the day was that despite the wandering spectators unfettered by marshals, the noise, the doctored greens, and the movable hazards—especially the excessive bouncing about of the llama—somehow the golf scores were often respectable, and low in many cases. Lem Barney, the Lion cornerback, shot a seventy-three, and his legendary predecessor at that position, Night Train Lane, shot a hole in one on the eighth hole. It was witnessed by a small knot of people who, seeing the ball land, take a big bite, and backspin into the hole, began leaping up and down.

Later, I asked Night Train, "What were your emotions when the ball ran in?"

The English language has always had a gentle love affair with Night Train. "Well, my commotions were that I had gone to the wrong club. I used a wedge."

"Wrong *club!*" I said incredulously. "My God, Train, you got a hole in *one.*"

"Yesterday I lost my nine iron," Train went on unperturbed. "Might have put it in someone else's bag. I should have gone to the nine iron." He shook his head sadly.

In the afternoon there was a considerable amount of aerial activity; besides Captain Phog's hot-air balloon, it included a flyover by two National Guard jets from nearby Selfridge Field, two stunt planes maneuvering loudly and threateningly over the golf course, a drop by two parachutists, and, perhaps most memorable, the catatonic arrival of a crop-dusting plane which roared down a few feet over the heads of the crowds on the fairways and let loose fog clouds of vapor.

"There was a little disappointment in that department," Karras told me later. "The real hope was to completely sock in the golf course with that crop duster—such a heavy cloud of fog that the golfers wouldn't be able to see each other. The pilot said he couldn't produce like that. Then the idea was to drop clouds of colored dye so that right before your eyes everyone would turn, you know, *red.*"

Throughout the afternoon helicopters dropped in and out of the tournament. Joe O'Higgins, the sheriff in the Dodge automobile television commercials, stepped out of one of them—the celebrity of the day, judging from the delighted shouts of the children and the thickets of paper thrust toward him to sign. But from time to time over the loudspeaker system it was announced that an even bigger celebrity than O'Higgins would be arriving. Tantalizingly, he was referred to as "The Big Man." "Get your autograph books ready!" we were informed by the amplifiers. "The Big Man is coming."

Finally, the helicopter floated in at about two P.M. An enormous circle of people waited for The Big Man to get out, craning their necks and calling, "Who is he? Who is he?"

The man who stepped out of the helicopter was indeed large, and he was wearing a yellow windbreaker with the words THE BIG MAN stenciled on the back. He alighted with a big grin and a wave. Everybody was shoving to see. "Who is he? Who is he?"

I did not recognize him. I went over and stood beside Karras, who was doubled up. "Look," he said, "the disappointment is just *intense.* 'Who is he? Who is he?' " His hand flew up to cover a giggle. "All these people shoving and pushing to see The Big Man, and then he gets off the plane and he's nothing. He's nothing at all. He's just fat. Oh, it worked just beautiful."

"Well, who is he?"

Karras looked at me, startled. "Oh," he said. "Why, that's Gene Mitchell. He's just a friend—an insurance salesman from Birmingham. He's a fat friend, that's all."

"A fat friend?" I repeated.

Karras said, "We were thinking of getting the rumor started that he was a big celebrity who had just gone through a big face-lifting operation and didn't *look* the same—you know, the new and bigger Mickey Rooney, or something like that. Johnny Weissmuller was going to go up and say, 'Mickey Rooney, as I live and breathe,' and shake his hand vigorously. But the trouble is that Mitchell doesn't look the part."

I agreed. People were drifting away. The "Big Man" excitement was over; there were other things going on. A cannon went off behind the first tee and someone yelled, probably a golfer bending down to put his ball carefully on the tee.

I wandered over to the eighteenth green to watch the foursomes finish. The chickens searching for picnic scraps moved among the spectators. I stood watching the late starters straggle in, coming slowly up the fairway. The revelry was beginning in the big tent. I could not stay for the entire awards dinner. What I saw of it was raucous with shouting and carrying-on, big hands reaching for yellow pitchers of beer set in rows on the wooden tables. Night Train Lane got the big prize for his hole in one on the eighth hole—a 1951 Oldsmobile, donated by a used-car dealer. Three other used cars were donated or auctioned off. Karras and Buterakos had planned to award an Edsel, which would turn out to be a six-hundred-pound woman of the same name, but like John Weissmuller's pet chimpanzee she had fallen ill at the last moment.

A high school kid drove me out to the airport. I told him about the cigar-smoking midget who had met me the afternoon before. He shook his head. "You're being returned to normalcy," he said.

# CHAPTER 11

In the spring of 1967 a movie producer named Stuart Millar called me and asked if I would join him for dinner with Marty Ritt, a brilliant director who had just completed *Hud*—a highly praised film set in contemporary times in the Texas Panhandle. Ritt, said Millar, was now interested in making a film about football, and the two of them wondered if I had any general opinions on such a project and, specifically, if I knew of any "properties" which they could use.

We met in a midtown hotel. I did not keep notes on the dinner, though I remember Ritt as a large and solemn man who saw football as the background for a deep and personal film study of a very "American" sort of tragedy. It would happen to an aging star (*Death of a Quarterback?*), played out against the violence and grimness of the sport, suggesting something of the correlation between the national character and ferocity; the whole thing would be very real and stark, with the sort of dramatic pertinence that had been done about boxing in *Champion* with Kirk Douglas. What did I think?

I remember being disappointed. I had hoped that perhaps they had called me because they were interested in the film rights to my own lighthearted study of football, *Paper Lion.* Apparently not. I remember saying to Ritt that I didn't know anything about the sort of thing he had in mind—that in my limited experience the atmosphere around a professional football team was buoyant rather than somber, and that I could not think of either Earl Morrall or Milt Plum, the two Detroit quarterbacks, as Willy Lomans. The really tragic people in football were the ballpark ticket-takers who were cooped up in their booths half listening to the great roars coming over the rim of the stadium and were never able to see a game.

The three of us sat looking at each other, turning our drinks in our hands.

Well, perhaps the tragic figures in football were the *owners,* I went on to try. Perhaps a film should be done about *them.* Here were these weird men who had pots of money and power complexes, which was certainly an American phenomenon, and look what they did with it: they bought football teams, though only one owner each year, out of all the franchises, would win a championship. The odds made it all so futile. Someone had once said something excellent about owners—what was it? Oh, it was awfully good. Yes: "What dark past would compel a man to arrange his life so that he could sit up in the back of the press box with a good-luck hat on his head and watch his team on their eleven yard line break the huddle with third down and thirty-five yards to go?"

"Or take Harry Wismer, the fellow who owned the New York Titans before they became the Jets," I went on. "On the Titans was a scatback—Tiller? Was that his name? Jim Tiller—and Wismer's wife was always crazy to see him run. He wasn't much good, but Wismer knuckled under, and he'd make the coaches send in plays for this guy. The trouble was that Tiller ran laterally and occasionally backwards, but rarely forwards. Still, he ran long distances, from one side of the field to the other, which was exciting, and Mrs. Wismer would sit next to her husband and cry, 'Oh, they're going to get him, they're going to get him,' and they would, and it was terrific for her. But what had driven her husband to accept this sort of thing? And what about her; what was their relationship? Highly tragic stuff."

We turned the glasses around in our hands some more.

"I guess it's not very filmic," I said finally.

I never saw Ritt again, but Millar stayed in touch, titillated by the notion of doing *Paper Lion,* and finally one day he called and said that he had signed to produce it in conjunction with United Artists.

Naturally, I was excited. In the beginning, I had the vague notion that perhaps I could perform in the film myself. I thought about it from time to time, daydreaming, and let Millar know that I was available—for a "draft," I think I described it. But Millar had other ideas. He felt that a documentary drawn straight from the book would not work, that the text was too static for filming. Some extra ingredients had to be added; specifically, to use a word that was bandied about constantly, the material had to be "Hollywoodized." To this end he hoped to find a big-name star to play my role in the film—dashing that forlorn hope that I might be able to play myself as well as anyone—which would help at the box office.

To attract an established actor Millar adapted the film script to give "fuller dimensions" to my character, and I found myself transmogrified from a somewhat shy and introverted reporter to a brash, rather kooky fan (one rarely had the sense that the character *was* a reporter, since he never carried a notebook or asked a question or even *listened*) whose motivation at one point was that he really believed he could make the Detroit Lion team—such a bizarre fancy that had I ever expressed the thought at training camp I would have been requested to catch the next train out. It was hoped that Jack Lemmon, the comedian, would be intrigued enough by this dipsy-doodle character to accept the role, but it turned out that he had other commitments and could not accept.

Millar looked around further and finally picked a young Broadway star named Alan Alda—a polished performer with a thin and wiry frame which looked vaguely athletic, perhaps a quarter-miler's, and whose facial features were thought by many people to bear the dubious distinction of resembling mine. I met Alda a few times. He was personable, and the football players liked him enough so that they felt easy joshing him ("Is that the fastest you can run?"), but his football experience was even more limited than mine. He had played two weeks in high school before his mother made him quit on the grounds that contact was bad for the braces on his teeth. He could never quite get over what he was doing—a feeling with which I could sympathize. He told me, "To think that three weeks ago in a touch football game in Central Park I was going after an eight-year-old quarterback. I got chopped in the larynx by his father. That was bad enough, but now I'm supposed to stiff-arm Karras."

Most of the filming of *Paper Lion* was done at a private school near Boca Raton, Florida. The winter months had gripped the Cranbook School in Michigan, the locale for the text of the book, so that Millar had to forgo the unique beauty of that opulent campus—the swans, the pine forests, the brick walks, and the halls and dormitories, with their fronts of ivy, and the quiet of the place, the sprinklers ticking back and forth on the lawns—all of which struck such contrasts with the physical intensity of a professional football team in training, and which would have been fine to suggest in the filming. With a schedule to keep, he was forced to look elsewhere, in the clement weather of the South, for a simulated training camp.

The Florida school he had found was set in flat, sun-parched barrens, palms set about haphazardly amid barracks-like school buildings, so that one had the sense that the classes were held outdoors, the instructor leaning up against the bole of a palm tree with his students around him. Next to the gymnasium was an outdoor swimming pool which was continually in use—whistles going, the constant thump of limbs against water, and, whenever one looked, a young face turning, streaming water, to suck in a tortured breath of air through a mouth grotesquely ajar, then facing down in the water again to pursue those endless laps—driven by new hope of one day winning a race and a tiny medal with a ribbon attached.

I went down to Boca Raton a few times to see what was going on. I had no official capacity with the film, though Millar was kind enough to show me the script every once in a while, and we fought about what was in it, especially a fabricated scene in which I knocked myself out running into a goalpost.

The first time I arrived, I could see a big crowd of Lions in football gear standing in the middle of the practice field. It turned out to have nothing to do with the film. The players were surrounding two linemen crouched opposite each other in their stances, as if on the line of scrimmage. Alex Karras was one of them; the other was Roger Shoals, an offensive lineman known as "the Turtle"—chiefly, I think, because his neck was so thick that it continued the dimensions of his head, a very large one, down into his body, so that he seemed to be peering out from the carapace of his shoulder blades. Apparently the two of them had bet fifty dollars that playing head-to-head the Turtle, who was an offensive tackle, could keep Karras from reaching a point seven yards behind him—the average distance a quarterback drops back to pass—within three seconds. The Turtle was sure enough of his abilities against the pass rush to put up twenty dollars of his own; the rest of the fifty was gathered from fellow offensive linemen who were skeptical but loyal enough to their own kind to back him.

Karras had not bet on himself; he said that was against his principles, which, as everyone knew, were rock-ribbed and airtight, but his side of the bet had been quickly covered by teammates from the defense.

Someone on the side barked out the signals, and at the simulated hike, the Turtle, with a hard concussive series of grunts, jigged back with quick ferocious steps and set himself up, hands cocked, for Karras's rush.

It was difficult to follow Karras's moves. Invariably, as one remembered from watching him in games, it seemed the opposing lineman's *clumsiness* that let Karras through, because the Turtle was left on one knee, off balance, grimacing in despair; of course what had put him there was something Karras had done to him in a quick blur of motion, a feint and heave. I could hear the crack of a hand on a helmet, and then Karras seemed to scuttle past in a maneuver that a master of Tai Chi, the most advanced and subtle of the Oriental martial arts, would have applauded. He reached the designated spot in well under the three seconds, almost as if he had scampered there unimpeded, and the players began to josh and rail at Shoals. Someone said he played his position like a guard on the taxi squad of the then enfeebled Philadelphia Eagles.

Karras saw me standing at the edge of the crowd and trotted up to say hello. His big peaceful face stared out of his helmet. "To think," he said, "that it's only taken two and a half seconds to destroy the confidence of a man built up over six and a half years."

Karras had come to Florida for the filming with suitable props: a director's chair shipped down with his name and four stars stenciled on the back; a red beret that he either hung off the back of his chair or wore at a jaunty angle—usually when he had his football uniform on, which gave him an oddly paramilitary look, as if he were a weirdly armored reconnaissance scout for the Green Berets. From time to time, during the shooting on the set, he took to shouting out the orders associated with moviemaking: "Slate it! Roll sound! Quiet on the set!" And especially, "All right, everybody, it's a wrap!"—the standard Hollywood phrase for calling it a day, which Karras would usually announce just five minutes or so after the day's shooting had *started.* He practiced an equivalently exquisite sense of timing with "Quiet on the set!"—bellowing it out when it *was* quiet, with everyone in their positions, and tense, and the camera just about to roll. "QUIET ON THE SET!" and everyone would jump and say, "Oh for Chrissakes, Alex."

The man most agonized by this sort of behavior was Alex March, the director. He was a lean high-strung ex–TV producer who had shifted to directing because he suffered such pangs handing over his shows to someone else to give them expression. He felt he could do as well, and for seven years he had been directing on his own, largely television dramas. He told me that in those seven years of directing, his voice had dropped practically an octave. *Paper Lion* was his first motion picture, and he expected that by the time he had done with it his voice would drop out of audible register, as if off the bass end of a piano.

"What's the trouble?" I asked. He had invited me over to his motel on the edge of the school grounds. He sat with his hands folded over his stomach, staring up at the corner of the ceiling.

"I love athletes," he began. "I'm a great fan. Once I went up in an elevator in the RCA building with Willie Mays. I was supposed to get off at the eleventh floor, but I recognized him and went all the way to the forty-fourth, where he was getting off, hardly even daring to look at him I was so excited. I feel the same way about great football players. But this film has been a nightmare.

"Football players are such opposites," he said mournfully. "They're big adults to look at, but really they're not: they're children. That was the first revelation. So I decided I'd *treat* them like children. But that didn't work. I tried to coax them. No. I yelled at them. No. In fact, I don't know *how* you handle them. Football players are supposed to be supremely disciplined people, since what they do is predicated on the notion of supreme discipline. But they're *not.* If I try to get them together for a scene, it takes hours. They mill around like cattle; they don't listen; they all talk at the same time. And Christ," he said. "The vulgarity. The incredible vulgarity. It's as thick as steam, and after a while you damn near get suffocated by it."

"What seems to be the main problem?"

"Well, for one thing I can't get them to *exert* themselves," he said. "We get the cameras trained on what is supposed to be a red-hot scrimmage, and it looks as though they're doing a mime, a gentle sort of ballet. Sometimes the defense pops; *they* do all right. It's instinctive for them, I guess; when they look across and see someone carrying the ball, they want to get him. Still, I can't get anyone to *sweat.* And no one will take out his false teeth. They all look scrubbed and clean. Hell, I don't think anyone even has to take a *shower* at the end of the day. After the morning's shooting, almost all of them lunch in the cafeteria in their football uniforms. Helluva thing to see a guy in shoulder pads tucking into a little cup of fruit salad. And of course the lack of exertion on their part shows up in the rushes. On the screen this training camp looks like everyone's getting ready for a pinochle tournament."

March told me that the first scene he had tried with the Lions was symptomatic. On paper it had seemed simple enough; it called for Joe

Schmidt to motion Karras out of a group of players running in from practice to tell him in a sentence or so that a writer from *Sports Illustrated* was turning up in training camp to join the team.

"Fifteen takes. To begin with, I couldn't keep the players—and they all looked scrubbed, not a grass stain on their uniforms—from looking into the camera as they ran by. Finally, after I got *that* straightened out, I discovered that as soon as they were out of camera range, they'd turn and hustle up behind me and the camera to watch Schmidt and Karras—ribbing them, obscene hand motions and so forth.

"I don't understand them. Their private *personae.* Christ! They go out all night and come dragging in at dawn. It's hard to imagine what they find in this strange octogenarians' town of Boca Raton. I think they go just out of habit, and lean up against buildings.

"And on the set. *Christ!*" Reflectively, he said, "You know, moviemaking is a dull business, really. I mean, it's boring waiting around for your scene, and then the retakes. So most of the people I know in show business find rather normal ways to pass the time—they play chess or cards or read a paperback or play liar's poker. But you know what these football players are doing?"

"I can't imagine," I said truthfully.

"A lot of them have got these magnifying glasses." His voice rose. "There's a whole rash of them around, and the players are always lying around in great heaps out there in the sun and trying to burn each other's body hair off with these magnifying glasses."

I expressed appropriate surprise, and then I asked if he thought any of his charges had potential ability as actors.

He was dubious. "Alex Karras could be a Nat Pendleton—a funny heavy. As for the rest of them..." He shrugged. "If they learn the lines, they sound like schoolboys. As for improvising—well, only the best actors can do that. But you know, sometimes I think they could do much better than they let on, that somehow I'm involved in a tremendous put-on. There's a terrible intelligence that shines out of their eyes, like the look you sometimes get from cats. For example, Karras had this line in which he had to mention Park Avenue. But he kept substituting other places for it: 'Hyde Park,' he'd say. So we'd start again. 'Dobbs Ferry.' 'Grosse Pointe.' I mean, what was he *doing?*" His voice was rising. " 'Memory Lane.' What did he have in mind? Did he have some sort of psychological block about Park Avenue? Take after take. Or a scene he had with John Gordy. Twenty-nine takes. They just giggled at each other."

March looked at his watch and sighed deeply. "Joe Schmidt's the only one who can handle them." He went on to describe one of the low points in his own attempts to keep order and decorum: the occasion of the big Jell-O fight between many of the players lunching in the school cafeteria. To no one's surprise, Karras was the instigator, apparently with a spoof of a television commercial current then, in which tea is shown being poured over ice cubes into a tall glass. "Harry, this iced tea is so good on a hot summer day," Karras was saying in the exact words of the commercial, "that I can't get enough of it." But he kept continuing to pour the tea until it overflowed the glass, spreading swiftly out across the cafeteria table and over the edge onto Roger Shoals's legs. "Just can't get enough of this super-tasting tea," Karras kept intoning. Shoals reached for his plate and, cupping his portion of Jell-O in his palm, he lobbed it onto Karras's lap. Karras retaliated with *his* Jell-O, and the contagion spread from table to table—largely, I was told afterward, because of the hugely pleasurable feel of Jell-O as a projectile. "There is a technique," I was told. "You can't close your fingers around it or it'll slip out between your fingers. Your true Jell-O shot is a lob. The Jell-O quivers through the air and lands just great. Beautiful!"

Because of the Jell-O fight, in which a lot else was thrown too—milk from jugs, pats of butter, rolls, a dish of mashed potatoes, celery stalks—Joe Schmidt called the team together that afternoon, told them that he was disappointed in them, and ordered them to behave like gentlemen henceforth. At the end of the talk, just as if he were appealing to their football instincts, he told them to dedicate themselves to the film, "to give one hundred percent to these motion-picture guys."

Poor March; he was a harried man. The team was at the Boca Raton location for almost a month, and on the last day of shooting a few of the players picked him up and threw him in the pool to celebrate the end of their stay there, much in the same spirit that the crew of an eight-oar shell picks up a coxswain and throws him into the river after winning a race. But March, who did not cotton to the idea at all, struggled desperately in the grasp of the players, cursing at them, and as he was tumbled into the water he fractured a couple of ribs on the side of the pool. "I'm broke!" he shouted, his mouth half full of water.

"He was real mad," one of the players told me. "He couldn't take it as a joke."

What the player remembered best about throwing March in was that the regular activity in the pool never stopped; the kids kept doing their laps, though they must have seen him—this man thrashing around, fully dressed, with his shoes on. They just kept going up and down, the swimmer in March's lane swerving slightly to avoid him. "Great dedication," the player said. "Man, that's *it*."

The morning after I had spoken to March, I saw him direct a few scenes, and I understood his torment perfectly. In the first one I watched, Pat Studstill, the team's flanker and punter, had one line to deliver—"I got a haircut," just a throwaway line for background effect, in essence—but he had stewed over it and practiced it, and when the time came he said, "Stand back, everyone; I'm kind of nervous." Then he delivered the line with such heavy, portentous emphasis that he seemed to be announcing that rather than a haircut he had a serious, very communicable disease. March threw up his hands. There had to be a number of takes to tone down Studstill's delivery.

Another instance of an ill-delivered line occurred in a scene in which Jerry Zawadzkas, a tight end, was cut down by Bruce Maher with a block, and John North, who coached the receivers, was supposed to yell out a reprimand and tell Zawadzkas to get off his tail. As a player, North had a reputation for being especially rough, with a lot of gold in his mouth as a result of reprisals, and he has always had an appropriately foul mouth to go with his deportment. But he found the camera completely intimidating, and at March's cry of "Action," he leaned forward and gazed out at where Zawadzkas had been dumped somewhat gently by Maher. "Gerald," he cried mournfully. "You're supposed to take the linebacker to the outside." Each word was carefully evoked from memory with immense formality.

"Son of a *bitch,*" he said later, with more characteristic fervor. "I've set this mothering industry back one hundred years." He was beside himself. " '*Gerald!*' Can you believe it? What the hell got into me?" He snorted scornfully. "Christ, I don't even call that guy 'Jerry,' much less 'Gerald'! I don't even call him 'Za... Za...'—whatever the hell his name is. I might call him 'you dumb Polack' or maybe 'you son of a bitch,' but '*Gerald!*' Christ!" He was shaking with dismay.

Among the Lions, however, one player had had considerable "practical experience," as he called it, in "motion-picturing." Night Train Lane, the greatest of the Detroit cornerbacks, was now retired and working in the Lion front office. I was delighted to see him again. He came running up in a bulky sweat suit. All bone and tendon in his playing days, he had now abandoned the training regimen that kept him slim and his weight had ballooned to over two hundred pounds, though it was not a disproportionate distribution of weight: he had simply turned into a big man. After the opposition began to beat him too often for him to continue as an active player, he stayed on with the Lions, working at one thing and another. He affected a pipe—a heavy, odd-looking meerschaum, a Sherlock Holmes type that weighed down one side of his face and gave him a somewhat strained expression. The Lions had him doing some scouting for them and gave him a little office at their headquarters where he kept his charts and scouting reports. Dick LeBeau, who collected Night Train anecdotes, told me that the place was full of craftsman's tools and slide rules, and that walking in there was like being in the chart room of an ocean liner. "The charts he kept on the players he scouted were so complicated that he had to be kept around just to *decipher* them," LeBeau said. "Either that or bring in a PhD. I once asked him what it all meant and he said it was nothing but a 'grading code,' but you could tell by the way the smoke poured out of his pipe when he showed you around his office and the way he'd reach down and touch one of those slide rules that he was pretty proud of how it all looked."

Also, at that time, LeBeau told me, Night Train was involved in "motion-picturing." During preseason training he was in charge of making videotapes of practice scrimmages to help the coaches pick up flaws. He worked on the top of a thirty-foot scaffolding set on the sidelines of the practice field.

"How were the films?" I asked.

"Well, they started out kind of blurry," LeBeau said. "Like he'd done them in a snowstorm. He had trouble with the sun at first, and he said he didn't know how to 'down-focus the meter,' which he said was very important. They got the thing working pretty good finally, and the players began calling him 'Cecil B. de Train.' "

The fact that he had been involved in the "motion-picturing" business gave Night Train a certain air of authority at Boca Raton. He took me over to look at the big Technicolor cameras on their rubber-wheeled sleds. "Look at these babies," he said.

"What would you point the camera at if you were in charge here?" I asked.

He squinted slightly. "The *best* thing to show in a film about football is what the people *don'* see, so in the the-ater they is surprised, and they say, 'Oh my, so *that's* what it's all about.' "

"What are some of those things?" I asked.

"The behind-the-scenes is what I'm touchin' on," said Train. "How to keep a team high on the steam. Now a very serious thing is the tapin' . . ."

"You mean taping ankles?"

"Correct," said Train. "A very essential business. Tapin' shot. That's what I'd do. Jes' get the camera in the trainin' room and crank away. A nice close shot of the fellow's *foot* and the trainer smoothin' the tape. You get a little scene like that an' you tell somethin' 'bout the danger—it *indicates* it—and it's interestin' 'cause the tape goin' around the ankle is so clean and smooth. And what about the fellow *doin'* the taping—what about him? Why, just what this fellow *says* is very important—puttin' the people he's workin' on at *ease,* if that's what he thinks is right, or maybe gettin' them riled up if he thinks they is shuffling too easy-like, maybe, or moseyin'. Why, we had this trainer on the Cardinals, Joe Dollar, who is a chiropodist in Florida now, and while he was doin' your tapin', why, this man would fin' somethin' to say, somethin' 'bout your ancestors, maybe, that'd snap you out of droppin' the ball durin' the game. He had a jillion lines. One time he says, 'Don' go down there with your head in the *crowds*'—he was talking about showboatin'. He was always sayin' little things like that to get you jes' right."

"That's very nice," I said.

"Another thing the movie man can focus on is the little things like the habits that a lot of ballplayers have, like chawin' tobacco. Just mosey the camera down into things like *that.*"

I pointed out that I had not seen much tobacco chewing among football players.

"That's true," Night Train said blithely. "You don' see so much of it around no more. But I remember this time when Joe Stydahar bent over with his chaw stickin' out of his back pocket, and Ben Sheets sneaked it out of there and took a bite out of it for a joke. Well, Ben Sheets was deadly sick and they had to pump it out of him. That's the type of thing I mean," he said triumphantly.

"Let me give you another. You have Erich Barnes down there on the field, the cornerback of the Cleveland Browns, and when he gets pass interference called on him he goes into a big confrontation with the referee. You see him down there hoppin' and jawin' to beat the band. That's when you get your camera crankin' on him, and you see Barnes leaning right up to an *inch* of that referee, and his mouth goin' at him. He's a mad rooster, but what is funny is that he can't *touch* that referee. If he does, it's a two-hundred-dollar fine, and Barnes, he *knows* that. So he may be awful mad, but he's not *that* mad. He got to keep his hands under control, and his feet too, because if he stomps on that referee's toe, even by mistake, he's goin' to be hurt plenty in the pocketbook. That's a fine thing to catch on the film—all this fire and fury, his fingers all jibbery wantin' to collect a referee, and yet that poor man is all flummoxed; he can't do *nothin'*. And the other fine thing on film is that the referee knows that *too,* so you see him standin' around as solemn as a church and 'bout as safe too, just achin' for that cornerback to stub him with a toe so he can balloon up as big as a thunderstorm and say, 'You *touched* me, man! Get on off this field and that'll be two hundred singles. You'll be hearing from the commissioner...' "

The other Lion who was having the time of his life in "movie-picturing" was, of course, Alex Karras. In fact, he began behaving like a star, but with all the pique of an ingenue. "Look at Friday Macklem," he said to me indignantly, pointing at the Lion equipment manager. "Not a damn thing out of him all season long. Players have to get down on their knees and beg for a shoelace. Now look at him—throwing jocks around, and sweatshirts, and yelling commands and looking worried when the camera's on, like he's got sixteen tons of responsibility. He's in every goddamn shot." I resisted pointing out that Karras's outburst was delivered as he sat in his own director's chair, with its four stars, wearing his actor's beret.

In fact, almost as soon as the filming began, Karras could see that potentially he was a good actor, as March had suggested, and that it could provide a funnel for his constant, near obsessive need to perform. We talked about it one afternoon after the day's shooting. Was it something he might consider after finishing football? He was skeptical, though intrigued.

The sun was overpowering, and we moved to the shade of a palm tree. He began talking about films. His favorite film was *Zorba the Greek,* which he had seen three times because, as he said succinctly, it was about ugly Greeks. The good-looking matinee idols disturbed him, and he felt that men like Tab Hunter and Rock Hudson—he referred to them as "those funny guys"—should be supplanted in romantic leads by potato-faced actors who looked like Wallace Beery. "Of course there are some scenes," he said, "that might embarrass audiences: say, a big, Beery-looking guy with whiskers making love to a Norwegian girl. We might have to hide him a bit. We might have to enclose the two of them in a sheet."

"What sort of roles do you see yourself playing?" I asked.

"Robin Hood," said Karras. "I've always wanted to wear a pointed green hat with a long feather in it. I also see myself as a Pépé Le Moko type who speaks a terribly thick foreign language. In the film I come into this room full of big high furniture where a beautiful Norwegian girl is struggling in the arms of a duke who looks like Rock Hudson. Church bells are ringing, and you can hear a big crowd shouting outside. Some sort of a revolution is going on. I lean up against the back of an armchair. I say something very suave. Nobody knows what it means. *I* don't know what it means. The duke looks over; he's puzzled. But whatever I'm saying in this thick accent, the girl says, 'Yes, yes,' and she pulls away from the duke and comes toward me. Her eyes are shining. She says, 'But first we will have a cocktail in the lounge of the Villa Caramba.' She has a sheet in a little handbag."

"Naturally," I said.

"But the role I really want to play," Karras went on easily, "is in a Western. First of all, it would have nothing to do with your usual Western. Not at all. I'd have a different sort of name. I wouldn't want to be called 'Slim' or 'Tex' or 'Wyoming Bill' or 'Monte.' Nossir."

"Well, what would your name be?"

" 'Ace Zerblonski,' that's what I'd like to be called."

"Ace Zerblonski? Why that?"

"There's been a big ethnic void in Westerns," Karras said grandly. "Ace Zerblonski would help fill it. And another thing: I wouldn't want to be one of your tall, gaunt Western stars, always looking into the sun and squinting. Nossir. To begin with, I wouldn't wear a cowboy hat. I'd be the first bareheaded cowboy star in the history of the cinema."

"What would you do about the sun?" I asked. "The desert sun gets awfully hot."

"Well," Karras said, "I'd have this little parasol—maybe a little Japanese parasol. It would be in a carrying case on my saddle if it was cloudy or I was traveling at night. Then when the sun came up, I'd take it out, snap it open—*click!*—and the people in the cow town would see the silhouette of this guy with a parasol on the horizon and they'd shout, 'Oh, for Chrissakes, it's Ace Zerblonski,' and they'd run into the meeting house and ring the bell.

"Besides, a parasol is a good prop," he went on. "All the best Western characters had their props. Bat Masterson had his cane; Dan'l Boone had his coonskin cap; Ace Zerblonski has his parasol. When the townsfolk see that parasol coming out of the tree line, everybody begins carrying on because they know that Ace is under that parasol and someone around there is going to lose their stuffings!"

"Is Ace a brave man?" I asked.

"Christ no," Karras said. "My style as a gunslinger is very different. I shoot people in the back."

"Oh, come on, Alex!"

"That's right," he said. "Just ease up to them from the rear and let 'em have it."

"Is that reliable?" I asked. "Don't you make mistakes that way?"

"All the time," Karras said quickly. "Sometimes I walk up to these people after I've shot them in the back and they're lying on their stomachs in the middle of the street, and I turn them over with my toe and I say, 'Oh Lordy, that's not Buck Jones *at all.* It's the *preacher,* isn't it? Amen! Damn shame!' I *brood* about mistakes like that. But in the long run, if you shoot enough people in the back, you're bound to get the one you're after. It's just a question of time. Of course it has a big effect on the cow towns in the area where I hang out. I've shot so many people in the back that the folks in those parts are always wheeling around to see if Ace Zerblonski is *behind* them. If a guy steps off his front porch and goes down to the saloon for a drink, he *revolves* down the street. That's one of the things you remember out there—these little cow towns where everyone's spinning around and walking quickly in circles. Then you know that Zerblonski's been through."

"What sort of a gun do you use?"

"It's very loud and powerful. Terrific kick at both ends. I have a great callus right here on my shoulder. But you know something? It doesn't bother the horse at all when it goes off. He's used to it. Doesn't even jump. Just ho-hum stuff for him. Of course, maybe he's deaf."

"What do you call him, this horse?"

"His name is Great Big Elephant. It's a very good name for my image," Karras explained. "It makes people think that I'm about a mile tall and dangerous, sort of like a rock slide. It has a nice effect. I mean, when the word gets around I'm coming into town they think I really *am* on a great big elephant. So they cry out, 'Martha, get the buckboard! Pack up the hens and chickens. We're pulling out. Ace Zerblonski is coming through the pass on his great big elephant!' "

"Had you thought of doing a television series about Ace Zerblonski?" I asked.

"No." Karras said. "I think of Ace Zerblonski as being in a mammoth super-Western one-shot that'll play in the drive-ins. The kids will look up from lying on top of each other in the backseats and see me on the huge screen in the night riding into town on Elephant and holding my little parasol, and they'll stir themselves and say, 'Jesus Christ! Put on your shoes, Kitty, here comes the Ace. Let's watch Ace Zerblonski.' "

The sun, orange and huge, was sinking toward the flat Florida horizon, and an evening wind began to rattle the palm fronds.

"Tough life, this. Show business is hell." He yawned. "It's hard to believe a guy can get through to the next day. I suppose I could get into it—I mean *truly* get into acting or something like it. When you play football, you always think of what's next. But it's never predictable. I always tell myself that when football's over I'm going to leave Detroit, pack up my family, move to Clinton, Iowa, and help my father-in-law run his bowling alley. Of course I could do something else," he said pensively. "But my father-in-law's bowling alley—that's solid. The days would be predictable. I could put my legs up on the desk and listen to the bowling balls rolling down the alleys. There would be things to do. That would be all right, wouldn't it?"

"I would think so, Alex."

We looked across the playing fields toward the school buildings. The whistles were still blowing by the outdoor swimming pool.

"They really work, those kids," I said. "Hour after hour."

Karras stirred. "When we're done filming," he said, "we're going to throw Alex March in that pool."

"That's absolutely predictable, is it?" I asked.

"Absolutely," he said.

# CHAPTER 12

That fall, Karras, swept by a sense of civic responsibility that somewhat startled those who knew him, became a head coach in the Bloomfield Hills Pony League, which was composed of a number of teams named after NFL franchises—the 49ers, the Rams, the Raiders, the Vikings, and so forth—and restricted to youngsters nine to ten years old. Originally, he had been offered the job of coaching even younger kids in the Bee League, where seven- and eight-year-olds played, but he felt there was probably "too much crying down there for me to take on the job."

Karras's team was the Bloomfield Hills Jets. His second son, Alex Jr., played on it, as did one of John Gordy's two sons and Joe Schmidt's son, Billy. It was an oddly frustrating experience for Karras. The Pony League teams played each other on Friday afternoons or on weekends, which meant that Karras, involved in his own turbulent football wars, was often away when his charges had their games. He did the best he could. As soon as his own game was over, he would hurry down the ramp to the locker room, lob his helmet into his cubicle, and reach for the phone to call home.

"Hey, Alex, that you? How'd the Jets do?... You *lost!* To the Chargers? What happened?... Six fumbles!" and he would sit and listen to his son's explanations, his face torn with despair despite the fact that around him his own teammates might be shouting and carrying on about their own victory, and that some fifteen minutes before, he himself had been scuttling around in a real-life adult backfield, reaching for the quarterback with self-satisfying success.

During the autumn, I came out to Detroit to watch the Lions play a few of their home Sunday games, and on one occasion I arrived a few days early in the hope of watching Karras's Bloomfield Hills Jets in action. Alex gave me directions, and in the late afternoon I drove out to the high school grounds where the Jets were going through their last drills before playing the Bloomfield Hills Vikings the next day.

I stood on the sidelines and watched. Wearing his golf hat, Karras reared above his team like a derrick. Almost immediately I could see that there were a number of distinctive characteristics about a Karras-coached team. After a run-through of each offensive play, the Jet center was required to form the huddle by stationing himself at the proper eight- or nine-yard distance behind the line of scrimmage, raising his arm aloft so it could be seen, and shouting at the top of his lungs "Hud-*dle!*"—apparently an attempt to get the players grouped quickly around their quarterback. It was a cry one could hear across a couple of fields, as echoing and forlorn as a loon's, and it indicated to anyone in the vicinity who followed Pony League activity that Karras was at work with his team.

I took a few notes. Almost all the players looked like choirboys, an appearance that was not even belied by the accoutrements of football warfare; they stared out from beneath the rims of their helmets with enormous gentle eyes, and their high voices, clear as whistles, were as unferocious as birdcalls in the evening. All of them were required to wear plastic mouth guards, which were attached to their helmets, and when they set them in place they seemed en masse to have regressed to the use of pacifiers.

Some of them, of course, did not like what they were doing. After every play involving contact, an inevitable grasping at imaginary wounds would occur, usually the elbow or wrist; or a sudden limp would devastate a player, and he would come hobbling up to Karras and say, "Sir..."

"Puffer, what the hell's wrong? You're wetting in there like a little girl. No one even hit you. Go on back."

"Yessir."

Not only was Karras tough on his charges, but predictably he was not above keeping his team on edge with his own brand of needling. At one point his quarterback, a youngster named Reardon, complained after an unsuccessful pass that he could not see his intended receiver. "Mr. Karras, I can't see Brookmeier. He's too small."

Karras blew his whistle to stop practice. "Brookmeier," he called out. A helmet atop a small boy turned. "Brookmeier, your quarterback can't see you. *Grow!*"

On another occasion, Karras called out, "I want the pass-return team over here. Quick!"

The youngsters milled around uncertainly.

"I want the eleven people who are on the pass-return team over *here.* You all know who you are."

A group began to form around him.

"Well, it's about time," Karras said. "Our special teams must have pride. Okay, let's hear it for the pass-return team."

"Yay!" they cheered.

"What is the best of the special teams?"

"The pass-return team!"

"Are you proud to be on the pass-return team?"

"Yessir!"

"Well, you dummies," said Karras. "There *is* no such thing as a pass-return team." The youngsters looked at him, betrayed, eyes solemn and large in the shadows of their helmets. Karras shook his head.

"All right," he called. "Everyone gather round." The entire squad moved in around the forlorn "pass-return" team, Karras in the middle, towering above them.

"Okay, that's enough practice for today," he said. "But first I have some questions. Who are you playing tomorrow?"

"The Vikings!"

"Once again."

"The Vikings!" they all shouted in unison.

"Who are a bunch of turkeys?"

"The Vikings!"

"Who are we going to slaughter?"

"The Vikings!"

"Dismiss," said Karras.

He watched them troop off toward the sidelines. A few mothers were standing in the gathering darkness. Back in the high school parking lot other mothers waited in their cars, the headlights on, and the youngsters moved reluctantly, as if what each had been playing at—aping an adult pastime of ferocity and hitting each other—should not properly conclude by going to one's mother, perhaps (the ultimate indignity) to be clasped briefly and asked if he was "all right" before being driven home, holding his helmet in his lap, in the family Chevrolet.

Karras, his son, Alex, and I walked to his car. "I'm wrung out from psyching my team up," he said. "There's nothing left for *me.* I'm playing Green Bay on Sunday. What kind of a game am I going to have against them? Jesus!"

"What sort of personnel do you have on the Bloomfield Jets?" I asked as we headed for home. "Certainly you've got a lot of football heritage," I pointed out, thinking of his son, and Gordy's, and Joe Schmidt's.

"They're okay, those kids," Karras said. "But the squad is very weak in reserves. Wait until you see them in action tomorrow. The rule is, they all have to play. Did you see the one called Puffer? Puffer is about one foot tall and he's all voice. He's very bright. If Puffer could play the game he talks, no one else would walk out on the field; they'd all go home and hide in their basements. He wears number one, and he's the single worst football player I've ever seen. I don't think he's made contact with *anyone* this year."

"What position does he play?"

"I think he plays somewhere in the line," Karras said. "It's hard to tell because he sidles away from the guy carrying the ball. He doesn't want to get involved. He wears glasses. He's *very* bright. He's going to be secretary of commerce one day. When I was playing football at his age, the kids had names like Slivovitz and McTawney and Bragodnic, really tough Polack and Irish and Eyetie names, and nicknames like Turk and Hammer and Jughead, and some of them had already lost their front teeth. Puffer," he said in despair.

From the backseat Alex Jr. said that a lot of the kids didn't really like to play. A couple of weeks before, the guy opposite him in the line of the Bloomfield Hills Raiders had said, "I'm really going to get you. I'm really going to push your face in the dirt." Alex had blocked him properly on the first play and the kid had broken into tears and gone back to his bench.

"I'll tell you one thing," his father said. "Those Raiders didn't *all* break down and cry. They beat us about one sixty-eight to nothing."

I asked, "How have the Jets been doing?"

"What's our record?" Karras asked, turning back to look at his son. "We beat somebody, didn't we?"

"Oh, Dad," Alex Jr. said from the backseat. "We beat lots of people."

"I have all sorts of problems as a coach," Karras went on. "My best player, a kid named Robertson, came up to me before the last game and said, 'Mr. Karras, I can't play.'

" 'What?' I said.

" 'I've got a French horn lesson at four-thirty on the day of the game.'

"Well, I near fainted away. A French *horn* lesson. We finally solved it. We moved the French horn lesson up a half hour and the teacher allowed Robertson to come dressed in his football outfit, shoulder pads and all. He sat in her parlor on a straight-backed chair with the music stand in front, and when the hour was up he took out the French horn mouthpiece, clapped in the football mouthpiece, and came running out to play. He had a *horrible* game. It's not the way to get ready for The Big Game."

I stayed for dinner at the Karras house, standing out in the kitchen having a drink with his wife, Joanie, while she occasionally turned a spoon in the stew. Drawings by the two youngest Karras children were pinned to a corkboard—square-shaped houses with big windows, and chimneys with lines of smoke coming out. I asked her how much she herself could get involved in football—whether she let it permeate her life as much as it did the males in her household.

"Oh, no," she said. "The wives and mothers have to stay on an even keel. They can't get wrapped up in games the way the males do—it would drive a household crazy."

Her husband was in the living room playing with the younger children. Was he easy to live with during the season?

"There are always the sullen silences if things aren't going right," Joanie said. "It's unpleasant to live with, but it's common enough. During the season, the first few days of the week are calm, but then the pressure begins to build. One night Al climbed out of his side of the bed, dragging the comforter with him. He draped it over his shoulder and looked at me sleepily and said that he was off to play the Green Bay Packers. That's because of the pressure. It's great that a football team spends the night before a game in a hotel, even if it's a home game. Why, they might jump up in bed and kick us wives to pieces."

"What about after a loss?"

Joanie turned back to the stew. "Oh, after a loss there's usually a half hour of blowing off steam when he gets home, but he feels fine after that. Once I remember I took the family to pick him up at the Detroit airport after a big loss, and we went to have supper at a Howard Johnson's with Nick Pietrosante, Jim Gibbons and his wife, and some others, and everyone was grousing and staring into their shrimp cocktails and really *beside* themselves, until finally Alex Jr., who was just three then, piped up and said, 'Well, back to the old drawing board.' No one could believe it."

After dinner, I left for my hotel. With The Big Game in the Pony League coming up, the Karras household went to bed early. When I returned the next afternoon, driving through a slight rain, I found the house full of tension. Alex Jr. stood in the hall, fully dressed in his football paraphernalia and wearing his helmet. His father was pacing through the rooms. Even Joanie seemed affected. She shook her head and told me that her days had been full enough of gossip and chatter about the NFL as it was, and now, like opening a closet door and finding someone standing there, the Pony and Bee Leagues had suddenly made their presence known.

"The kids have their ups and downs about it," she said. "One time young Alex came to me and said, 'Mom, I have a bad shoulder. Do I have to go to practice?'

" 'Yes, Alex,' I said. 'Put on your uniform. Think of your father. He played five games with two torn cartilages . . .'

"You know what young Alex said to me? He said, 'Yes, but he had novocaine.' "

Joanie stayed home with the smaller children. Peter Karras had gone off earlier to play in *his* league. Alex Jr. sat in the backseat of the car. "Are you going to give us a big pep talk, Dad?"

"Why, what's wrong? Didn't you like the one I gave you last week?" Karras turned laboriously from the wheel, maneuvering his big shoulders around so he could glance briefly at his son.

Alex Jr. did not answer. He was looking out the window at the passing scenery. "Mr. Stump usually gives the pep talk," Karras told me.

"Who's Mr. Stump?"

"He's the defensive coach. His first name's Dick, but I call him Mr. Stump. I give it a 'Mistah Stump!' " He cried out the name in the car like a sea captain calling for his boatswain's mate. "Mistah *Stump!* Sometimes I think Mr. Stump is putting everybody on with his pep talks." He shook his head. "Wait till you hear him. Couple of years back *I* gave a pep talk before my old school. At Iowa. They had the worst team that year. I went back for a homecoming, and they asked me into the locker room before the game to talk to the team. So I thought, Shall I give them a real Win-It-for-the-Gipper sob talk, or a big long Vince

Lombardi scream and knock over a few lockers and act like a gorilla? I gave them neither; I looked at my feet a lot and mumbled a few things. What I remember is that there was a black guy right in front of me—Levi Williams, hell of a good tight end—and while I talked he had on this big grin, like I was telling him the funniest thing in the world, some great honky joke that really grabbed his ass. I couldn't figure him. So the team went out on the field and they got beat something awful. A real horror. But this fellow Williams came up after the game and he *still* had this same tremendous grin on his face—and hell, he'd really been *laced* out there; Iowa was beat about forty to nothing. I said, 'Hey, man, you all right?' He told me that he liked what I'd said in my pep talk. I said, 'Hell, man, you got beat forty–nothing.' He said, 'Hell, man, you *not* give that talk and maybe we get beat *eighty*–nothing.' He was one grand man, let me tell you."

When we reached the playing field it was overcast and threatening rain. Karras had left his rain gear at home; he was wearing the golf hat that read JEWISH OPEN and brightly polished cowboy boots. Alex Jr. stood beside him and looked across the field at the Vikings. "They're all big," he said.

Karras collected the team on the high school gym steps for his pep talk. "We better hold on here a bit," he said. "No one seems to be here," he explained to me. "Just reserves. Where are my stars? I'm missing my quarterback and my best running back. No sense in panicking; they're only half my starting backfield. The quarterback is probably washing dishes... Mistah Stump? Do you have a few words for us?"

His assistant coach stood up. He was a big man who wore a trench coat, and he had a Coke in one hand. "Men," he said. "We're going to win this one... and we're going to win it big. I don't want crumbs. I'm not interested in crumbs. *You're* not interested in crumbs. I want the whole slab of bacon." He took a swig of his Coca-Cola. "I want you to hit them out there. We want blood, sweat, and tears—otherwise you can go home. This game isn't milk and cookies. Nossirree, it's blood and *guts*." He sat down.

"Thank you, Mistah Stump," said Karras. He rose for his own pep talk. "Boys, I'm tired of losing. Are you?"

"Yes!"

"Now, the Vikings have lost three games this season. After we're through with them this afternoon, how many games will they have lost?"

Everyone shouted, "Four!"

"I want this one. Do you?"

"Yes!"

"Now, tomorrow's Halloween. I don't want anybody thinking about Halloween. I want you to think about winning and hitting the other guy and bringing home the bacon. Right?"

"Right!" they all yelled.

A latecomer came hurrying up wearing his helmet, his mouthpiece inserted, and a big number one on his jersey.

"It's Puffer," said Karras. "Boy, are we glad to see you."

Puffer removed his mouthpiece. "Did I miss anything?" He had a clear, bright voice.

"You missed Mistah Stump's pep talk. And mine," said Karras.

The boys began milling around. There were only a few minutes to go and they began aping their elders' pregame rituals—boxing each other on the shoulder pads and running in place. Puffer stood off to the side. I watched him, a small vigorous figure with a pale intelligent face and a spotless uniform. He was chattering away to himself. "Puffer is here," I heard him whisper. "They'll tremble in their boots when they hear that Puffer is here." He looked across the field at the Vikings. "They're not so big," he said. "Puffer is going to stomp them and ring their bells." He walked over to his coach. "Mr. Karras," he said, tugging at his sleeve and looking up. "Their shirts are going to run *red with blood* when Puffer gets ahold of them."

"Yes, yes, Puffer," his coach replied.

"Mr. Karras, their brains are cooking with the awfullest fear."

"Puffer, sit down and calm yourself."

"Mr. Karras, when I tackle them, I'm going to put their lightbulbs out."

"Sure, Puffer. Now just don't burn yourself up thinking about it. Save yourself."

Puffer sat down on the gym steps, his hands in his lap. Across the field the referees' whistles began to shrill. The team was quiet suddenly as they trotted across to their bench. Their captain, the middle linebacker, a youngster named Simon, chugged out under his oversized helmet to the center of the field for the coin toss. Karras had instructed him what to do. "He's a good player," he said to me as we stood in front of the bench. "He's three feet tall and he weighs thirty-three pounds, but he sticks like a burr."

Apparently the team lost the toss, for the referee signaled by extending his leg that the Jets were to kick off, and then, turning and catching an imaginary ball, indicated that the Vikings were to receive. But when Simon came trotting back to the bench, he allowed that he had actually *won* the toss.

"Wha'? Wha'? Well, then, why the hell are we kicking *off*?" cried Karras. He looked betrayed under his golfing cap.

"It's psy... psy..." Simon stuttered.

"Are you trying to tell me there was a *psychological* reason?" Karras exclaimed. "Jesus Sweet Christ!"

To avoid hearing more, Simon turned and scampered out to his team, drawn up in a line and waiting for him to kick off. At the referee's whistle he ran forward and, perhaps frantic in his anguish at having made a tactical error, sent a wobbly kick down to the ten yard line, where it bounced and eluded some potential receivers who looked forlorn and not especially anxious to fool with it until finally the least nervous of them picked up the football and ran it up to the twenty-three. Simon was one of the tacklers.

"Nothing wrong with that," Karras said, looking pleased. "Shows what a heady team leader can do."

The Vikings moved for a few first downs before kicking eighteen yards, and then the Jet offense took over.

Karras sent in the offensive plays by shuttling quarterbacks. It would have given him the greatest sense of power if they ever turned out to be what he expected, he said sadly. He would instruct his quarterback to call "the power left on 'go,' " pat him on the back as he ran out for the next play, and stand peering forward through his big spectacles in the hope of seeing his orders translated into a recognizable physical facsimile. Instead, the play itself would convolute and heave, with perhaps a fumble for good measure, and when the quarterback arrived back on the sidelines Karras would ask, "Now, damn it, what in God's name was *that?*"

"Oh, sir," the quarterback would answer, "they're kicking us and *everything!*"

The second time the Jets got possession of the ball, they did better. They made a first down, but then stalled with fourth and six to go. Since the team was on its own thirty-five, the situation seemed to call for a kick, but Karras sent in an end-around play. "I don't believe in punting," he told me. "These people can kick the ball just about fifteen yards. Only the very suave coaches call for a punt. The Viking coach punts. The Viking coach is very suave."

His tactic worked; the end around went for twenty yards and the Jets had a drive going, supported with high-pitched yells from the bench. Before every play the Jet center raised his loon-like yell of "Hud-*dle,*" and finally after one distant grouping down at the far end of the field, we saw the Jet players run a short plunge and then leap up and down, barely discernible in the gloom. We had scored. All of the Jets began slapping each other's palms as they trotted back toward the bench, a massive imitation of the familiar ritual practiced by their elders involved in a score. The try for the extra point failed, but there was still general jubilation.

"Damme, Mistah Stump!" cried Karras. "Have we got ourselves some champions?"

Mr. Stump's face glistened happily in the rain.

After receiving the kickoff, however, the Vikings began marching steadily for the Jet goal line. Seeing his defensive charges wilt before the

Viking onrush, Mr. Stump was beside himself; he took off not only his trench coat but his suit coat, so that in the considerable chill and rain he was wearing no more than a sleeveless white shirt, patched against his body, and a black string tie, looped loosely to his neck from nervous tugging. "Come on, Jets! You gotta have guts to play this game," he cried. He leaned over the border of the sidelines, jackknifed, as if he were poised on the edge of a swimming pool. "Oh no! Make him go inside of you." He turned away and strode frantically in front of the bench.

"Mistah Stump!" cried Karras. "What is transpiring?"

Stump shouted at Karras. "What can you do? You ask them to move just a little bit to the outside, maybe a step or so, and they shift twelve *yards.*" He turned back to the game. "Plug up those holes. No more *flinching,* damn it!"

His cries were to no avail. The Vikings scored on an end run. Their extra point try failed as well, and the score was tied six to six.

The time it took the teams to make the two scores used up almost the entire first half, which in the Pony League consisted of two ten-minute quarters. With all the emotion and concern invested in the game, it seemed we had just barely settled down before the referee came over to Karras on the sidelines and said, "We've got one minute to go to the half."

"What are you on, Greek time?" Karras said querulously. His team had possession of the ball and was moving in Viking territory. The two men glared at each other. In the background the cry of "Hud-*dle!*" arose. "You heard what I said," the referee remarked. "One minute." He was wearing all the proper accoutrements of his profession—the striped shirt and the whistle suspended from a bleached cowhide lanyard. A bead of rain wobbled on the brim of his cap. "You want me to say it again?"

There it was: they had just a few seconds in which to establish the adult prerogatives—in the case of the referee, who probably taught math in the third grade, his authority in a profession in which the man he was trying to face down was probably the most famous tackle in the country.

Karras stared at him and found nothing to say. The referee turned almost immediately and trotted swiftly toward the Jets, now breaking the huddle and moving up to the line of scrimmage. "What's with that guy?" Karras muttered. "What's wrong with Greek time? Hey?"

In the second half the teams began to slip in the mud. I was hoping to make some notes about the playing of the Detroit Lions' progeny—Bill Schmidt, the Gordy boy, and young Karras—to detect whether they reflected their famous parents on the field, whether one could tell from the boys' mannerisms—the hunching of shoulder pads under a jersey, the position of the hands on defense, the profile of their stances—that a Gordy was out there, or a Karras, or a Schmidt. It turned out to be impossible to tell, not only because of the mud and gloom but because at nine or ten the boys' frames were as thin as ropes and bore no resemblance to the quick heft their fathers carried around. As Karras said of them, "They get into positions like snakes."

The teams churned back and forth, neither scoring. Behind the Jet bench a few girls stood watching the game, shifting their weight from one long, thin leg to another. "Is that your brother?" I heard one of them ask in disgust. "He fell down. He's gross."

"It's raining. Why not?" said the other defensively. "But he *is* gross," she added reflectively. She bent and began speaking earnestly into the face of an Irish setter, cupping its head in her hands. "I'm going to petrify you tomorrow," she said. "I'm going to leap out at you with a Halloween mask. Are you prepared to be petrified?" The dog moved its tail uncertainly. His haunches lowered and he began to tug against her grip. She let go. "Stupid," she said to him. "Big stupe." She stood up. "What's going on? Who's ahead?"

"Who knows?" said the other girl. "Maybe it's a tie. Your brother fell down again."

I moved out of earshot as the team toiled on in the semidarkness. Behind us a group materialized and stood at the bottom step of the stands in back of the bench. With a start I recognized Joe Schmidt, the Lion coach, standing under a large black umbrella, his face impassive. He was there to watch his son. The rain began to pelt down harder and his wife moved in closer to share his umbrella. I wondered whether Karras was aware that Schmidt was watching. Rumors had it that recently the two were not on the best of terms.

With only a few minutes to go in the game, Karras called out, "Has anybody not played yet?"

A number of hands went up along the bench.

"Jesus Christ, Mistah Stump, we've got about ten of them," Karras said grimly. "Mistah Stump, begin sending in the reserves!"

His assistant substituted at every opportunity. The last one sent in was Puffer. A small tidy figure with the big number one on his back, he ran out with quick, busy steps that carried him along quite slowly. Karras watched him go. "Okay, Puffer!" he called. "Turn out their lightbulbs."

"See if you can figure out where Puffer plays," he said. "It's somewhere of his own choosing."

I watched. The Vikings were on the offense at midfield, and when their fullback moved forward with the ball I could see Puffer receding from the play, falling back from the line into his own backfield. I was reminded of a shorebird, one of the plump plover family, retreating up the beach from a line of surf.

Still, Puffer's presence on the field did not result in any change in the score. In the gloom, the game finally ended in a six–six tie. On the sidelines Karras asked, "Is that the end? Okay, everybody. Go over and shake hands with them."

The players began walking slowly back toward the gym, winding down, I supposed, their emotions about the game. I moved along with them, my notebook open and smudging slowly in the faint rain. I could not resist leaning down and asking the superficial questions that reporters put to players in postgame interviews. "What about the Vikings?" I asked Morton, the Jet center. "What sort of a team?"

He looked up, startled. "Well, they defense good," he said, aping the locker room banalities of his elders—his voice husky from the effort he had put into crying out "Hud-*dle!*" "They're a real good ball club. They come off the ball real good."

The boy walking along next to him said, "We proved one thing, though: the Vikings put on their legs... er ah... at a time."

"You're saying that they put on their pants one leg at a time?"

"That's right," he said. "They can be beat. We just didn't get enough points up on the board."

"What was the problem?"

The boy shuffled along. "We couldn't get enough points up on the board," he said again, keeping to that familiar platitude, so incongruous because it was delivered in a high-pitched fluting voice. "They defense good." Then he began to have trouble. "Er ah... Brookmeier... and then there was that time... well, *you* know, when... and what about when... and he *kicked* me, that big guy... and the rain..."

"But most important...?"

"We just couldn't get those points up on the board"—this clear and positive.

I fell into step alongside Puffer. "Puffer, what is your opinion of the Jet coaching staff?"

"I think Mr. Karras is the new Chubby Checkers," he said, in reference to the somewhat stout pop star of the day. I jotted this comparison down in my book. I continued. "Puffer, did you put out any lightbulbs?"

He did not answer. He walked with his head down. My heart sank.

"No," he said softly. "I ran away."

I had no idea what to say. "It's all right, Puffer," I said finally. "One day you're going to be secretary of commerce."

He stopped and looked at me out of the depths of his helmet. "Isn't that funny," he said cheerfully. "That's exactly what Mr. Karras tells me."

# CHAPTER 13

In the long run of the history of the NFL, John Gordy may be remembered less for his considerable skills as an offensive guard (selected three times for the All-NFL team) than for his contribution as a prime mover in the formation of the present-day version of the NFL Players Association. There had been a Players Association before Gordy got himself seriously involved, but it was thought of as being little more than a social club. Representatives elected from each club would meet once a year to draw up a list of grievances, largely to do with minimum salaries and cases regarding complaints about injuries. These would be presented, usually by letter, to the owners, who would sulkily acknowledge receipt and promise to get back in touch with the association. That was about it.

What led to the strengthening of the association's hand was the attempt in 1963 by the Teamsters Union to organize the football players. Their chief organizer was Bernie Parrish, the former Cleveland Brown defensive back, described by Gordy as being as aggressive and determined off the field as he was on it. In addition, said Gordy, he was very, very bright. "What he wanted to do originally—backed by Harold Gibbons of St. Louis and the Teamsters there—was to organize *all* of sport," Gordy told me. "The whole works—baseball, hockey, Roller Derbies, what have you—into a sort of conglomerate. He came to see me about this in Detroit. At that time I was the vice president of the

Players Association. I was skeptical and told Parrish that I thought that football had its own problems and should concentrate on setting its own house in order."

Parrish went back to St. Louis without Gordy's support. At this point, the Teamsters apparently thought better of their conglomerate plan and Parrish was sent out to concentrate solely on organizing football. He traveled to the NFL cities and began getting affirmations from the members of a number of teams. Gordy received a progress report in Detroit which dismayed him. Unable to understand the value of a matchup between the Teamsters and the players, he decided that if the drift of the NFL players continued toward absorption by the Teamsters, he would resign his vice presidency. He announced his intent at a meeting in Hollywood, Florida, where the NFL players' annual golf tournament—just the sort of a social occasion the organization had become known for—was scheduled. Gordy stated his reasons for resigning so effectively and with such concern that the entire roomful of players rose up, and by the time they were done Gordy had become their new president—with a mandate to struggle to keep the players out of the Teamsters.

At first it did not seem an easy fight, because the Teamsters listed a lot of pie-in-the-sky demands that they claimed would be pressed on the owners. In vying for the players' support the Gordy group was much more contained, not wanting to make promises they knew they could not deliver on. Eventually, a poll of the players of the league showed a ninety percent vindication of Gordy and the Players Association, and a vote *against* professional unionization. The latter, Gordy had always felt, was a concept that football players regarded as antithetical to the sacred notion of being rewarded solely on how well one played the game.

But the owners were fair targets, and in January 1968 the association flexed its newfound muscles and hired an obscure Chicago labor lawyer named Dan Shulman, an energetic and cheerful public relations man from Houston, Texas, named Tom Vance, and Mal Kennedy as a business manager. These were the civilian advisers; Gordy's negotiating committee drawn from the players consisted of himself, quarterback King Hill from the Eagles, fullback Ernie Green from the Browns, tackle Bob Vogel from the Colts, and Dave Robinson, the Green Bay linebacker. As the chief negotiator, Gordy worked at such a pitch that he remembers seeing his family only about twenty times between January and the day in July when the issues were finally resolved.

Twenty-one conditions were presented to the owners. Some of them involved small beefs such as an increased out-of-town meal allowance, and permission for players to purchase two good tickets before the public sale began. The three main demands were a $5,000,000 contribution to the pension fund, a $15,000 minimum wage for a season's work, and $500 per game for preseason exhibitions.

"The pension payment was the biggest bone," Gordy told me. "What we were trying to do was to make football's pension plan equitable with baseball's." At that time baseball owners contributed $4.1 million each year, whereas the NFL owners put in about a quarter of that figure. They had found out that Frank Howard of the Washington Senators, who played in the majors for ten years, would be getting a pension of $1,287 a month when he was sixty-five, while Gordy, after the same number of playing years, would receive only $656. "Those figures are memorable, let me tell you. Even at the age of fifty Howard will be getting paid five hundred dollars, and I won't be getting anything. I remember at one of the players' meetings the salary and pension potential of a guy named No-Neck Williams who played with the Chicago White Sox was a chief topic, and when they heard what he was getting, there was a vote to beat him up and take his share!

"Of course the owners' position was that they couldn't afford our demands. But we'd done a careful study, using the Green Bay books, which are open to scrutiny since they're a public corporation, and it was fair to assume that the costs of other operations in the NFL were similar. We knew that profit estimates in 1972 totaled forty-four million dollars. Our position was that if the owners were making a ton, we wanted a *quarter* ton.

"So we sat down with them. My background in negotiating was simply zilch, and none of the other players—King Hill, Ernie Green, Bob Vogel—knew very much either. What we *did* have was an instinctive ability, and of course a firm belief in our cause, which was to do something for the players. The most important thing to remember was not to say too much. There was an awful lot of psychological maneuvering. I always tried to have some great superstar sitting behind me, so that when the owners began lambasting me they'd look up and see Bart Starr sitting in the shadows, glowering at them.

"The owners' negotiator was Ted Kheel, the great labor dispute arbitrator, and he is simply the best there is. Damn, he was so bright, and he could tie you up in knots. He knew every trick there was. So the best thing to do was to retreat, play dumb, not say much and always fall back on football, which is what I *did* know, and leave him hanging. It must have been exasperating for him—to offer these seemingly plausible and articulate observations, beautifully put together, and requiring *some* sort of response, and have them go winging past this guy sitting opposite with his mouth hanging slightly open, a real dumb-ass; his brilliance must have seemed so *wasted.* But I had to be so careful. There was hardly a sentence I could say that Kheel couldn't turn around somehow."

I once had the opportunity to ask Kheel about the negotiations and Gordy's part in them. He was very complimentary about Gordy's abilities. It was not surprising, he said. "Time and time again I've seen guys come out of the rank and file, completely untrained, with such intuitive ability as negotiators that they can hold their own, and even sometimes outwit the professional lawyers opposite them. Gordy was one of those people, and he also had the qualities of a natural leader. I once told him, 'John, you have the makings of a great union leader—you're absolutely unscrupulous.' "

"What did you mean by that?"

"Oh, I didn't mean it unkindly," Kheel said. "All I meant was that Gordy was able to say something he didn't really believe, in order to enhance his bargaining position."

I said that Gordy had talked about silence being a weapon.

"It *is* a weapon," Kheel said. "It requires great discipline, because the temptation to resist answering what the other fellow is saying is enormous. But if you can stick to it, it's effective because the other side doesn't know whether you're speechless or have something to hide."

I reported this later to Gordy; he laughed and said that "speechless" was the correct word for the state he was in most of the time.

"What about the owners?" I asked him.

"Kheel did almost all the talking for them. In fact, Coach Lombardi, who was representing Washington then, paid Kheel the highest compliment by referring to him as 'Coach.' But the owners—I'm excepting Lombardi—weren't any good. Many of them had always talked to their players as if they were talking to dogs—*nice* dogs—and had no idea how to deal with them as equal negotiators. It was like coming down to breakfast to find your Labrador sitting tending the toaster and he asks you to pass the jam. Of course, Lombardi was not like that. He was the toughest to sit across the table from, because I thought he was the greatest individual in professional football. I'd been coached by him once in a Pro Bowl game and had seen that amazing ability to take athletes and give them momentum, to channel and maintain their abilities. Now here I was opposite him and still feeling this awe, and knowing I couldn't act scared. That was another reason I was so quiet—I mean, suppose I opened up my mouth to say something to Lombardi and out came this little canary noise?

"Well, the negotiations went on and on, and I began to learn the language. But it was awfully taxing on everybody, and boring. I remember that at one of the player-rep meetings Tom Vance, who was doing public relations for us, suddenly noticed Dick Butkus from the Bears motioning him over. Butkus shoved a pad of paper at him and whispered, 'Draw me a squirrel.' He'd heard somewhere that Vance once went to art school or something.

"Vance said, 'What?'

" 'A squirrel. Right here on this pad. I mean it. Right here.'

"So Vance took his pencil and laboriously, because he was out of practice, drew a squirrel. All this while somebody from the Players Association was droning on with his lecture. Vance said he was nervous as hell because Butkus kept leaning over the pad to see how the drawing was coming out.

" 'Well, there's your squirrel.'

" 'Draw me a rooster,' Butkus said.

"Poor Vance said, 'Oh, come on,' but Butkus insisted, getting quite noisy about it, and Vance drew a rooster, and then a pig and a large cow, and he was working on a horse when the session finally adjourned and Butkus let him go.

"But most of the time, of course, it wasn't anything like this at all; it was very serious stuff, and nip and tuck too. The licensing fees we'd arranged for players endorsing products came in just in time to pay off our office and telephone bills. The final stumbling block was the pension plan. In July, just before the training camps were to open, the owners made an offer. They'd accepted the other twenty points, though all of them with compromises, but not our demands on the pension deal. When they finally made an offer, I turned it down. I felt the players would want me to. It was quite a step, because it meant that as head of the organization I could face ten to fifteen years in jail for calling a work stoppage and defying interstate regulations. But we polled the players and discovered that they were behind us. The owners retaliated by closing the training camps. They remained closed for ten days, until finally we met again in the Waldorf Astoria and the owners agreed. It was over! We'd got the three big things we wanted. The minimum wage was hiked to twelve thousand dollars a year for a two-year player and thirteen thousand for a three-year player. We finally got good money for playing in exhibition games. And the great thing was that we got a three-million-dollar pension plan, which just about doubled a player's pension benefits. There'll be increases in the future, but it was a start. What a relief!

"The best part was when Coach Lombardi took me aside and patted me on the back and said that I'd done a helluva job. That meant everything—it's one of the great times in my life, though I've never figured out whether it was because it was all over and I could start thinking again about simple things like knocking a man down with a cross-block, or whether it was because of the pat on the back from that man. Anything he ever said, he *meant.*

"It *was* an honorable agreement, and it was good for football. It cost the training season ten days, which wasn't much of a price, was it? I mean, that's not too much for getting good security for players when they get older, do you think?"

# CHAPTER 14

Despite his efforts on the pension plan, and his concern for players once their playing days were over, Gordy had ambivalent feelings about old-timers, at least regarding reunions and becoming part of the ritual of nostalgia. Alex Karras felt the same way.

"I've never even thought about being an old-timer," Gordy told me a year after he had left football. "When you quit, it's hard enough to learn how to be a fan, much less an old-timer. Besides, who wants to go to reunions?"

"What's the problem?" I asked. "Wouldn't you enjoy seeing your teammates again?"

"I'd be scared of the failures," Gordy said. "Life ain't easy, and once out of a football uniform they might all look so *vulnerable.*"

Karras had a more particular reason. It was his fantasy that an old-timers' reunion would be crowded with wizened and shrunken men who would stare at each other and read each others' name tags, squinting forward to see, and then one of them would sing out, "You're the guy I knocked the crap out of in nineteen thirty-six, and I can do it again." So the two of them would go off in a corner and throw pathetic cuffs at each other with arms like sticks until finally the waiters would sigh and step in and lift them up and put them down in their chairs for The Big Meal, which was applesauce and zwieback. The old-timers would eat in silence. Then someone would say, "Ah, Tittle, you were never any good." The great quarterback would look up from across the table, pick up a piece of zwieback, and take careful aim. The throw, across four feet of tablecloth, would miss. The old-timers would look up, but their attention span was short, and quickly the scrape of knives and forks would rise again in the quiet dining room.

I was under no such compunctions, myself. So when an invitation arrived to attend a Lion alumni reunion I packed a bag and went to Detroit. The occasion was held in a large, dimly lit clubroom in a hotel in a Detroit suburb. Everyone wore plastic-encased name cards. Some of my contemporaries were on hand: Terry Barr, Night Train Lane, Tommy Watkins, and Darris McCord (who told me regretfully that his hayrides were a thing of the past). Wives were there, and some lively dancing was done to a three-piece orchestra that played in a corner of the room.

The more venerable old-timers sat at tables around the dance floor, gossiping and looking out at the younger people like parents chaperoning a high school dance.

I wandered around. I overheard Night Train telling a Polish joke. "Why don' Poles ever commit suicide? Because," he said, "outhouses ain't above two stories high." He slapped his knee. "It's all right for me to tell jokes like that," he confided to me. "I'm an ethnic."

I sat down at a table next to Jim Steen, the president of the Lion alumni association. He introduced me around. "...Dutch Clark? You heard of this great one?"

"Certainly," I said.

"Look at ol' Dutch," Steen said with tremendous affection. "He was the greatest runner that football ever had."

I stared across the table at a kindly-looking man, his jaw working just slightly on gum, tieless, with a yellow shirt buttoned up to the neck and ill-fitting glasses that with a recurrent gesture he would push back up to the top of his nose.

"He was the slowest runner you ever saw, but every step meant something," Steen said. "Isn't that right, Dutch? There was a standing joke: if you missed a block for Dutch, you didn't have to worry because by and by he'd be back, still on his feet, and you'd have another crack at helping him. Isn't that right, Dutch? He was the passer for us—wore wool gloves, which made Potsy Clark, the coach, good and angry. He'd say, 'Get those gloves off, Dutch; how the hell can you pass with those gloves on?' And Dutch would say, 'Potsy, my hands are cold.' Isn't that right, Dutch?"

Clark finally stirred. He had been listening to these rapid-fire comments with no show of interest or reproach, as if it were an established part of his social existence to be forced to sit within earshot of people telling stories about him. Clearing his throat, he said softly, "My fingers were all broken and white and stiff, so I wore gloves. I couldn't pass worth a damn."

"He's the number one Lion," a wife at the table said loudly.

"Naw," said Clark. "I had a bad left eye. On defense I played safety, and they used to shoot down on my blind side."

"The worst guy on pass defense was Father Lumpkin," someone said.

Dutch Clark said, "Quite right. He couldn't cover *anybody* on pass defense. A pass would get completed in his area and he'd stand there holding his head in his hands in horror. He got confused; he was too independent-minded, I think. But on offense he was great." He pushed his glasses back up to the top of his nose.

"Why was he called 'Father'?" I asked.

No one seemed to know for sure. Someone said, "Well, he was certainly no priest. Off the field he was sort of meek and quiet, a slim-built guy; maybe that was why. He was also called 'The Ramblin' Wreck' because he came from Georgia Tech, and he *looked* like one, too. He had a cauliflower ear, and toward the end of a game he'd rip off his helmet and play without it. He couldn't find one that fit. Maybe it hurt that ear of his."

Clark said, "He was a great blocking back. He was a rassler and he loved to knock people down. We never had huddles in those days. I called the plays at the line of scrimmage, and Father Lumpkin would turn around and look at me with this pleading look, as if to say, 'Please call the one where I can run and really give the other guy a lick.' Oh my, he loved the offense."

"What did he play on defense?"

"Linebacker. He was fine on running plays because it gave him a chance to knock people down. When he wasn't knocking people down on a football field, he was off somewhere *rassling* them down. He'd disappear, and Potsy Clark would yell like hell, and Father Lumpkin would turn up in Charleston, rassling someone. He did what he felt like. He was finally dropped from the Lions because he wouldn't give up professional wrestling."

"What I remember about him," Jim Steen said, "was that during the season he never wore socks. He taped up his ankles on the first day, and then wore that tape until the last game. When the tape got dirty, he just slapped on some more."

"He was quite a character," Steen's wife said. "He came and stayed with us once. He slept on top of the covers in the guest room. I know, because I went in there to wake him up for breakfast and he was lying fully clothed and with his hands folded over his stomach, like he was lying on a slab. But it took him forty-five minutes to come down for breakfast. What do you suppose he was doing up there?"

None of us could arrive at an answer.

"He never got hurt playing without that helmet?" I asked.

"Probably," said Clark. "But people *had* to play hurt in those days—at least when I began—because there were so few players that you *couldn't* substitute. On the Portsmouth Spartans we had a fourteen-game schedule and fourteen players. Why, I remember one time we were playing the Philadelphia Yellow Jackets, or the Staten Island Stapes, one of those teams, when this kid called Harry Ebding, who played end for us, got hit so hard in the eye that it just absolutely swole up with blood so he couldn't see. So at halftime somebody ran down to the drugstore to get some leeches—"

"Leeches?"

"That's right, leeches to put on that kid's swole-up eye so the blood would get sucked out and he could see good and proper."

"Lord Almighty," I said.

Everyone at the table looked puzzled that I should be startled by this information.

"Well, we *had* to get him out there," Clark said, pushing at his glasses.

A thin slight man named Aid Kushner, who had been the trainer for the Lions in the late thirties, said that the best thing for swelling had always been ice; he didn't want any leeches around, nossir, and he could remember when Lloyd Cardwell had gotten his face busted up by the Bears and they had used the snow off the field to pack the bruises and he'd finally gone back out and played a whale of a game.

"I don't think today's players can play through pain the way they used to," he said. "People don't walk enough; too many escalators. They get hurt easy. There are a lot more injuries now because the players don't go the full sixty minutes and aren't physically prepared."

Leon Hart, the great Lion end, leaned forward and said that *chance* had a lot to do with injuries, that he had once been injured running up out of the dugout in Baltimore for the pregame introductions.

A wife said, "Yes, I heard that."

"It's true," he said. "Coach Buddy Parker wanted me to play in that Colt game real bad. I had pulled hamstrings, but he decided to chance putting me in the starting lineup. We were supposed to run out between a line of girls with pompoms. When I heard my name over the loudspeaker, I took that first step up onto the field from the dugout, and the muscle popped. I couldn't even get to the center of the field; the next guy being introduced ran past me. I hobbled to the sidelines and told Parker. He said I must be the first guy ever to be injured in the introductions."

After the chuckling and nodding had stopped around the table, I said that I was curious about what it was like to play both ways for those sixty minutes, and wondered if players who had done so had a preference.

Jim Steen said that since hitting was the name of the game, linemen usually preferred defense, because they could freewheel and really sock people.

Leon Hart disagreed. He said that he always thought of the offense as being constructive, something that had been carefully put together to perform a function; there was great pleasure when it worked as it was supposed to, and it was terrible when it was destroyed. "I just don't approve of ripping things apart," he said. "That's the trouble with defense—it's destructive. It made me uncomfortable playing it."

This struck me as a sensitive observation, and admiringly I wrote it down on a napkin so I could remember it. But later, wandering around the room, I heard Hart telling someone, "There's only one way to tackle quarterbacks, which is to come in high on them so you have the chance either of, *one,* destroying their passing sight, or *two,* you might break an arm."

Toward the end of the party, Hart saw me standing at the edge of the crowd watching the dancing. He came through the press, a huge-shouldered man who wore thin steel-rimmed spectacles. "Hey, I've got something to tell you about."

We sat down at one of the tables. "God, the football stories are great," I said. "Dutch Clark told me that they're all the same, but that every year they get better."

Hart laughed. He said he had been listening to an awful lot of them because he was an official of the NFL Alumni Association, which represented old-timers like Dutch Clark. "That's what I wanted to talk to you about," he said. He told me that the Alumni Association was involved in a bitter scrap with the Players Association and the owners.

The gist of the fight was that nearly six hundred NFL veterans—many of them in the Hall of Fame—were barred by a technicality from participating in the benefits, especially pension benefits, enjoyed by the members of the Players Association, which, ironically, many of them had helped found. The bylaws of the Players Association stipulated that the only players eligible for the pension and benefit plans agreed to by the NFL owners in 1959 were those who had played for the five years from 1955 to 1959 inclusive—which denied benefits to any players who retired before 1959.

"Why that particular date?" I asked.

Hart leaned across the table to make his voice heard above the dance music. He said that he had always assumed the date was arbitrarily set, probably by an actuary, and chosen because of the funds available at that time and the economic conditions that prevailed. But of course these had changed enormously since then. Television income and the rising popularity of the sport had substantially increased the resources for pensions, but the 1959 date had remained the same. The NFL Alumni Association had been formed in 1968 to do something about it, but they had been largely rebuffed. The only help the Players Association had offered was to organize an exhibition *basketball* game to raise money so that the old-timers could start their own pension plan.

As a result, the old-timers had decided to bring legal action against the NFL owners and the Players Association. Some months ago they'd had an emotional meeting at which Rocco Cavelli, a 350-pound former middle guard who had played for the Philadelphia Eagles and then the Boston Yankees, and was nicknamed "The Walking Billboard," had jumped to his feet and cried, "Let 'em have it! Sue! Throw the bomb!" and the cheering had started, and someone else had cried, "Let's go for six," and another, "Clothesline 'em!"—a series of football exhortations erupting from men so excited that they had regressed to the phrases of the profession of their youth.

The Alumni Association was going to have a meeting in Las Vegas a couple of weeks later, Hart told me, at the same time that the defendants in the suit, the Players Association, would be meeting just across the street. Hart thought I might be interested in coming out. Many of the great names of football would be there—Marion Motley, Alex Wojciechowicz, Bruiser Kinard, Dante Lavelli, Eddie LeBaron, a whole bunch of them—and the confrontation with the younger stars would be dramatic.

"Will I get the chance to hear some stories out there?" I asked.

"Will you hear stories? Holy *God!*"

When I returned to New York I called John Gordy to tell him that I was going out to Las Vegas for the meetings, and to see what he had to say about the cutoff date and the dilemma of the old-timers. He groaned and said that while it seemed paradoxical that the great stars of the past were not benefiting, the fact of the matter was that to have the pension plan include them was not actuarially sound. The report from Ed Garvey, the executive secretary of the Players Association, was that the players would have to bargain for an additional ten million dollars to fund such a program. The money would have to be paid out immediately, since many of the beneficiaries had already reached retirement age, whereas the 1959 cutoff date allowed the money in the pension fund to work for twenty years or so and pile up interest before it began to be tapped. Besides, it didn't seem to him that present-day players should be responsible for their elders; why not the owners, the twenty-six millionaires, who had made such a lot of money off them in the old days? But hell, he was out of it now; maybe the situation had changed. He had passed on the leadership to John Mackey of the Colts and the others I'd be seeing out in Las Vegas.

The NFL alumni were meeting in Caesars Palace. When I arrived, I noticed that the team representatives of the Players Association were across the Strip in the Flamingo, and that much was being made of their stay. A floodlit sign announced their presence, and each player had his name on an individual sign set into the grass in the traffic island in front of the hotel.

About forty-five of the NFL alumni had turned up at Caesars Palace, many with their wives. When I met them, I discovered that the topic of the moment was not the organization's legal action, but its pride in the singing voice of Rocco Cavelli, "The Walking Billboard," who had been persuaded to perform during the Frank Sinatra Jr. supper show at one of the hotels on the Strip the night before. Someone had tipped off the management that he had a fine voice. At first, there was consternation that the stairs leading up to the stage would not bear his weight, which was 350 pounds, so he had sung from his table, in a sweet soaring voice, picking up in quality and volume after a somewhat nervous and quavering start. "D'ja hear Rocco last night?" I was asked by an old-timer on the way through the hotel to the alumni breakfast. "Well, man, you sure missed something great!"

The breakfast was held in a purple-carpeted meeting room with high ceilings, a buffet table set at one end and large round tables set for eight or ten places, on each a centerpiece of an individual long-stemmed rose in a thin glass.

Leon Hart took me over to a table and introduced me around: to Alex Wojciechowicz, the center famous for his absurdly wide stance over the ball, who had been one of the Seven Blocks of Granite from Fordham whom everybody, to my relief, referred to as "Wogy"; Ray Monaco, who was an ex-Redskin; Bill Dudley, who played his famous years with the Steelers; Marion Motley, the great Cleveland running back; and two or three players' wives. Other people came and went, sitting down with their coffee cups and listening to the stories, perhaps contributing some, before moving to another table where the same sort of conversation was going on. Motley was the only black in the room, and I realized how few old-timers *would* be blacks because of the discriminatory practices of their times.

The conversation started up again after the introductions. They were talking about the hardest hitters they had faced. Motley said that Chuck Bednarik of the Eagles was a bitch, and so was Wojciechowicz (who looked across at him and grinned), but the worst was Tom Kennedy of the New York Giants. "He followed me everywhere. When Otto Graham called a trap play in the huddle, I always said, 'Oh no,' because I knew that I'd find Kennedy waiting for me in the gap. What a war we had! In his house, which is in Maryland somewhere, I'm told Kennedy has a photograph hanging on the wall showing the two of us in a play in which I knocked out all of his front teeth. He's got this brass plate underneath which reads 'Marion Motley Knocking Out My Teeth,' with the date. He was a rough one."

Someone across the table said, "You had a rough one over there in Cleveland in that guy Chubby Grigg, that three-hundred-pound tackle. Why, he'd have your brains out if you *looked* at him."

"You know something?" said Motley. "You know who kicked the extra point in Philadelphia for the Cleveland Browns in the championship game?"

"Wasn't it Lou Groza?"

"Groza had hurt himself. He picked up a fumble and headed for the goal line. There were some people in front of him." Motley got out of his chair to demonstrate. "He wanted to move *this* way, and then he wanted to move *that* way... but what happened was he didn't go any way at all. He crumpled like a napkin was thrown down." He threw a napkin on the table. "He pulled some muscles, so he couldn't kick. The guy who came in for him was Chubby Grigg, that's who."

"Is that so? That guy who weighed three hundred pounds could *kick?*"

"That's so."

Ray Monaco said, "Big mistake for a lineman to pick up the ball like that. I remember a guy called Eddie Ulinsky, an offensive guard on the Browns, who picked up a fumble in a game against Washington, and he got hit by every Redskin there was—just *bam bam bam bam*—and after it was all over he pulled himself up and he said to this running back, 'Man, I know you get *paid* for running the ball, but Jesus *Christ!*' "

The laughter rose around the table. Motley slapped his knee and revolved the cigar between his teeth.

"What did Ulinsky weigh?"

"Oh, he'd go two hundred and thirteen pounds. Six-footer. Maybe a touch shorter. He was bald-headed the first time I ever saw him, which was when he was barely twenty-one. Big hairless bastard. Excuse me, ladies."

Wojciechowicz stirred and said that he could remember the one time he had tackled Motley. As he told the story, he spoke about it as if Motley were not sitting across the table, referring to him by name rather than addressing him personally: "What happened was that they gave the ball to Motley and he came right up through the middle, just *pounding.* I was playing linebacker off to the flank, and I knew I was going to have to tackle the bastard from the side. That's not good for me; I like to kill a man from the front. That's the way to handle power—to whipsaw these power runners like Norm Standlee and Motley and get 'em under the neck, and backwards they go. Of course, if you hit 'em in the shoulder or the knee, then *you* get killed." He wiped his mouth with a napkin. "Well, as I was coming at Motley from the flank, I kept thinking, How'm I going to *do* this? Where am I going to hit him? So I got to where I could throw myself in front of him." He looked up. "How much did you say you weighed?" He seemed to be noticing Motley for the first time.

"Two forty."

"Well, I'll tell you something. After I made the hit on Motley, I didn't want to get up. I lay there and I thought, Well, I've heard a lot about Motley and now I know why."

Motley nodded as if to thank him for the compliment, and said, "At two forty I was the oldest and biggest guy on the team. I started when I was twenty-six."

"Bigger even than the defensive tackles?"

"Well, Lou Rymkus was the biggest of the tackles and he weighed two thirty-two. I was the biggest guy until Ernie Bland came along and then Chubby Grigg."

"Ernie Bland," someone said with a sigh of recognition.

"He was what?"

"Oh, he ran about two forty-six, around in there."

"I'm told he was living around Baltimore and died recently of bladder trouble. I never seen a guy so afraid of a woman. A woman would come around training camp and the big man would hide behind a tree and peek out like a buffalo was waiting for him."

I sat enthralled. There seemed to be a number of distinctive characteristics to the ritual: each storyteller always got undivided attention from around the table; no matter how preposterous or exaggerated the tale might seem, there was never any dissent or wonderment, but rather an occasional remark of "That's right" and a nodding of heads in accord; the players described in the stories were usually identified by their weight, invariably to the last digit—such as "Well, Mayberry, who was two sixteen, maybe two seventeen on a cold day..."—and everyone would nod because they had a clear physical picture of the player involved. The stories usually divulged that the old-timers had all played on both offense and defense, which was the custom before the platooning system, and many of them had played both ways for the full sixty minutes of a game. They were very proud of that fact. Ray Monaco told me during a pause in the storytelling that at a football players' golf tournament in Fort Lauderdale, Florida, a foursome of three old-timers and one young player, Chuck Mercein, a Yale graduate who played with the Packers and then the Giants, had got to talking about playing "both ways," and Mercein piped up and admitted that he didn't know what "both ways" meant. Gary Fincemelti, an enormous old-timer who had played defensive tackle and offensive guard for the Eagles, was so upset by this ignorance that he hit two drives into a pond, missed his third attempt completely, and left the golf course to go somewhere and sulk.

Mayhem was almost invariably an ingredient of the stories. "It took thirteen years before I lost any teeth," Wojciechowicz was saying. "It happened in an exhibition game against the Chicago Bears in the Milk Fund game in nineteen fifty. I was with the Eagles then. Chuck Bednarik, who played middle guard, came down with the flu, and Greasy Neale took me aside and said, 'Wogy, old man, it's going to be like the good old days; you've got to play sixty minutes, both offensive and defense, but remember that it's only an exhibition game and you can pace yourself.' Well, I did a damn fool thing. I told Ken Kavanaugh about it, who was playing offensive end opposite me, thinking maybe they'd go easy on me, and he went back to the Bear huddle and they ran every play at me, until finally their fullback Osmanski came ripping through and his elbow caught me in the mouth and out came two teeth.

I still had to go the sixty minutes, but everyone had their adrenaline going by then and we beat the tar out of them. I had the best game I ever played. I tried to kill Kavanaugh and everyone else too." He slammed his fist into his palm. "I *love* to play tough against the Bears."

"That guy Ed Sprinkle of the Bears was a tough one," Motley said. "I fixed him one day. Coach Paul Brown warned us about him. 'He'll hit you anywhere and anytime.' Well, early in the game Sprinkle hit Tony Adamle a terrible blow on the Adam's apple and then ran off the field laughing."

Everybody nodded.

"That's right. He was holding his sides he thought it was so funny. Well, when we got back on offense, I told Otto Graham in the huddle to call a pass play which would put me into Sprinkle's area. It was just fine. I got him and *tried* to get him in his Adam's apple but something went wrong and I got him far south of there, if you catch my meaning. Excuse me, ladies."

After the chuckling had died away, someone said that the guy who really got Sprinkle was Charley Trippi of the Cardinals, who got so angry that he pulled Sprinkle's helmet off with one hand, just like lifting the lid off a pot, punched him with the other, and then walked off the field.

From the other side of the table Leon Hart cleared his throat and said, "Well, you all remember who gave Charley Trippi *his*—John Henry Johnson, that's who. What a head-hunter he was. He hit Trippi with a roundhouse right, his arm extended, and the plastic surgeons had to redo the whole of Trippi's face—jaw, nose..."

Beside me I heard a wife suck in her breath.

"You know, there's a fine line between being *nasty* and being *dirty*," Hart was saying. "I don't know whether Sprinkle was nasty or dirty, but John Henry was just plain dirty. There was a time in San Francisco when I caught a pass, and some defensive guy got me by the ankle and I was dragging against him. Out of the corner of my eye I caught sight of John Henry coming for me, getting set to clobber me with that roundhouse right, so I shifted the ball to under my left arm and as he came in I gave him a short pop with my right fist and down he went before he could get that punch of his uncorked. Really coldcocked him. The referee said, 'Okay, Hart, that'll cost you fifteen yards.' I cried out, 'But didn't you see what he was going to do to me?'

"'Sure,' said the ref. 'And I probably would have done the same thing you did. But you did the hitting, so it will cost you fifteen.'" Hart laughed. "I'm probably the only guy who ever carried the ball on a play and got penalized fifteen yards for unnecessary roughness."

"The hell you are, man," Motley said. He was beside himself with delight. "The same thing happened to *me.* In a game against the Redskins. Can you believe it. The gun had gone off at the half and I'd run the ball out-of-bounds and I was turning around to give the ball to the referee." He jumped out of his chair to demonstrate. "The play was *dead,* but Eugene Pepper was coming at me, hell-bent, and he was getting ready to hit, first with his elbow, then with his fist. Like this. Well, I countered before he could do anything, and I hit the nose guard of his helmet and broke all my knuckles."

On the other side of the table Bill Dudley rocked back and forth in his chair. "That's right. You got thrown out of the game!"

Motley turned his cigar in his mouth. "Ox Emerson came in for me, and he had a big heyday."

"What did Eugene Pepper weigh in at?" someone asked.

"Oh, two thirty—right in there."

"That was like Pepper," Dudley, who had played with the Redskins for a short stint, said. "I mean, to try to smack Motley when the play was dead. His timing was always way off. He was the guy on the team who was supposed to pretend to be hurt so that they could get the clock stopped. But his act wasn't any good—it looked like he was having a convulsion—and his timing was terrible. He'd fake his injury just after the gun had gone off and the game was over."

"That's right."

"Or he'd be thrashing around on the ground and the ref would come rushing up and ask, 'Are you hurt?' and Pepper would forget and say, 'No, of course not.' "

Wojciechowicz leaned forward, the ballroom chair creaking under him, and said, "You know, sometimes you *got* to crack someone. When Hunk Anderson came to the Lions from the Bears in thirty-nine, and co-coached us with Gus Henderson—this was before I went to the Eagles—he said there was only one way to handle the Bears. He ordered us to slug them for the first three plays of the game—every lineman in front of us. We did it. You could hear the punches, *bam bam bam* all the way down the line. We got penalized three times fifteen—forty-five yards—back to our thirty-five yard line, but that's as far as the Bears ever got that day. They were supposed to be the big bad bears and we were supposed to be the meek pussycat lions, with our paws up, and they were *surprised.* Bulldog Turner, Joe Stydahar, Musso, all those big people—they couldn't believe it. They kept ducking. We beat them ten–nothing, right there in Chicago!" He made a convulsive motion in his chair which jarred shivers across the water in the glasses, and the ice clinked. "Golly, I *love* to play against the Bears."

An announcement was made that the room down the corridor was ready for the meeting, and that it was time to get down to business. The players around the table rose and stretched.

It was a closed meeting, but that afternoon I was invited to the final session. Jim Castiglia, a former back who had played with the Redskins, Eagles, and Colts, spoke from the rostrum. First he mentioned and commended Rocco Cavelli's singing performance at the supper show, and Cavelli, an enormous tub-like man, rose to raise an arm in acknowledgment to shouts of approbation. Next, the Wogy Award was given: a bottle of bourbon to Buck Evans, the oldest veteran in the room. The award seemed to serve no other purpose than to indicate the warmth and goodwill for the white-haired, slightly stoop-shouldered gentleman. He was a Harvard man, class of '23, who had played with the Bears. He had an old Bear game program with him which he had shown me before the meeting. In it was a column of news notes from around the football league, and we had both admired the fact that the Dayton Triangles had a Chinese player who was called "Sneeze" Achui. Evans rose and addressed the group from the rostrum, speaking in a soft stutter; he said that he was going to be seventy-three in April, which was as good a time as any to start thinking about a pension. He grinned and said that he hoped that everyone would oblige and arrange one for him. He sat down to a storm of applause.

Jim Castiglia then reviewed their meetings and the progress of their struggle with the Players Association. He was confident, he told them. Four years ago the Alumni Association had twenty-one members; now they had eight hundred. Their cause was justified. There was so much money in the NFL pension fund that the opposition was thinking of lowering the retirement age to forty-five, at which point a veteran who had played ten years—subsequent to the cutoff date of 1959—would receive in the neighborhood of *fifty thousand dollars* annually! And yet the old-timers, who had formed professional football and played for twenty dollars a game, were left out in the cold. It was a mockery. If Vince Lombardi hadn't died, things might have been different; he had pounded his fist and told the owners that they *had* to include the older fellows. Well, now the Alumni Association had taken things into their own hands. They would prevail with their legal action. "The vehicle is there," Castiglia said. "It's on the expressway."

When the meeting broke up, a few of the old-timers asked me to join them for dinner, but I said I was going to see some friends from the Players Association.

"You going over to the other place!"

"Just to visit," I said.

"We've met them. All they think we want is a handout. They don't care. All they want to do is finish up their meetings so they can go out and play some golf and get some desert sun so they'll look better for the girls they'll find in the evening."

"Aw, the kids can't concentrate right anymore," another old-timer said. "How can they? Got all these goddamn billion-dollar contracts, and they wear hats indoors and buckles on their shoes and clothes fitting for a whore. Why, I saw Dan Pastorini, that kid who plays quarterback for the Oilers, over in the lobby of the Flamingo Hotel, and he was wearing these two- or three-inch stilts on his shoes. Now why? He's a big tall boy in his bare feet. What in tarnation is he wearing that kind of shoe for—less'n he wants folks to take him for a basketball player."

"Hey, do you know who he reminds you of?"

"Who you talking about?"

"Pastorini..."

"He reminds *me* of someone?"

"That's right. He reminds you of Bob Waterfield in his good years quarterbacking the Rams, that's who. He'll be a great quarterback if he survives."

"Now don't you be telling me who reminds me of who! A kid who walks around on built-up shoes reminds me of *no one!*"

I went across the Strip to the Flamingo. Evidence of the presence of the Players Association was everywhere. Placards on wooden easels directed the press to different conference rooms. Some of the players were in the casino. Bill Curry of the Colts was wearing a buckskin jacket. Pastorini of the Oilers did indeed have stilts on his shoes, which raised him up to six-four or five. He was wearing a gold chain around his neck.

I sat around for a while with a group of them. The matter of the Alumni Association grievance was not even on the Players Association agenda. "What's wrong with you guys?" I asked. "What they're asking, as I understand it, might cost everyone playing maybe ten dollars or so more a month."

None of them seemed to know much about the alumni demands. "They should get it from the owners," someone said.

"These people are all your old heroes," I said. I said Karras told me that he kept a picture of Bronko Nagurski on his dresser.

"Is he over there—Nagurski?"

"No, but Marion Motley is."

Bill Curry remembered that Motley had been one of the coaches in the East-West game some years before, and he had taken Ken Willard aside, a very bright undergraduate who had been an All-Scholastic fullback, and said, "Young fella, you got your foots lined up all wrong."

"That was Ken Willard's introduction to professional football," Curry said, not unkindly.

Ed Podolak, the great running star of the Kansas City Chiefs, asked, "Hey, did they tell you how they played both ways and how they folded up their helmets and stuffed them in their back pockets?"

They looked out at the action around the tables.

When we left for dinner, everyone walked very slowly through the gaming room, like cowboy stars, and the young girls looked up from the keno tables.

# CHAPTER 15

One day Karras and Gordy turned up in the apartment and began talking about the differences between the teams of the National Football League. They were in town for a game; the Lions were going to play the New York Giants the next day up at Yankee Stadium. John Gordy's contention was that the personality of each team was so marked that a player could tell by remembering the feel of a game just who the opponents had been. The Giants were invariably neat and surgical; so were the Baltimore Colts. The great Giant teams of the past decade had the additional characteristic of playing somewhat undistinguished games, and then making long, improbable, but precisely executed run or pass plays in the waning moments which produced a win for them. On the other hand, some teams tended to possess simple brutal philosophies: the Rams and the 49ers, for instance; also Minnesota and Atlanta, probably because of the hard-hat attitude of Norm Van Brocklin, the coach who had put together both clubs. With his teams, both offense and defense tended to run straight over people. The Chicago Bears were that sort of team too, their defense notoriously rough, and invariably big and quick-tempered, conceived in the George Halas mold and perpetuated by the "Monsters of the Midway" sobriquet which conditioned them to think of themselves as brutes both on and off the field.

"The Bears hang out in Chicago bars you wouldn't advise your worst enemy to go to," Karras said.

"That's right," Gordy agreed. "They spend their time seeping up ill will. They're the most vocal and loudmouthed of the teams out on the field—just a stream of vilification. There's method to all that yelling, too: shouting like that across the line can break the rhythm of the quarterback's signals, and it's effective, especially against teams which use staggered rhythm calls. It makes opposing linemen jump offside."

"The Monsters of the Midway...helluva name," Karras mused. He shook his head.

"On the field they're even rude among themselves," Gordy went on. "Really cussing each other out. It was a terrific thrill to beat that kind of team, to shut them up—like beating up the bully down the street."

"What about Green Bay?"

"Green Bay is the team I always love to play," Gordy said. "Except that they win. You never get the sort of physical beating you take playing the Bears or the Rams or the Falcons, because Green Bay's mark is finesse and perfect execution, and you never seem to get bruised by it. On pass rush they get around you and you never touch them. They get by you somehow, and you look around and the Green Bay front four are sitting on the quarterback with these big grins. Or on a running play, you're out in front running interference, looking for someone to block, and Ray Nitschke filters through behind you from his linebacker's spot and gets the runner down, leaving you thundering along thinking the play is still alive and just aching to knock someone down. It's very embarrassing. You come back to the huddle, really puffing hard, and someone gives you a scornful look and says, 'Hey, give the ball to Gordy, he's really tearing up the ground with his cleats. He's running forty yards on every play!'" He laughed. "No, Green Bay was good. It was always terribly frustrating to play Green Bay because I always felt we should come out on top. We always seemed to lose to them in some jerk way."

"That's right," Karras said. "Green Bay is like Notre Dame was when I was playing in the Big Ten. When we played Notre Dame, we annihilated them, and at the end of the game we'd come off the field feeling good until we looked at the scoreboard and saw we'd lost. It worked the other way, too. When we played Purdue, they just beat the crap out of us. We'd walk off the field feeling maybe we'd been beaten one hundred to nothing—but we'd won. That's how Green Bay is. You beat them physically, but they always seem to beat you on the scoreboard.

"I'll tell you another thing about playing at Green Bay," Karras went on. "The showers are cold. They get you up there into that freezing frontier town, beat the crap out of you, and then make you take a cold shower. Three years in a row they haven't had any hot water. Of course I've been in some weird visitors' showers in the NFL—some of them have showerheads that must have been set for midget women wrestlers, the water hitting you about navel height. Everybody on the team has to crouch like baboons on the tiles to get any water."

"Baltimore is a team like Green Bay," Gordy said. "You always have the feeling that you are being treated kindly until you get on the team bus to go out to the airport and realize that you've been whomped."

Gordy went on to say that some teams had schizoid personalities. Kansas City had a deft brush-block offense which seemed to leave the opposition still on its feet after a play, standing around and wondering what had happened; yet its defense was massive and corrupting.

"What's the key to stopping a clockwork offense like that, and Green Bay's?" I asked.

"There was only one thing to do with those great Lombardi offenses," Karras said, "and that was to gang-tackle and try to mess up that mechanism by going for the ball in swarms."

I asked about the Philadelphia Eagles, who had been in the doldrums for a number of seasons. Both Karras and Gordy agreed that the one distinguishing feature about playing the Eagles was that fistfights were almost sure to erupt.

But doesn't a team character change as its personnel changes? I wanted to know. Were the Eagle players doomed to fistfights year after year?

Both of them demurred, pointing out that obviously while a team had its ups and downs, its character remained surprisingly constant. For example, Green Bay had always been the scourge of the Central Division under Vince Lombardi; they never played a bad game. But Lombardi was gone, and the Packers had begun to lose. But they still had that grand aloofness that Coach Lombardi had instilled in them, though from time to time it would crack, and across the line the Lions would hear the bickering and the name-calling that suggested that the team's composure was deteriorating. "It's such a sweet thing to hear a Packer linebacker bad-mouth one of his people," Karras said. "Especially at Green Bay. We'd never heard anything like it before. They beat you with this terrific superior aloofness, like they'd all been born in some great palace somewhere and it wasn't worth considering that they might lose. They were elite."

"But the point is," Gordy said, "the Packers'll never lose that elite character, unless there's a huge shift of ownership or they get moved to Orlando, Florida, or they trade everyone who's ever had a sniff of it; they'll have their bad seasons, like now, but the team character will remain, and it's very valuable. A lot of it has to do with that crazy town up there that they all work out of. And the support they get from their fans."

"What *about* the fans?" I asked. "What was it like playing in Chicago, for example? Do they behave like the team?"

"The Chicago crowd is unbelievable," Gordy said. "For one thing, Wrigley Field seats are built right up to the edge of the field, so they're all on top of you. They really let you have it. I don't know what sort of language they learned at their mothers' knees, but this isn't it."

"They're very good on your background," Karras said. "They told me about things Greeks did that I didn't even know."

"There was this one time," Gordy went on, "when Erich Barnes, who was playing corner for them then, intercepted a pass out by the pitcher's mound, and when I rushed over to tackle him he ducked his head and I went sailing over him and got him solid in the head with my knee. It must have looked like I'd kneed him on purpose, because the

Chicago bench emptied and we all had this big shoving match out there on the field, the kind of thing that usually happens in Philadelphia. A photographer snapped a picture of me with my fist under George Halas's chin, just a freak picture that made it look like I was going to punch that nice ol' man. Well, he's a *tough* old man, but sure as hell I never wanted to hit him. That's how it looked, though, and it got published in the papers. The Chicago fans have the memories of elephants, and the next time we played them, you wouldn't believe the abuse..."

"Five years after my suspension for gambling," Karras said, "they still remembered. I'd run out on the field, and I'd hear these cries drifting down: 'Hey, you Greek fat-ass. Wanta place a bet for me? Who you betting on today?'"

"Is there no recourse?"

"Oh, I'd yell back at them sometimes. 'I'm betting on your mother,' I'd shout. I don't know quite what I meant by that, but it seemed to disturb them. I'd see them rocking back and forth up there, their fists up."

Gordy got up out of his chair. "Hey, you remember that time when the Chicago crowd came running out on the field, and everybody started to slug everybody? It was catching, like some sort of quick-moving disease. Jim Martin was standing over on the sidelines. He was our placekicker, and he'd been in the Marines, and he was a Notre Dame man, and he was a little crazy, too. While he was watching what was going on, a cop came up alongside, Martin saw him, turned, and hit him with a short, stiff right hand. Absolutely great punch. The cop went *boing* and down he went. I don't know why Martin did it—maybe because he'd always had a hankering to hit a policeman and it seemed as good a time as any. Playing in Chicago always drives you a little nuts anyway."

"Fans have always scared me," Karras said. "I don't know anything about sitting in the stands. I've only been up there a couple of times in thirteen years. I sat there once at a baseball game with four men and I was scared to death. Beer drinkers."

Gordy said intensely, "It's the frustration. They take out their frustrations through what we do on the field. They can't go around hitting people. They're scared to, or they don't want to—it's barbaric—so they pay football players to do it. But the trouble is that the game doesn't really rid them of their frustrations. I'm not even sure that a *win* satisfies them, but a loss makes them grotesque. They wait for you at the end of a game. They hang over the fence, their faces twisted with hate, and shake their fists—these *little* people."

He was visibly upset. He began pacing around the room. "You can feel the mob rule ticking in these people. I don't ever want to look at them—bent double over the fences screaming down at us. That's what scares me more than anything: a mob scene. In Mexico once, when I was there with my family, they were having an election and a riot started. It was just at the time of those 'Yankee Go Home' scenes. They came pouring down the street. I was in the car with my family. Man, I wanted *home.* I was scared to death. I started up the car, but they closed in around us. I could see that they had no control over themselves. Man, I was through, I was just *finished.* A man started pounding on the window. I had no choice; I rolled it down. He leaned in, a big, swarthy guy. I shrank back, and he said, 'Hey, Joe, you wanta buy some watches at the market?' "

Both Karras and I laughed, but Gordy's face remained grim. "No, no," he said. "This is very serious. The snowballs come down with rocks in them. I've seen these guys who are sedate businessmen, and they've got a Caddy out in the parking lot and a big house in Grosse Pointe to drive home to, and a wine cellar, and all they have to worry about are their golf handicaps—and I've seen these guys hanging over the runways with the hair hanging down in their eyes, and their faces blood-red, screaming insults, like you were a bug and they wanted to exterminate you...

"It's like they have no concept at all of what a football player goes through out there. I remember I got hit in the throat one time, going down after a punt. It was against the Giants, the team we're playing tomorrow. I went down on both knees and put my head on the ground, and it was as if somebody had cut me open and taken everything inside of me and pulled it out of my open throat. I was hit right in the Adam's apple and I had nothing left. I wanted to go straight to the locker room and take off my football equipment and never ever, *ever* hit anybody or be hit again as long as I lived. Well, no sooner had I got myself supported to the sidelines when the ball changed hands and I had to go back out there again. I remember thinking if only all those people knew what it was taking me to get myself back out there . . . Or the time I hit Eddie Meador of the Rams; as I blocked him I pinched every nerve I've got in my body. Goddamnedest thing! I was knocked out, lying flat on my back on the ground, and my arm was frozen, *pointing straight up,* the nerve locking it there, like I was pointing up at God or something. What do you suppose the people in the stands thought? They probably thought I was pointing at a pigeon. 'Look at that lazy dumb-ass lineman lying on his back and pointing at pigeons.' When I came to, I still couldn't get the arm down. It was locked, absolutely numb, and when I walked off the field it stuck straight out in front of me like a Hitler salute."

Karras and I were laughing again.

Gordy was beside himself. He strode about the room. "No, no, no, no, it's terrible. When something like that happens to you, and the pain, and all the grief of losing, you come off the field and you want to get to your family, and you hurry through the tunnel to get away from the crowd, and you hear them screaming at you, and you think about where you can go to eat in a place where nobody knows you, and all the time you're wondering how you can be *hated* so much for going out there and trying your best."

He collapsed in a chair; it squeaked sharply under his weight. He put his legs out in front of him. "Aw, to hell with it. The crowds shouldn't mean that much anyway. They have nothing to do with the great satisfactions of football either. Jesus! Sometimes it's fun to see that mob take it on the chin. Do you remember the game—I think you wrote about it in *Paper Lion,*" he said, looking at me. "The one in Baltimore where in the last minute of the game Lennie Moore of the Colts made this fantastic touchdown pass against Night Train Lane?"

"Yes," I said. "And Earl Morrall came on for the Lions and—"

Karras stirred in his chair. "Christ! I'll never forget it. Lennie Moore went six yards in the air *parallel* to the ground, I swear. He caught the ball just on his fingertips, the most fantastic catch I ever saw in my life. I ran down the field. I couldn't believe it. Neither could Night Train. His whole spirit left him; he turned *white.* And then this whole ant army of Baltimore fans came down on the field, and they knocked Train over and they were yelling and screaming. The announcer came on the public-address system. It was almost impossible to hear him, and he was saying, 'Okay now, you've got to get off the field. This is Baltimore's greatest hour. Please don't ruin . . .'

"Well, man, I was hot. I got to the sidelines and these three Baltimore fans started giving me the needle. One of them called me a 'fat-ass something-or-other' and I took my helmet and hit him *whap* in the head with it. He went down, and one of the other two guys pulled a knife. I stared at it bug-eyed and began swinging my helmet back and forth to keep him away from me. Jimmy Butsicaris was there, a friend of mine from Detroit. He came rushing up and pretended he had a gun. He put his hand in his overcoat pocket and shoved it out with the index finger forward and said, 'I've got a gun, you mothers.' They turned and ran. Christ, all he actually had on him was a *bench pass!*"

"Remember Gil Mains?" Gordy said. "He just waded into the crowd. He almost killed one of them."

"What was going on out on the field?" I asked.

"There were still twenty seconds left," Karras said. "When they finally got the crowd moved, Baltimore kicked off and we had time left for one play. There was only the slimmest chance of winning it—being what? Five points down?"

Gordy nodded.

"Out of the corner of my eye I could see Coach Wilson," Karras continued. "He was behind a row of fans on the sidelines, jumping up and down like a kid trying to see over a fence. The poor guy couldn't even see what his own team was doing. As for me, I didn't care about the game. I was still running around holding my helmet by the strap trying to bop the guy who'd pulled the knife on me. The whole place was going crazy—the damnedest sound."

"That's right," Gordy said. "The acoustics in that stadium are weird, and it funnels the sound right down to the field. The 'Baltimore Boom.' Sometimes it's so loud that the quarterback has to scream in the huddle."

"And then suddenly all that noise stopped," Karras went on. "It was like all those mothers had been throttled. There wasn't a sound. I pulled up. I thought maybe I'd gone deaf. Just like that—*blam!*—the whole place went silent."

Gordy could hardly contain himself. "Christ!" he said. "I was out there." He spoke in awe, as if he still could not believe it. His voice squeaked. "There were six seconds left after we'd run the kickoff back," he said. "Earl Morrall gave us the pass play in the huddle. We went up to the line, and I had Art Donovan to contain, and Willie McClair, playing offensive tackle for us, had Gino Marchetti. Man, that's a tough game for both of us. At the snap, Donovan and Marchetti did a loop—what they call a 'twist' at Baltimore—and they ran *into* each other. Well, that neutralized them just for a second, and then they came on—too late. Morrall hit Jim Gibbons over the center and he got to the sidelines and ran into the end zone and scored as the gun went off. Willie and I looked all over for penalty flags going down. No flags!

"Christ, we'd won it. But then came the scary part. There was that quick awful silence. The crowd moved onto the field again, and it was like they were coming for us. We jumped up a few times in the air when Gibbons scored, but then we stopped. No cheering by us, nos*sir.* You had to weave your way through them to get back to the locker rooms. They wouldn't move. If you got near them on the field they'd elbow you, and you'd look into these crazy, mad, *quiet* faces, and it was the scariest thing in the world. You have to step down into the baseball dugouts at Memorial Stadium to get to the tunnels that lead back to the locker rooms. The crowd was so thick and surly around the dugout steps that I asked a cop to help me through. The guy *shoved* me into the dugout, real hard, and I smacked up against the dugout wall. A policeman! I didn't say anything. The whole town was furious. They had to drive us to Washington to catch a plane back to Detroit; they were afraid to take us to the Baltimore airport. Oh, yes, we stuck it to the crowd that time."

We sat there, turning the scene over in our minds, and then Gordy said, "Of course, the same score that stuck it to the Baltimore fans made the people in Detroit go crazy with delight in front of the TV sets—spilling their beer and leaping up and down and scaring the hell out of the family cat. Well, I don't care if they're Baltimore fans or Detroit fans—they *all* scare the hell out of me."

# CHAPTER 16

The next day, for that bleak mid-December meeting between the Lions and the Giants, the producers of *Paper Lion* wired up Gordy and Karras with microphones, and from time to time the tape machines were turned on to eavesdrop on them. The hope was to get authentic background sounds for the film. The tapes were later transcribed by a pair of embarrassed secretaries—the language is constantly blue and violent—though they turned out to be useless for the film. A year later, the producers were kind enough to send the material around for me to listen to.

I found it fascinating, perhaps because I am an eavesdropper at heart. I despair not knowing what is being said just beyond my hearing—what it is that has produced a roar of laughter in the far corner of a cocktail party. At spectator sports I find myself feeling the same way—in baseball wondering what is being said at the conference on the pitcher's mound, or in football what the coach is whispering to the quarterback on the sidelines. Football is particularly frustrating since so much of the game is verbal: voice signals, both offense and defense huddling to talk things over, spotters and assistants outfitted with microphones and headsets, hurried conferences at critical moments, and especially the exchanges that must erupt between men in close quarters under violent stress—all of which, to the despair of the football fan, goes on out of earshot.

The fidelity of the Karras-Gordy tapes is extraordinary, recording not only the immediate sounds of the two players' voices, but also the quarterback's commands, the defensive signals, the constant warnings from the officials ("Linemen, keep your hands in!"), smatterings of conversation on the bench, and the concussive sounds of the plays themselves—the grunts, the crash of padding, the sharp, near-expiring gasps of players smacked hard to the ground, along with an occasional word of comment between the combatants.

In the background, the roar of the crowd, varying in its intensity, provides a strong clue to what is happening on the field, further illuminated by the public-address system over which the stadium announcer's voice, shredded slightly by the wind, intones: "Tarkenton's pass... complete to Crespino... brought down... by LeBeau... first and ten... on the forty-three." It is easy, listening to the tapes, to conjure up a visual picture of the proceedings.

Also in the background, providing a wrench of authenticity, are the occasional jangled and tinny strains of a banjo-dominated musical group known as "Your Father's Moustache." The Christmas season was almost at hand, so on the tapes one hears the startling contrast of "Jingle Bells" and other such carols plinking over the brutal yawp and heave of the proceedings on the field. By some mysterious and perverse edict, Your Father's Moustache—a small collection of portly musicians housed in a little shelter down at the bleacher end of the field—has been playing at the stadium for years. I suspect that if a change were made, if their plinkety-plinks were supplanted by more traditional band music, a great outcry from the traditionalists would go up and they would come to the support of Your Father's Moustache with all the zeal of a dowager dog-owner defending the character of her ancient mongrel.

That is an odd corner of Yankee Stadium: above, the bleachers with its raucous citizenry (invariably fights break out); the Moustache group playing in front of the bleacher wall; and in front of *them,* down on the field, long lines of patients in wheelchairs who are trundled in by attendants at the beginning of the game to watch from behind this corner of the end zone, the worst vantage point in the stadium. Invariably, just at the beginning of the fourth quarter, whatever the situation in the game, the patients are wheeled out. They seem to go without complaining, with rarely a head turned to watch as they are rolled away, or a cane raised in protest. Perhaps they consider it a relief to get away from the sounds of bleacher strife and the ragtime assault of Your Father's Moustache.

When I told Karras I had the tapes, he said that he doubted they'd be of much use, pointing out that he rarely talked to the linemen opposite him. He remembers his private wars with Jerry Kramer, for instance, the offensive guard of the Green Bay Packers, as being absolutely silent struggles. He recalls only one instance when they had words—a weird occasion when the left side of Karras's nose guard, or "cage" as the players refer to it, came loose and somehow, as the two of them bulled at each other, *hooked* into Kramer's cage, so that their two helmets were stuck fast, the players jammed up against each other, their faces within inches, staring at each other, with neither able to pull himself loose.

"It was crazy," Karras said. "We must have looked like a terrible, snake-like animal, two-footed at each end, some kind of big inchworm writhing about."

"And you had words during this?"

"Damn right. Kramer kept shouting, 'What the hell are you doing?' I guess he thought I'd hooked up to him on purpose. He looked a little scared. I mean, we were really stuck."

Finally, Karras was able to disengage himself by skinning out of his helmet and backing away, leaving it hanging off Kramer's nose guard like a huge morsel dangling from his jaws. "Yeah, he talked that time. He still thinks it was a sly maneuver I cooked up to intimidate him."

"So other than a rare case like that the offensive guards keep their mouths shut?" I asked.

"My brother Teddy," Karras said, "played offensive guard like Jerry Kramer, and he once told me that he never said anything to the guys opposite because generally they were twice as big, being defensive tackles, and twice as strong. He said, 'Why should I say anything? They'd kill me.' Once when he was with the Chicago Bears, he was playing against Big Daddy Lipscomb, the huge lineman who was with Pittsburgh then. Big Daddy was one person it was *good* to talk to, because maybe you could tone him down a bit if you said, 'Hi, Big Daddy, how are you today?' and a lot of friendly crap like that. So Teddy was trying it. 'How's the family, Big Daddy?' he'd ask, and in the meantime Big Daddy was just kicking the crap out of him, and Teddy'd say, 'Oh that was good, Big Daddy. I've never see such moves. *Gee,* you're good.'

"Finally, on this one play, Big Daddy went offside and he just killed Teddy, who was still down in his stance. He hit him alongside the head so hard— *WHOP!*—that Teddy thought he had forgotten to put on his helmet. He went back to his huddle and asked, 'Where's my helmet?' His teammates looked at him and said, 'It's on your head, man.' So on the next play Teddy's temper got lost, and when Big Daddy came at him, he hit him alongside the head with a right hand as hard as he could. It didn't even budge him, but Big Daddy must have felt it because he said, 'I'm going to get your ass.' Teddy said, 'Any time you want to fight me, Big Daddy, I'm ready. Any *time!* I'm tired of your bullshit. If I ever catch you off this field, I'll kick your ass.' After he'd said it, he felt like slapping himself in the face. It was like he was listening to somebody else talk. Big Daddy looked at him, leaning in to be sure he'd heard right, and then he said, 'Well, I'll see about *that,* boy.' Teddy heard himself replying—and he couldn't believe what he was saying—'Don't call me "boy," you son of a bitch! I'm *Karras!*'

"Well, in the hotel after the game Teddy was coming down to the lobby from his room. He was alone in the elevator, and at the tenth floor the elevator stopped, the doors opened, and standing there was Big Daddy. When Teddy saw him, he turned and faced the corner of the elevator like a dunce in the schoolroom. The elevator gave this big creak when Big Daddy stepped in. He's huge! Big Daddy said, 'How you doin', boy?' Teddy said, 'Fine, Big Daddy. How's the family?' He could hear Big Daddy breathing—high up back of his head! The elevator started down. Teddy couldn't believe how slowly it was moving, especially with all that weight of Big Daddy in it. Well, Big Daddy made him sweat for nine floors. Then, just as they got to the lobby, he said in this deep voice, 'I know that's you, Karras.' Teddy just about went to his knees, he was so frightened, but then Big Daddy started to laugh, and so did Teddy, a real high-pitched laugh of relief, and it was all right."

John Gordy was not sure about the value of the tapes either, and questioned what could be gained by wiring up players. He remembered that a scientist who was doing a serious paper on what he called "impact structure"—a study of the kinetic violence of football, how hard players hit each other—had come to Los Angeles for a Pro Bowl game. He reasoned that the middle linebacker probably dished out and took more punishment than anyone else, so Joe Schmidt, then an All-Pro at the position, was persuaded to play the game rigged up with a number of measuring devices. According to Gordy, the trouble was that Schmidt had a terrible game, or perhaps opportunities to make primary tackles were rare that day. At any rate, he did not make one solid tackle, and when the tapes were transcribed on graph paper, much like a seismograph chart, hardly a wiggle showed up to suggest the concussive nature of football. "The scientist read his charts," Gordy said, "and as far as he could tell from them *ballet* was just as full of contact as football."

Of the two tapes the movie producers sent me, the Karras transcript is the more extensive. Gordy keeps his mind largely on the business at hand, while Karras characteristically lets his faculties freewheel somewhat more extensively, though much of the verbiage is directed at himself. "Stay tough" is a constant self-goad. Still, there are certain outside catalytic forces which command loud verbal observations—European placekickers, for example. Karras is roused to a sort of wild, half-serious frenzy by the steady encroachment in football of European players whom he refers to as "tiny, foreign soccer kickers" who are summoned from the bench (the coach calls out, "Hey, Boris...") and prance onto the field in their spotless uniforms shouting, "I am going to keek a touchdown. I am going to keek a touchdown." On the tapes the first words Karras speaks to any member of the Giant team are addressed to Pete Gogolak, the Hungarian-born placekicker, who appears for a field-goal attempt early in the game. The monologue is not without bite. Of course the quarterbacks (in this case Fran Tarkenton of the Giants and, later in this game, Earl Morrall) are traditionally targets for Karras's comments, and there is always abuse for opposing linemen unfortunate enough to have been raised in the South. Karras has always felt that southerners, being overly sensitive to criticism, can be intimidated by verbal attack.

The Lions won this game rather handily, scoring two touchdowns and a field goal in the first half and thereafter never being seriously threatened. They received the opening kickoff, Mel Farr carried nine yards on the first play, and the team went on from there to score. Karras spent this first offensive drive on the sidelines, of course, and since he does not see well, much of the early section of the tape consists of his asking, "What's going on?" "What was that?" "Did he pick up any yards?" "Who's that?" "What down is it?" "Was that Amos Marsh who ran the ball?" At one point, he stumbles into a fellow player on the sidelines who accidentally steps on his foot. There is a sharp cry and Karras's voice says, "Oh Christ, my foot's gone, and I haven't even been on the field yet."

"You all right?" a voice asks.

"Yeah, yeah."

In the background, another voice says, "Alex, they ought to give you a white cane so you can tap your way up and down the sidelines."

Then the Lions kick off, and the tape picks up the creak of Karras's gear as he trots out onto the field.

KARRAS:
*(Steady roar of crowd in background. Voice of middle linebacker, Mike Lucci, calling defensive signals: "Four four three; blitz; blue!" Crack of hand*

*slaps as defensive team breaks huddle*) Come on, come on. Start it good. Fix 'em. (*Concussion of play; heavy breathing*) Jesus! Again! My foot's smashed again! Oh my! Christ! First play and my foot's smashed. Christ! I'm a hundred and twenty-three years old. Keep moving. Keep moving. (*Lucci's voice calling next play: "Four three; blue."*) Play tough. Let's go, fellows. (*To himself*) Killer, here we go. (*Concussion of play; grunts*) Beautiful! Jesus Christ! Beautiful! Good position. Yumyum. Who ran that ball? Young rook? (*Lucci's voice: "Four three; blue."*) Once more. Yeah. (*Enticingly*) Come on inside here, baby. (*Crash of gear; heavy breathing*) Okay, okay! Nice. Nice. That was beautiful. He tried to come out and he had to go back in. (*Voice in background: "Yeah, yeah, I know." Announcer's voice: "Gogolak for field-goal attempt."*) Now who are you? I said who are you, you little pisser. You from Rumania? Latvia? No? Well, then, are you from Finland? You lending *class* to the league? From England? That's why you're in here? Lending *class?* (*Concussion of play; heavy breathing; stadium announcer's voice: "Gogolak's attempt failed. Detroit's ball on the Giant twenty."*) Go on back to the bench, you little pisser. Hey! Unscrew your foot and stick it down your throat, that's what I said, you little Slovakian pisser. Jesus!

(*Creaking of gear as trots to bench. In background, tinny band plays "Jingle Bells"*) Nice going. We're gonna get some points. (*Cheering the offense*) Run, Melvin [Mel Farr, Detroit running back], run, baby, run, you mother, beautiful. Man, look at that offense move! Mel Farr's the sweetheart. He'll go a thousand yards this year. Man, it's raining touchdowns. I can't believe it. Who scored that touchdown? (*Voices: "Kickoff team get ready."*)

(*Back on defense, Lucci's voice: "Four three; red."*) Okay, killer, stay tough. Here we go. (*Concussion of play: heavy breathing*) Oh, you mother! You stomped my foot. You took care of my toes! Christ! (*To Lucci, hurt on play*) Hang in, Looch. Get up, Looch. Hey, Looch! (*To John McCambridge, defensive end playing alongside*) Hey listen, Johnny, Looch is staying in, but he's hurting. I'm gonna play a little tight there, right? (*Lucci's voice in huddle: "Four four; blue."*) Right. (*To himself*) Okay, killer, here we go. (*Referee's voice: "Watch your feet; watch your feet!"*) Yeah, yeah, yeah. (*Another play; heavy panting*) I shoulda had him. Jesus! Oh Christ! I had the mother. I shoulda had him. Jesus!

(*On next play Karras tackles Giant quarterback*) D'ja like that, Fran? Hey, Fran, d'ja *like* that? Hey, Fran? Hey, Fran? Hey, Fran, watcha think? (*Announcer's voice in distance: "... tackled by Karras."*) Oh yes. Oh my.

(*On bench*) Sweet. Sweet. It's like a bunch of bees out there. Really swarming. No fun being a halfback today. Gang-tackling. Real bunch of bees. They'll try to run some fast screens. Is there any water? Water? C'mon. C'mon. Lace their ass out there! Lay it on them! (*Band plays "Rudolph, the Red-Nosed Reindeer" in background*) Run, baby, run. I'm going to tell you something right now; it *nice.* It's nice sitting here in New York on a wood bench in the sun with your team doing fine. (*Unidentified voice: "Man, I got a good bunch of Tarkenton that time. How's your man coming?"*) He comes strong. They were right during the week with those scouting reports. Dess [Daryl Dess, Giant offensive guard] uses that forearm. He's good. He's rough to get by. They got anybody to come in for him? Some kid from Tennessee? (*Crowd noise rises*) Christ! What was that! Horrible!

(*Back out on defense. Lucci's voice: "Four four three; blitz; red." Referee's voice: "Watch your feet!"*) Stay tough. Yumyum. (*Crash of play*) Double twist! Great! Great! (*Calling to linebacker*) Good position, baby. Beautiful. (*Unidentified voice: "Okay, let's keep 'em back in the toolhouse."*) Hey Jer [Jerry Rush, tackle playing alongside]. Jer, there's a little trap on me. (*On next play, Karras reaches Tarkenton again*) Hiya, Fran. Howdee*doo*dee Fran. Hey Fran, you like it out here, hey Fran? Hey Fran baby? Nice. Nice. (*Lucci's voice: "Four two; blitz; blue."*) Double twist! (*Lucci yelling: "Open right! Open! Open!"*) Hold him up! Get that guy. (*Loud applause and shouting; distant cowboy yell*) What happened? What the hell happened? What's going on? Christ! Hold him up for Chrissakes. (*Snorts violently*) Come on, boys. One more play. (*Play called in huddle*) I screwed up on that one, Jer. Should have had the son of a bitch. Give me room and keep outside this time. I'm going to play him a little tight. Come on, Jer. (*Concussion of play; thudding; heavy panting*) Nice, nice. Yes. Yes.

(*On way to bench; announcer's voice: "... brought down by Karras."*) All ri-ight. Right at me. Way to go, Paul [Paul Naumoff, outside line-backer]. Yumyum. Real sweet out there. Isn't it the quarter yet? Run, baby! Beautiful! Get some points. Christ! (*Tries to clear throat*) I got this upper respiratory problem. I got a headache I wouldn't wish on Khrushchev. Killing me, just killing me. What down is it? Third? Third and what? (*Announcer's voice, with slight Continental inflection: "... carried by Farr."*) D'ja hear that? (*In heavy British accent*)... bawl kerried by Melvin Fah of England. That's what I like. A lot of class in football! Carrying British stadium announcers. Quite! Splendid! What the hell is wrong with Amos [Amos Marsh, Detroit fullback]? Tired? I wish I could get tired anytime I felt like it, walk off like that and sit down. Put him back in. Get the *force* out there. *Got*-damn. No more scrambling, gang. Let's lay it on them. Block that man! Knock his dick off. (*Ragtime band in background: "You've Got the Sweetest Little Baby Face"*) Keep it up. Oh my. That's lousy. That's horrible! (*Announcer's voice: "... tackled by Lockhart."*) One foot. One little foot. That's all they had to make. (*To himself*) A foot. You know how big a foot is. (*Announcer's voice: "Fourth and one."*) Twelve inches. Couldn't make *twelve* little inches, so I've got to go back to the pressure cooker. (*Crack of gear as runs back onto field*) The pressure cooker. Christ.

(*Announcer's voice: "That's the end of the quarter."*) Hey, you hear that announcer from England? Quatah! Quatah! What class! (*To new Giant guard*) Hello! Who are you? I'm a hundred and twenty years old. Y'all from Tennessee? You one of them cotton-pickin' hillbillies? Well, fry my ass, I do de-clare. What's a li'l ol' Southern boy like you doin' out here in this mess? Y'all lookin' to get your dick knocked off? (*Line judge calls: "Offensive linemen, keep those hands in. I'm going to call it on you. That's a warning." Concussion of play; Karras gets to Tarkenton*) Hi*ho*, Fran. What are you doing on the floor? (*Announcer's voice: "... brought down by Kar-*

*ras.*") Hey Fran? That's some li'l ol' Southern boy you got yourself for pass protection—mah *good*ness! (*Lucci calls play: "Four three; blitz; blue."*) Hello, hello. You still in here? Goodness. What you breathin' so hard fo', li'l boy? (*Concussion of play; heavy panting*) What's that for? Ref! What you throwing down that flag for? Wait a minute! (*Yelling*) He was on the ground already! Holding face mask? Oh that's horrible, ref, that's a horrible call. He was on the ground. The play was over! (*Players arguing*) Shut up! I'll talk. Shut up for a minute. I'm the captain. I'll talk. Don't tell me *not* to talk. (*Voices calm him down; one says, "I'm with you, Alex."*) Okay then. (*Calmer*) Okay. Okay. (*Lucci calls defensive huddle: "Four three; blitz; blue."*) Okay, Jer. Let's get them (*Crash of contact*) You *held* me! You held me, you motherfucker! You hold me again and I'll punch your goddamn hillybilly head off. Get off me, you piss-ass hillbilly. (*Heavy breathing*) Motherfucker! (*Next play; crash of gear*) Nice. Nice. Come to me. That's it... go to your knees!

(*Announcer's voice: "Fourth down." Lucci's voice: "Double twist. Special set." On way to line Karras and Rush hold whispered conversation about which will be primary attacker in looping maneuver by two tackles*) Me first? (*"Sure, you."*) You? (*"No, you."*) No, *you* go ahead. (*"Quit kidding, Al. You go."*) Okay, man.

(*Signals called; crash of play*) Man, you hillbillies can't block worth... hey... hey! He's *clipping,* hey ref! (*Whistle*) Damn right. Give 'em five yards. Five more. That's right. Five *more.* Hey, hillbilly, you're doing your team real good in there. A fifteen-yarder. Yumyum. (*Lucci's voice: "Safety blitz."*) Jerry, your man is pop-blocking, isn't he? (*Muffled reply: unidentified voice: "It's what? It's what?"*) Safety blitz. Safety blitz. (*Crash of play; whistles; referee's voice: "Get your hands off him, number seventy-one. You're hitting him late. That's a warning, number seventy-one."*) Christ! (*To himself*) Must have heard that a billion times. "Get your hands off him." "Don't spear him." "You're hitting him late." "That's a warning." Goddamn quarterbacks. What are we supposed to do: stand around and *gawk* at them sons of bitches? (*Lucci's voice: "Double twist. Special set. Reverse." Crash of play; grunts*) Hey, Mike! Did you call the twist? Yeah? Well, I didn't twist. No. I didn't hear. That's my fault.

(*Back on bench*) No, coach. I didn't hear. But I'm glad I *didn't* twist. I got him. He came right to me. (*Announcer's voice: "Farr carried the ball; tackled by Lockhart." Players begin yelling along the bench*) Flag's down. Damn right. Cheap shot. Give them fifteen yards. If I did that, they'd give me twenty-five yards. Hell, they'd throw me out of the park. Hey, *water.* Let's have some water up here! (*Drinks; spits*) Hey, Looch. We've got the game. Ease up on the blitzes. Let the linebackers help out with the backs. (*Lucci's voice: "Okay. I'll talk to Jim [Jim David, defensive coach]." Announcer's voice: "Two-minute warning."*) That's good. The soup is getting cold. (*Band begins playing "Four-Leaf Clover." To show discontent with Giant head coach Allie Sherman, crowd begins to sing "Goodbye, Allie" to tune of "Good Night, Ladies." Singing drowns out band, though plinkety-plunk of banjos still discernible*) Man, they can boo here too, can't they? Listen to them. The great American fickle fans. Hey, Carl? The Giant team is second in its division, isn't it? Six wins, six losses, and they're second in their division! Damn tough division, this Eastern Division, whooo-eee!

(*Back on defense. Lucci in huddle: "Double twist; outside double."*) Yeah, yeah. Okay. Play it tough in the middle. (*Concussion of play; grunts*) That's a wham, baby. (*Breathing hard*) That's a wham on me. They really came down on me. But it's okay. That's the way to hold up. Hustle all the time. (*Lucci in huddle: "Double twist; special set."*) Okay. The soup's getting cold. Time for the big reach. (*Referee's voice: "You guys are playing a tremendous game. Don't spoil it. Keep your hands in." Unidentified voice: "Aw, man, git out of here." Lucci's voice: "Over right! Over right!" Concussion of play; Karras reaches quarterback*) Howdy, Fran. Why, it's *not* Fran. Who've I got here. Earl? That you? Earl Morrall. Well. God*damn.* How sweet it is.

(*Gun goes off, ending game. Karras trots to bench. Unidentified Lion says, "Hey, Alex. You still wired up?"*) Huh? (*"You still got a microphone on?"*) Yeah. (*"Well, can I tell you something?"*) Yeah. Go ahead. (*"Yeah?*

*Where do I speak? I mean, I want them to hear this."*) Right here. You speak right into my chest. (*"Okay, Alex. I wanted to say what a shame it is, being wired up and all, that today, of all days, you had to have the worst goddamn afternoon of your career. I mean, man, you stunk!"*)

The laughter goes up, and on the tape the listener can hear the creak of Karras's shoulder pads as he takes a retaliatory cuff at his persecutor. The voices of the autograph hunters take over: "Hey Alex, would you sign this 'To Tracy'? And maybe put 'A swell guy' after it. Right here on this napkin."

The Gordy tape is substantially the same—the exhortations, the panting, the violent shifts of mood, though Gordy coughs more and spends most of his time on the bench trying to clear his throat and nostrils. He says far less on the field than Karras, presumably because his work, leading the interference, leaves him spent at the end of each play, so that he gasps out his sentences as if trying to speak while being garroted. His accent becomes far more Southern than it is in usual conversation, and his grammar sometimes collapses. At one point, suddenly aware that the microphone has picked up an ungrammatical entreaty to the defensive unit ("Hey, big D., don't give them nothing"), he lowers his voice abruptly and says, "I wonder if I could correct that. Please substitute: 'Please, don't give them *anything!*'" At another point, he shouts out, "Get them motherfuckers," and immediately says, "Get *those* motherfuckers... sorry, and maybe you'd better leave out the last part, too."

GORDY:
(*On sidelines, to Karl Sweetan, Lion quarterback*) Hey Karl! They're stunting off that four four. Anything in the four or five hole is no good. Is there any water? Water! (*Hawks and vomits*) Christ! (*To himself*) How come I got to throw up during the game? Happens every damn time. Pass the word down. Everybody hustle. Hey, are they going to try a field goal? (*Frantically, to Jim David, Lion coach*) Hey, Jimmy! It's going to be a fake. Honest to God. This guy I was out with the other night said that

they had practiced the fake field goal all week. Honest to God! (*Stadium announcer's voice: "Gogolak's attempt fails... Detroit's ball on the twenty."*)

(*Creak of gear as Gordy runs onto field for offensive series*) Okay. Four good downs here. Let's go (*Sweetan's voice calls play in huddle: "Opposite right thirty-four on two." Sharp handclaps as huddle breaks. Line judge's voice: "Keep your hands in. Last warning." Sweetan's voice at line of scrimmage: "Four. Set. One nine A. Hut! Hut!" Crash of play; tremendous grunts from Gordy*) Oh Jesus, no! (*Loud yell from crowd; referee's whistle; big pileup. Referee's voice: "Okay, everybody relax, except you with the ball. Relax. Relax. Detroit ball." Gordy spits*) Christ! Where was the MBU on that. Jesus! What the hell. I got to take the guy in the gap. (*To Ed Flanagan, Detroit center*) Come on, Ed! Get him inside, hey? Okay. Let's get a good play. Let's get some blocks. (*Following next play, to Chuck Walton, Detroit offensive tackle*) Hey Chuck, what was that? A four four. Want me to take the guy in the gap? Call me a signal, because he can keep you from getting out. Or I'll call "George." (*His voice hops and breaks*) Then you can step out. If you call the signal, say "left" or "right" in case I forget which direction I'm supposed to go. (*In huddle*) Okay, babies, let's go. (*Concussion of play; sharp, staccato grunts from Gordy as he runs; crash of his block*) Christ! Get off my hand. You stepped on my hand. Oh, Jesus, you broke my hand! (*Heavy swearing*) My fingers are all gone. My hand's broke (*Unidentified voice: "Shake it off, Bear."*) Did you see what that guy did? He went and stomped on my hand. (*His voice calms*) What did he want to do that for? (*Ragtime band in background: "Hello, Dolly." Sweetan calls end sweep in huddle; his voice sounds healthy and chipper above Gordy's puffing. Tremendous grunts from Gordy as play commences and he pulls to run interference*) Huh huh huh huh huh huh huh huh huh... (*Crack of gear as throws block*) Crap! Nowhere! Jesus! I should've had the guy. (*To Amos Marsh, Detroit running back, on way to huddle*) Hey, Amos. I thought I had him. I blew it... I blew it... if I had a little more in me I would have had him, but I didn't... my fault. (*Blows nose; Sweetan calls running play in huddle; concussion of play*) No. No. Please no... Please! (*Detroit fumbles; great roar from crowd as Giants recover*)

* * *

There is one greatly poignant moment on the Gordy tapes. Following a running play, in which Mel Farr's signal to carry the ball is called, a sudden, sharp scream erupts over the crash of padding and the heavy grunts of the players. Gordy's voice cries out, "Mel, what's wrong. Mel! What's *wrong!*"—a voice so tragic with concern that, listening to the tapes, one conjures up a quick image of a crippled running back lying askew on the field with Gordy standing over him in despair. In the background, Farr's voice is barely understandable, but it is reassuring; he is all right. Gordy's reaction is startling: his voice shifts abruptly from anguish to rage. "Bastard! Don't you be yelling like that. You mothering bastard. Don't you *ever* yell like that. Don't you ever scare me like that, you bastard!" The temper of his voice then shifts once again, as in his relief he suddenly sounds close to tears: "Mel, baby. Please don't scare me. What the shit am I going to do without you out here, baby?"

Farr's reply is audible. Startled by Gordy's outburst and the sweep of its emotion, he says in a high, almost querulous tone, "Damn, John, I don't know. I don't know."

Both Karras and Gordy came around to my apartment to hear the tapes played on the machine. It was the following year. The effect on them was quite different. At the time Karras was still in football, so the sounds—that shredded roar of the crowd, the tinny background music, the whistles, the thuds, the signal calling—were as uninteresting to him as a phonograph record of barnyard noises might be to a farmer. Most of the time he stood at the window and watched the big tankers easing up the East River toward Hell Gate. "Any bodies float by?" he asked.

"I suppose so," I said. I was changing the tapes on the machine. "I've never seen any. Traditionally, most of them are outfitted in cement boots so they go to the bottom quick and stand there."

"Well, look close the next time you see a bunch of floaters going by and you'll see they're all old washed-up football players. They can't afford cement boots. And they'll all be linemen," Karras said. He stared moodily down at the currents and sighed. "Quarterbacks and tight ends die comfortably, in big beds, and the Irish setter is whimpering on the other side of the door, and someone is mowing the great lawn outside the big mansion. But the linemen give it up in these little rooms in the poor sections. They wake up on a cot in a room the size of a closet, and they look at their pushed-in kissers in the little mirror, and they pull their old football jerseys with the number on the back out of the bottom drawer of the beat-up dresser, and they put them on and go up to the bridge there—what's the name of it?"

"That's the Triborough."

"The Triborough. And they drop off the Triborough and float down here." He leaned forward. "There goes one. That's Ed Glurk, number seventy, good journeyman tackle for the Eagles in the fifties. Always was a nice guy. Look how he rides nice and high in the water. Just behind him, that's Al Wojciechowicz—good Polack kid who played guard for the old Yankees. He's got his jersey on inside out. Look at him turn in the water. He always had classy moves. Now who's that coming along now?" His voice rose in mock excitement. "Why, is that John Gordy, that old has-been from the Detroit Lions, number seventy-*five?* Why, I do declare I believe it *is*..."

"Can it," said Gordy. Hunched over the next tape, he turned the volume up on the machine and the roar of the crowd in Yankee Stadium shivered in the room.

For Gordy, out of football for a year, the sound track re-created scenes for which he had such nostalgia that the muscles began working in his throat and I thought he was going to cry. Afterward, he took the tapes and edited a composite for his own use. I thought of him occasionally, sitting in his small New York apartment (he had left his family in Detroit and was involved in the bitterness of a divorce action) playing his tapes, the volume up on his machine, lost in the re-creation of that cold December afternoon in Yankee Stadium.

What did it give him? I asked.

Oh, it took him back. "But the main thing," he said, "is that I am in awe of myself. I think, 'Jesus, what it took to go through that.' I'll tell you something: it makes me feel proud."

"Do you play the tapes a lot?"

"From time to time," he said. "Sometimes I play them for other people. Sometimes alone, when I'm down. It has a big effect on the girls." He laughed and shook his head. "It fills them with awe, too; they look at me different after they hear them. This man went through *that?*"

# CHAPTER 17

Just about the furthest thing from my imagination was that I would ever again hear firsthand the sort of sounds that we had listened to on the tape recorder in my apartment. When I left the Lions, I thought I was done with it forever. Friday Macklem, the equipment manager, had given me a few mementos of my experience there: a couple of gray sweatshirts inscribed DETROIT LIONS in blue on the front; a helmet with the Lion decal on each side, which I hung above a door in my apartment. Occasionally I wore one of the sweatshirts around the apartment. Once, on a cold fall day, I put one on, with a couple of sweaters over it, and went out to Central Park for some exercise.

The best type of communal exercise in the park if you don't want to jog around by yourself is to play in the pickup touch football games, which are quick, often violent, and very competitive. Many of the players wear cleated football shoes, and often the faded jerseys of their college football days. The procedure to enter such games is to stand along the sidelines, especially if the teams playing are not evenly matched, either in numbers or ability, and when you can get someone's attention, to call out, "Hey, you want anybody?"

The Central Park touch football games are imbued with ritualistic procedures. Such a request is never acknowledged as far as one can tell. The heads turn and look, like cattle at a sudden noise, and then the huddle forms and the game continues. But the request has been absorbed. After a while, unless you have an obvious physical problem, such as being on crutches, the heads will come up and turn toward you once again, and a voice will sing out, "Hey, you!"

Almost invariably the new player trotting in, lifting his feet high to try to give the impression he was once a college hurdler, is placed at center. It is the position of least authority on the field. The key figure is, of course, the quarterback. Since all the plays are improvised on the spot, it is he who instructs the others, and if he is a good quarterback, with a sense of public relations, he involves all of them in the possibility of glamorous participation in the play: "Harry, you go long; I'll be looking for you. Tim, cut across diagonally on a fly." To a stranger wearing a number on his jersey: "Ninety-eight, you go ten yards down and circle like this." He kneels down and scrabbles a design in the dirt. "Pete, hold the rush up and then slide off *here* for a safety valve, just in case I got to unload the ball. On two."

This last is directed at the center, the only instruction he will get, unless possibly: "Try to hold up that big guy, for Chrissakes. He's coming in like an express train."

For the new player at center, the position affords the others on his team the chance to judge the way he moves, his ability to catch the ball, if he should get the opportunity, and whether he seems to know what he's up to. There is always the chance he'll be promoted.

In my case, our team's quarterback had to go home ("I've got to take the goddamn kids to the goddamn zoo") and a man wearing a heavy knit sweater said to me, "Hey, do you want to run a few plays?"

"Sure," I said easily. "Just a couple."

In the huddle I said, "Look here, let's do this. Harry, you go way long. I'll look for you. Tim, a diagonal cut. Ninety-eight, ten yards or so, and then buttonhook. Pete, a little blocking and then slide off to the side in case I got to get rid of it. On two," I told the new center. A squat figure in heavy dark glasses, he was wearing a Beethoven sweatshirt and had been standing on the sidelines for ten minutes.

The play worked. Tim's diagonal cut carried him out beyond a defensive back who was probably thinking of something else, perhaps that he ought to be getting home for lunch, and as our man ran between the two piles of coats and gear marking the goalposts, someone said, "Man, hell of a pass."

It *had* felt good, a clean spiral and a good trajectory, and I had come up on my toes to savor the last steps of the receiver's run. I felt warm, so I trotted to the sidelines to remove a sweater. As I started to skin it off, I thought, Well, why not, so I took off both of them, revealing the gray shirt with DETROIT LIONS on the front. It was sleeveless and I felt the cold prick the skin of my arms. Still, I should have known better than to think the shirt would make an impression on my teammates; they could not help noticing it, but there were no reactions, no gasps, no double takes, no one saying, "Well, for Chrissakes, why didn't you let on?" One of the players said, "What's the play, man?"

"Harry," I said in the huddle. "Why don't you go long. I'll be looking for you. Tim, take that diagonal cut of your..."

The huddle broke.

Somebody on the opposing team wearing a tattered gray fedora stepped in front of Tim, arched his neck, and, reaching high, pulled in my pass. He ran a few steps and fell down. Our defense held, and I was allowed to continue. This time, on the first play, the man in the Beethoven sweatshirt let his man brush by him. As he came on, I retreated, backpedaling to keep away from arms that reached for me like a film monster's, until I was leaning so sharply backward that when I released the ball, it rose almost straight up in the air. It came down in the hands of the man in the fedora, who caught it in full stride and ran for a touchdown.

A change was made, initiated by the éminence grise on our team, the slightly built man wearing the heavy Shetland sweater which exuded a slight but noticeable odor in the huddle. I noticed that everyone deferred to him. Perhaps he owned the ball. He said, "Hey, Tim, why don't you take over for a few plays." The Beethoven man was shifted out to flanker to take Tim's place, and I, wearing my DETROIT LIONS shirt, went back to center. It was very cold. I stayed until I felt I could say with a certain amount of grace that I was required elsewhere. "I've got to go to the goddamn zoo," I said, and trotted off the field to the warmth of my two discarded sweaters.

# About the Author

George Plimpton (1927–2003) was the bestselling author and editor of more than thirty books, as well as editor of the *Paris Review* for its first fifty years. He wrote regularly for such magazines as *Sports Illustrated* and *Esquire,* and he appeared numerous times in films and on television.